Usable Pasts

Traditions and Group Expressions
in North America

Usable Pasts

Traditions and Group Expressions in North America

Edited by
Tad Tuleja

Utah State University Press
Logan, Utah
1997

Utah State University Press
Logan, Utah 84322-7800

Typography by WolfPack
Cover design by Michelle Sellers

Cover illustrations. Front cover above: Deborah Anders Silverman. Steven
Cleves Weber Collection; photo courtesy of David Cook/ Fine American
Art. George Lewis. ©The Church of Jesus Christ of Latter-day Saints;
courtesy of the Historical Department, Archives Division; used by permis-
sion. Jim Gambaro. *Front cover below:* Clark Kelley Price; ©The Church
of Jesus Christ of Latter-day Saints; courtesy of the Museum of Church
History and Art; used by permission. Courtesy of the Royal Canadian
Mounted Police. Joel Saxe. Deborah Anders Silverman. Bert and Brenda
Lazar Collection; photo by Martha Lochert. George Lewis. *Back cover:*
Minerva K. Teichert; ©The Church of Jesus Christ of Latter-day Saints;
courtesy of the Museum of Church History and Art; used by permission.

Library of Congress Cataloging-in-Publication Data

Usable pasts : traditions and group expressions in North America /
  edited by Tad Tuleja.
    p.   cm.
  Includes bibliographical references and index.
  ISBN 0-87421-226-X (paper)
  ISBN 0-87421-225-1 (cloth)
  1. Minorities—United States—Social life and customs.
2. Minorities—Canada—Social life and customs. 3. Ethnology—
United States. 4. Ethnology—Canada. I. Tuleja, Tad, 1944- .
E184.A1U83   1997
305.8'00973—dc21   96-51304
                                                        CIP

With gratitude to
George Carey
and
Brooke Thomas

The past isn't dead. It's not even past.

—William Faulkner

Contents

Acknowledgments

The seed of this book was sown some years back at the University of Massachusetts at Amherst, where a midlife critical assessment of my writing plans was turned in a fruitful direction by two fine teachers. George Carey of the English department gave me an unforgettable introduction to the dynamics of folklore, and Brooke Thomas introduced me to anthropology in a marvelous potpourri called "Biocultural Processes of Change." Both were sources of warm encouragement, and it is as much because of their kindness as because of their example that I am pleased to be able to dedicate this volume to them.

At the University of Texas at Austin, I have been fortunate enough to work in a program whose founding luminary was the don of performance folklorists, Américo Paredes. My thanks to the university for its generous fellowship support and to the folklore and anthropology faculties for their insightful and spirited collegiality. With regard to this project in particular, I am grateful to Steven Feld for commenting on the introduction and for guiding me through the "authenticity" debates, to Douglas Foley for his helpful reading of my yellow ribbons essay, and to Roger Renwick for a stimulating introduction to folklore theories. Frances Terry, bless her, has held the fort together.

Versions of three of the following chapters were previously published. George Lewis's chapter appeared under the title "The Maine

Lobster as Regional Icon: Competing Images over Time and Social Class," in *Food and Foodways* 3 (1989): 303–16. Part of Jerrilyn McGregory's work was published as "'May the Work I've Done Speak for Me': The Migration Text of the Lucky Ten Social Club" in *SAGE* 9 (1991): 10–13. A version of my chapter on yellow ribbons appeared under the same title in *Journal of American Culture* 17 (1994): 23–30. We thank the journals' editors for permission to print revised versions of these articles here.

This volume has profited much from the kindness of strangers—those anonymous reviewers whose gentle (and not so gentle) proddings have helped us to sharpen its focus and clarify its intent. I thank them, whoever they may be, for trimming our sails. In addition, I am grateful to four identified readers. Judy McCulloh gave helpful comments on the manuscript in an earlier incarnation; Pat Mullen's mastery of the scholarly literature helped us considerably in polishing several of the essays; Barre Toelken's generous reading clarified the advantages of our eclectic approach; and John Alley's input as executive editor of Utah State University Press has served us as a paragon of editorial professionalism. My appreciation, too, to the press's director, Michael Spooner, who was kind enough to invite our submission in the first place.

For years of personal and professional support, I am especially grateful to Angus Gillespie and Jay Mechling. As editors, they were rash enough to include my first scholarly paper in their anthology on American wildlife; as colleagues and friends, they remain two of the reasons that I still look forward to scholarly conferences. To Andrée, as always my lift and my keel, *te embrazo* on our twentieth and my thirtieth.

Making Ourselves Up: On the Manipulation of Tradition in Small Groups

Tad Tuleja

In a justly influential book published in 1983, Eric Hobsbawm and Terence Ranger coined the phrase "invention of tradition" to describe the appearance within modern states of novel, symbolic, generally normative behaviors that served to "establish continuity with a suitable historical past." Such invented traditions, they claimed, responded to rapid social repatterning by fixing some areas of social life as comfortingly "invariant." Thus "customary traditional practices" were revived, and new ones devised, to provide a refuge from the dizzying pace of modern life.[1]

Because Hobsbawm and Ranger were interested in how British colonialism managed transactions of symbolic capital, they depicted tradition invention as primarily a "top down" or nationalizing phenomenon, an elite practice designed to bring homogeneity and continuity to imperial disparateness. "Traditions are commonly relied upon," Michael Kammen has observed, "by those who possess the power to achieve an illusion of social consensus, [invoking] the legitimacy of an artificially constructed past in order to buttress presentist assumptions and the authority of a regime."[2] Hence the political and social conservativeness of new traditions—amply demonstrated by their proliferation in uneasily democratizing 19th-century Europe and in the United States in the equally unsettling period of the New Immigration. Because this nationalizing pattern had simultaneously to accommodate and to conceal diversity, morevoer, invented traditions were typically "vague as to the nature of the values, rights, and obligations of the group membership," even while specific practices endorsing cohesion—such "symbolically charged signs of club membership" as saluting the flag and rising for the national anthem— became compulsory in both Europe and America.[3]

In North America, such traditions were being invented generations before the expansive age of Victoria and Cecil Rhodes. As Henry Steele Commager pointed out a quarter of a century ago, the search for a "usable past" was ubiquitous in the period of Manifest Destiny, as Americans foraged diligently to supply a "suitable" history to a country that was told repeatedly—and not only by Europeans—that it lacked one. "Nothing in the history of American nationalism," Commager wrote, "is more impressive than the speed and lavishness with which Americans provided themselves with a usable past: history, legends, symbols, paintings, sculpture, monuments, shrines, holy days, ballads, patriotic songs, heroes, and—with some difficulty—villains." By century's end, what Henry James called the "undecorated walls" of American culture had been symbolically plastered with instant memories: a broad sweep of affective signifiers including (to name only a handful) Plymouth Rock and Lincoln's log cabin, the first Thanksgiving and Nathan Hale's last words, Old Hickory and Old Ironsides—and slogans from "the whites of their eyes" to "the home of the brave." As David Glassberg has shown in a definitive study of American historical pageantry, the vaunted "traditionality" of such signifiers was turned at the start of this century to multiple public ends, from boosterism and moral education to urban reform; an underlying intent of this progressive-era pageantry, according to *The Century*, was "to cement the sympathies of our people and to accentuate our homogeneity."[4]

An appropriate intent, no doubt, for civic celebrations. But traditions may also be deployed on a smaller scale, by people for whom "homogenizing" impulses may be far less secure, and securing, than they are for municipal or imperial administrators. It is a necessary modification of the Hobsbawm and Ranger thesis, therefore, to say that the politically powerless may also have the power to invent, to apply the creative impulse to their own private heritages, and in doing so to keep their own walls vibrantly renewed. Ethnic groups, regional groups, organizational and occupational groups, families: all such groups may find themselves creatively utilizing "past practices"—both inherently aged ones and deliberately aged ones—as manipulable markers of a common identity.

Such smaller groups are the focus of interest in this volume. A collection of case studies from the increasingly diverse mosaic of North American society, *Usable Pasts* explores the manipulation of "micro"-identities, to see how tradition invention may articulate on subnational scales. The focus here is nothing so grand as an American or North American style, but the ways and attitudes of distinctive smaller units: Boy Scouts at a single California campsite, the women members of a Philadelphia social club, Jewish elders on a single Florida beachfront. In the last section, we do adopt a national perspective, but even here the thrust is diffractive rather than totalizing. Robert MacGregor's work on the Mountie uniform and mine on yellow ribbons show how certain North Americans, not all U.S. citizens or all Canadians, negotiate symbols that are charged with nationalist import.

Since we hope that this volume will prove of value to students, not merely to specialists in folklore and expressive culture, a preliminary word on terminology may be in order. When we speak of "traditions," we do not mean something so ostensibly stable as "the old ways" or the practices that have been "handed down from generation to generation." Hobsbawm and Ranger's fundamental insight was that practices commonly understood as primordial often betray, upon inspection, a recent origin—and that they have been "traditionalized," that is, artificially aged, to serve elite agendas. A vigorous scholarly debate has followed that insight, with folklorists and anthropologists as well as historians contesting "authenticity" and questioning whether an invented tradition can be considered "genuine." While resolving that debate is beyond the scope of this volume, we do want students to appreciate that in current scholarly discourse, "tradition" does not necessarily imply a venerable lineage.

Although the practices we consider here are viewed by their participants as traditional, not all of them have validated "pedigrees." It might be fruitful to think of them, therefore, as expressions less of "heritage" than of style. Anya Peterson Royce suggests this term as a substitute for tradition because it allows for an appreciation of personal choice and diachronic change, which tradition—the more traditional term—does not. When we speak of traditions, then, we mean currently practiced expressions of group style that may or may not come trailing ancient glories.[5]

The term "invention" is likewise problematic. Like its more astringent avatar "constructed," the term "invented" has come to smack of falsity, inviting the delicious glee of the scholarly debunker. We hope in this volume to avoid that particular indulgence, playing down the negative connotations of "invention" by stressing instead the flexibility that its etymology allows for. Latin *invenire* gives the sense both of "finding" and of "finding out." In its reflexive form *(se invenire),* it means "to show oneself," to put oneself forward as something discovered or revealed. In all of these senses, invention suggests the creative impulse. Simon Bronner has that impulse in mind when he discusses the "interdependence of creativity and tradition" and when he refers to folklore, nicely, as "manipulated knowledge." For something to be manipulated, invented, or even reinvented means only that it is the product of human agency, of the bricoleur's skill. Aesthetic purism may find that skill objectionably "crafty." The essays here, to the contrary, applaud its potency.[6]

Presences and Premises

Scale is one basic difference between the groups examined here and those examined in the Hobsbawm and Ranger volume. But it is not only that the groups themselves are relatively small, subnational entities. The specific practices explored here are also "minor." Since I am as fascinated by local knowledge as Hobsbawm and Ranger were by nationalism, I asked contributors to address well-articulated "socionemes"—not the Navajo "way of life," but Navajo weaving; not the entire Newfoundland "heritage," but a single public ritual. The implicit theoretical bias is self-consciously ethnographic. I believe that what Lévi-Strauss called the science of the concrete is still the best avenue into the patterns of a data-busy world. Thus I asked contributors to keep their eyes on the ground, so that—to borrow Thoreau's lovely phrase—each closely observed fact might flower into a truth.

This is hardly a novel slant in folklore studies. In addition to the glosses embedded in book-length ethnographies, the professional journals abound with illuminating case studies that follow a similar "flowering fact" approach. Isolated gems in this copious literature— to take a random quintet of North American examples—focus on topics as varied as the Italian American funeral, interior decor among Greek Philadelphians, Slovak and Ruthenian Easter eggs, the "experience narratives" of black railroad porters, and the border *corrido* among Texas Chicanos.[7] Recent years have also seen several collections of thematically related case studies. Of particular value to Americanists are works on food and festival, festivity and ritual, regional cultures, ethnic "symbols and strategies," organizational cultures, and Elliot Oring's standard volumes on groups and genres.[8] We offer *Usable Pasts* as a contribution to this literature.

If the spirit of Hobsbawm is frequently evident in these pages, it is joined by two other, equally significant presences. One is that of Frederick Barth, who in 1969 sparked a paradigm shift in social theory by countering the commonplace, and seemingly common sense, notion of ethnogenesis as an ancient, virtually biological process. In reframing ethnic formation as a social and political dynamic, rather than a racial category, Barth posited boundary maintenance as a motivating factor and suggested that group identity evolves not in vacuo but in constant response to external pressures. Hence no matter how isolated a group might appear to be, its traditions and self-ascriptions develop within communicative fields and are inevitably mediated by a "conversation of images" across borders. Stern and Cicala make this Barthian point nicely when they observe that ethnic identity is "precarious" and that it emerges only in "concrete social relationships." After Barth, one emphasizes the "between-ness" of social identity.[9]

A similar interactive tack informed the work of this volume's third animating presence, the communicative or process-oriented folklorists who revolutionized the field in the 1970s by privileging "context" and "performance" over static texts and by defining culture as a dynamic of endless self-fashioning. These "young Turks"—now the profession's senior scholars—first garnered attention in 1972, with the Texas-bred manifesto *Toward New Perspectives in Folklore*. That volume, in a remarkable series of theoretical position papers, introduced Dan Ben-Amos's notion of folklore as "artistic communication in small groups," Roger Abrahams's sense of folk performance as the management of "social misalignment," Richard Bauman's concept of "differential identity," and Dell Hymes's insistence on the "expressive, or stylistic, dimension" of "communicative events." Common to all of their papers was the premise that the "lore" of social groups was not a thing but a practice—that, to borrow Barre Toelken's rightfully popular term, it could only be understood as a function of dynamics. That premise also underlies the essays in this volume. Like *New Perspectives*, it avoids presenting a single theoretical position and offers instead a diversity of approaches—but a diversity that is united in the conviction that folklore is alive, is a malleable, mobile expression of social identity.[10]

The essays themselves are organized into four sections, for each of which I provide an introductory headnote. In the first section, contributors examine the links between traditions and the creative manipulation of ethnic consciousness. The second three essays concern the expressive traditions of "intentional," or consciously chosen, group memberships. The next four address the role of "place lore" in the dynamics of regional identity. The volume closes with two studies of national traditions. The trajectory thus is roughly from narrower to broader, although the taxonomy, I readily admit, is hardly airtight. Indeed, the fuzziness of boundaries is an inevitable consequence of the multiple allegiances that always inform human loyalties and that have become miasmically complex in the modern world. Differential identities today are the result not only of intercultural exchange, but also of a plethora of opportunities for social alliance that a media-saturated (if personally thirsty) world affords.

To take only one example from this collection, the African American church women discussed by Jerrilyn McGregory appear here in the "ethnic" section, but we do not suppose that their African American heritage fully defines their expressivity. They might as readily have been placed in the "intentional" section (as members of the Lucky Ten Social Club), in the "regional" section (as proud daughters of their Virginia homeland), or in categories that are not foregrounded here, defined for example by gender, genre, or age. And yet none of these pigeonholes would have fully encompassed them, any more than does our calling them African Americans. Taxonomy is always a form of ideal typing, more to be recommended for its suggestiveness than its precision. Accepting that fact, indeed, underscores our collective intention—our conviction that social identity is a patchwork affair, a process of making and remaking not only our "selves," but also the communal matrices from which they emerge.

A Conspicuous Variety

In examining that process through these essays, several lessons stand out. First, perhaps, is the "variety of stylistic resources" that smaller groups may employ in the manipulation of their identities. The potential range of such resources is extremely wide. In fact, what Hobsbawm and Ranger called the "signs of club membership" may include virtually any expressive common endeavor that a group sees as uniquely its own. Any "socionemic" variable may mark identity.[11]

The fourteen essays presented here, for example, reveal almost as many different manipulable resources. The inventory includes parodic theatrics among California Boy Scouts and Newfoundland businesses; legendary history among martial artists, Mormons, and Texans; various artifacts of popular culture used to negotiate the meaning of the down east lobster; personal narrative among Appalachian migrants; weaving among the Navajo; song among urbanized African American church women and elderly Jews; a revamped calendar custom among Polish Americans; food as a contestable symbol along the Mexican border and in Maine; military dress in the Royal Canadian Mounted Police; and patriotic display as an invented tradition of the Gulf War. Max Weber seems to have had it right. "Any cultural trait, no matter how superficial, can serve as a starting point for the familiar tendency to monopolistic closure."[12] In the post-Barthian era we may question his notion of closure, but his fix on the variety of markers remains instructive.

A second, related lesson is the value of conspicuousness. Weber was also prescient in this regard. Among the traits that he saw as commonly employed ethnic markers were seemingly trivial features that he called "perceptible differences in the conduct of everyday life." Of special importance, he wrote, are "precisely those elements that otherwise might seem to be of small social relevance, since where ethnic differentiation is concerned, it is always the conspicuous differences that come into play."[13] Hobsbawm emphasized the concrete particularity of class signifiers in his discussion of proletarian football and costume styles.[14] Thorstein Veblen made very much the same point in his famous critique of Gilded Age conspicuous display.

The essays here support this socio-aesthetic insight. They imply that identity markers are commonly chosen not for any motivated (political, social, religious) reason, but for their more arbitrary feature of mere visibility. For symbols to serve simultaneously as community glue and boundary markers, they must be at once expressive, publicly expressible, and mnemonically markable. The implication is that the cause-and-effect relationship between symbols and meanings may in fact be counterintuitive. As Durkheim hinted in discussing clan totemism, symbolic display may actually generate, not merely reflect, the emotions symbolized.[15] The cowardly lion becomes ferocious with the acquisition of a medal; we become Texan by the pulling on of cowboy boots. Barth suggests just this counterintuitive truth when he notes the importance of visible as opposed to merely cognitive "assets": "People's categories are for acting, and are more significantly affected by interaction than by contemplation."[16] Thus it is predictable that seemingly insignificant markers like strip steak, handcarts, and yellow ribbons signify better than their attendant abstractions what it means to be Chicano or Mormon or American. You are, in other words, not only what you eat, but what you are visibly *presented* as eating to the outside world.

Factors of Exchange

This suggests a third major lesson: the importance of communication and contrast in establishing identity. Notice that Barth counterposes contemplation not to action, but to interaction. His point is that social identity always involves *exchange;* contesting ascriptions is a necessary feature of differentiation. Thus while one may fruitfully begin from the native's point of view, these essays remind us that a native perspective alone is insufficient. Even within relatively "isolated" folk groups (Navajo weavers, central Texas martial artists), mainstream and tributary cultures flow together—especially, perhaps, in media-rich North America. Inevitably, identity manipulation goes on within what Steven Feld has called a "dialectic of accommodation and resistance" so that the facts that flower into truths more closely resemble wild pansies than hothouse orchids.[17]

One interesting variant of this process is a strategy that might be called *parodic parry*, in which negative external ascription is creatively resisted by being turned back, with satirical exaggeration, against the attacker. In this example of "producerly" behavior, the "pure fool" appears as smarter than the master, and the despised minority ends up mocking the mockers.[18] Royce cites the colonial American appropriation of "Yankee Doodle" as a classic example of this parrying process; Paredes notes a similar apotropaic defense among Mexican Americans; and Widdowson has given it the useful label "functional reversal."[19] The technique has also been in evidence as part of African Americans' defensive arsenal; here Stepin-Fetchitism is the modality of survival. In this volume, Peake shows how Navajo weavers play creatively with "red man" stereotypes; Byrne reveals how "Newfie backwardness" becomes an appropriated device for "gullibilizing" tourists; and Montaño demonstrates that along the Rio Grande, the manipulation of an alleged gastronomic "impurity" can transform stereotyping into a badge of racial solidarity.

The exchange factor also operates *within* group boundaries, as members continually reassess not only their commonalities, but also their place as individuals with multiple allegiances. The internal contestation of identity and identity markers inevitably colors the representation of "group" identity, and it is well to remember this obdurate social fact as a way of avoiding the reification of "collective consciousness." So, for example, Lewis shows how the iconic lobster reflects social fissures within Maine itself; Eliason makes an equivalent point about the Mormon pioneer, and Grider about the supposedly pan-Texan Alamo. McGregory describes a range of personal testimony styles among Philadelphia club women; Silverman recounts debate among Polish Americans, and Byrne among Newfoundlanders, over the wisdom of promoting oneself through "ludicrous" display; Peake cites a Navajo weaver who rejects his people's pictorial weavings as "not Navajo"; and MacGregor and I explore the public contestation of "unifying" symbols at, respectively, the Canadian and United States national levels. There is ample evidence that differential identity is continually refashioned, even within groups that an outsider might see as homogeneous.[20]

Another pattern by which identity borders are negotiated may be seen in the availability of *public* images for group display. The role of the mass-media in disseminating cultural stereotypes—in imposing both hegemony and homogenization—is obvious enough to any student of American history, yet the reverse process has not been widely noted. Certain essays here suggest that the creative ingestion of mainstream images by small groups may be just as forceful a feature of our social life as the more frequently discussed "cooptation" of the subversive. Mechling, for example, shows how California Boy Scouts draw for their invented traditions on the electronic gauze of prime-time TV. A similar exchange between folk and mass culture is evident in Eliason's focus on the popular history of the Mormon hierarchy; in Silverman's discussion of the public and private versions of *po dyngusie*; in Lewis's work on the ubiquitously advertised lobster; in Peake's essay on the interplay between personal creativity, tribal tradition, and market forces in Navajo weaving; and—perhaps most blatantly—in the two nation-level studies, MacGregor's discussion of the "Kamell Dung" flap in the Canadian press and my look at media-saturated yellow ribbon display. In all of these cases, group tradition is less etiolated than invigorated by contact with what Sir Hubert Parry, almost 100 years ago, called the "boundless regions of sham."[21]

This would hardly be worth mentioning had not folklorists engaged in such bitter debate for so long over the "spurious" versus the "genuine" in traditional practices.[22] Combatants in this debate's largest arena have, like Hobsbawm and Ranger, questioned the extent to which authenticity is dependent on age; in a smaller arena, scholars have addressed discordance of value as well as lineage, seeking to distinguish "natural" folklore from the mass-mediated sub-variant denounced as "fakelore." In America, the family feud between Richard Dorson and Benjamin Botkin was only the opening salvo in this wrangle.[23] A more recently placed disciplinary battle marker was the founding at Bowling Green State University of "popular culture studies"—a field that ought to articulate intimately with folklore, but that is often as marginalized from its debates as folklore itself has been marginalized within the professional disciplines of literature and anthropology.[24] Students of tourism have also entered the fray, debating to what extent the "staging of authenticity" debases or reaffirms cultural identity.[25]

The fascination of such contestations aside, it is clear that the laurels being sought here matter little to the "folk." Scholars may rail against the contaminating influence of mass culture, but few small group members seem to share their outrage. They use "spurious" and "capitalist" resources with the same delight as "genuine" and "resistant" ones in the creative reconstitution of their group expressions—and they do so without losing a sense of their own distinctiveness.

At the White Top Folk Festival in the 1920s, for example, it was musicologist Charles Seeger, not the "hillbilly" musicians, who banished steel picks from the concert stage. In the 1976 building of a Hawaiian oceangoing canoe, those most concerned about its authenticity were not the Hawaiian crewmen, but white academicians.[26] Similar patterns emerge from the studies presented here. Mechling's Boy Scouts gleefully incorporate commercial jingles and *Gilligan's Island* characters into their cherished customs and traditions. Silverman's Polish madcap, Chester Tarnowski, sees nothing amiss in "going on the Dyngus" in a clown suit. In Eliason's essay, the Mormon Church's "Days of '47" parade, creatively responding to an increasing tourist presence, is now devoted almost as much to "fun" as to sacred history. Tourism also elicits stylistic innovations from Peake's Navajo weavers and Lewis's coastal merchants, who must play with market imperatives in order to survive. In all of these cases, the folk groups, negotiating with the regions of sham, are reinventing rather than foresaking their traditional expressions.

As far as the instrumental value of traditional practice is concerned, in other words, pedigree seems to matter very little. Devotion to taxonomy should perhaps be understood, then, as an occupational disease of professional folk watchers. As Kathleen Stewart has shown in a pointed critique of nostalgia, and as Charles Keil observed in a famous exchange with Richard Dorson, hypostasizing the "folk" as somehow beyond the taint of modernity may be part of the bourgeois project of "folking them over."[27]

Shaping the Past

A final lesson of this anthology is implied in its title. Among the cultural resources available for creating a usable past is the very idea of the past itself, the idea of common heritage and shared memories. That such memories are often constructed (and therefore "spurious") no more saps them of constitutive strength than an exposé of Parson Weems's cherry tree story would invalidate it as a usable legend for American nationalism. Voltaire mused that history was the fable we agree on. But as the "we" changes, so do the fables. If Faulkner was right that the past is neither dead nor past, it follows that making histories means making them up, recasting the lines (or lyings) as we go along.

This fact has been broadly noted in the social science literature, and a handful of examples will suffice to make the point. Richard Tapper, discussing rival histories in the Middle East, suggests that the stories of common origins recounted by most groups "represent no pure line of descent," but rather a "disputed and changing ideological charter" that responds to both internal and external politics. Ana Maria Alonso shows how the burrs of the Mexican Revolution have been smoothed out by the "state cannibalism" of ruling elites. Ted Swedenburg reveals a similar sanitization in Palestinian fighters' memories. Barre Toelken shows how selective dramatization in Western family memories helps to "highlight tensions over race, land, acquisition, gender"—and, ironically, to create a sense of shared "normalcy." George Lipsitz demonstrates how working-class New Orleans blacks reimagine a collective past as "Mardi Gras Indians."[28]

The essays here that most obviously reflect the notion of history as a manipulable resource are Green's work on the legendary past of Won Hop Loong Chuan, Eliason's study of Mormonism's hagiographic trek narrative, and Grider's analysis of the Alamo legend in local politics. These three studies reveal most patently the truth of Faulkner's observation. In less obvious ways, however, the other essays in the volume also make the point. As Byrne demonstrates, the debased heritage that Canadians ascribe to "Newfieland" is richly modulated by the ritual Screech-In. Maine's class tensions, Lewis observes, grow directly out of the historical moment of the Gilded Age, when non-Mainers appropriated the state—and its supposedly "typical" food—for their own leisure. The Appalachia remembered by Williams's migrants resonates like a fictive paradise lost whose memory is talismanic against the depradations of modernity. In Peake's essay, Navajo weavers' appropriation of modern images into their traditional designs enables them to come to terms with the onus of change; they fix modernity by weaving it into the fabric. In McGregory's essay, the "origin myth" of the Lucky Ten club members enshrines their childhood home as a locus of meaning. Among the Jewish singers described by Saxe, the past is both anecdotally and aesthetically present as a landscape of loss. Silverman stresses the fact that Dyngus Day parties emerged as a direct response to the destabilization of community, to the perception that the Polish past was in danger of vanishing. In Montaño's essay, the Anglo myth of "greasers" and "chilis" is transformed through the conscious embrace of a "degraded" heritage. Even Mechling's Boy Scouts, with an understandably meager sense of history, employ images of a "golden age" in their reconstructions. By absorbing *Gilligan's Island* into their skits, they evoke the instant tradition of America-in-reruns. In this they invite comparison to Eliason's Mormons, who also take an attractive past at two removes, by recapitulating a recapitulation.

Finally, as MacGregor and I show on the national level, history plays a defining role for many North Americans—whether north or south of the St. Lawrence—in views of official institutions and public displays. White Canadians' vociferous objection to changing the eighty-year-old Mountie uniform may be seen as an attempt to stall history by denying the reality of Asian immigration. Similarly, the adoption of the yellow ribbon reframes a painful past so that, at least symbolically, historical loss is redeemed. In all of these cases, a usable past confronts, and comforts, the present.

Particularity and Resistance

In explaining why so many small countries—Ireland, Finland, Hungary—have generated more than their share of folklore collectors, Alan Dundes cites a "psychic need" for national identity—a need that acquires urgency in political crises. The lesson here—that external pressure can make folklore "matter" reactively—is as old as the discipline of folklore itself. German *Volkskunst* began with Johann Gottfried Herder, who romanticized Teutonic peasants as a corrective to Napoleonic hegemony. Slavic folklore study began as a reaction in turn to Teutonic hegemony, the Finnish *Kalevala* hurled a gauntlet at Czarist history, and the Celtic Revival crescendoed with the Easter Rising. Our own Paul Bunyan stories, as Dundes points out, were first widely read on the eve of World War I, when Fortress America, threatened by German U-boats, began nervously to recognize her world political position.[29]

Reactivity also works on the subnational level, as the history of sectionalism, from Bosnia to Quebec, makes painfully clear. Richard Maxwell Brown marks the social and psychological implications of this lesson when, in speaking of North America's recent resurgence of sectional sentiment, he calls the New Regionalism a "quest for identity" aiming to "check the nationally homogenizing tendencies of modern technology."[30] Although there is more to homogenization than technology, Brown's fundamental point is on target. The fortress may be Brother Jonathan's front yard, besieged by the cultural power of John Bull. It may be broken Dixie, reimagining the Old South in the wash of Reconstruction. Or it may be young blacks redefining themselves as African Americans by donning dashikis and other accoutrements of a heritage denied. The players change, but the marking process remains familiar.

In that process, as these essays show, the past becomes usable not for itself, or even for the present, but for the future. One wears a dashiki or a kilt not for nostalgia's sake, but to recover from amnesia, to resist homogeny, to create a "counter-memory" that can facilitate self-recovery.[31] As David Thelen observes, this means that the "truth" of a tradition is less important, instrumentally speaking, than its authenticity to us as a resource for making ourselves up.[32]

On the national level, as Hobsbawm and Ranger showed, the making up more often than not serves unifying ends. As the scale gets smaller, the opposite impulse often comes to the fore. The manipulation of traditions that we see in small-group activity—both "spurious" and "genuine"—attests not, as Durkheim might have supposed, to the power of cohesion, but rather to the fruitfulness of particularity within the wash of the whirled. And the fruit borne is as often resistive as playfully accommodating. The Navajo weaver who shrugs off the "proper" (that is, Anglo) spelling of Farmington as irrelevant, the working-class Mainers who white out the lobsters on their license plates, the Vietnam veteran's wife who reads the yellow ribbon as a peace symbol—all are repositioning themselves vis-à-vis received tradition by—as Jay Mechling observes of his "producerly" Boy Scouts— "developing their own cultural resources for resisting control."

Hence another counterintuitive truth. Folklorists, pundits, and tourists alike often consider tradition a stable entity—the "slow drip" of Robert Redfield's little community—which can only be debased or polluted by contact with outsiders. But actual communities, as distinct from ideal typed ones, do not exist, much less thrive, in hermetic bubbles. They exist in the world and of it, to their great good fortune, and as the case studies in this volume amply indicate, they can be animated rather than crushed by outside irritants—moved to rechannel the streams of their peculiar expressivities by the very forces that threaten to stop their flow. This is not to minimize the hazards of cultural homogeny, but only to highlight the benefits of creative response.

Traditional practices, then, enable us to present ourselves, in a fluctuating present, *to* ourselves, at precisely the moment when universal culture—the culture of "Cocacolonization"—seeks to palliate, and thus obliterate, stylistic distinctions. In this atmosphere, to embrace an ethnic or regional or intentional style becomes, far more than a quirk of identity, a centrifugal empowerment. In their zest for the particular, the actors here enlist "survivals" in a quest for personal communion, for collective identity—and for survival itself.

Notes

1. Eric Hobsbawm, "Introduction: Inventing Traditions," in *The Invention of Tradition*, ed. Eric Hobsbawm and Terence Ranger (Cambridge: Cambridge University Press, 1988), 1–10.

2. Michael Kammen, *Mystic Chords of Memory: The Transformation of Tradition in American Culture* (New York: Knopf, 1991), 4–5.

3. Hobsbawm, "Mass-Producing Traditions: Europe, 1870–1914," in *Invention of Tradition*, 263–307; and Hobsbawm, "Introduction," in *Invention of Tradition*, 10–11.

4. The locus classicus for the phrase "usable past" is Van Wyck Brooks's spirited attack on the "commercial tradition" in American literature: "On Creating a Usable Past," *The Dial* 64 (April 11, 1918): 337–41. Henry Steele Commager turned the phrase to quite different ends in *The Search for a Usable Past and Other Essays in Historiography* (New York: Knopf, 1967), 13–16. See also David Glassberg, *American Historical Pageantry: The Uses of Tradition in the Early Twentieth Century* (Chapel Hill: University of North Carolina Press, 1990), 5, 41.

5. Notable contributions to the debate over invention and "authenticity" include Jocelyn Linnekin, "Defining Tradition: Variations on the Hawaiian Identity," *American Ethnologist* 19 (1983): 245; Richard Handler and Jocelyn Linnekin, "Tradition, Genuine or Spurious," *Journal of American Folklore* 97 (1984): 273–90; Regina Bendix, "Folklorism: The Challenge of a Concept," *International Folklore Review* 6 (1988): 5–15; Regina Bendix, "Tourism and Cultural Displays: Inventing Traditions for Whom?" *Journal of American Folklore* 102 (1989); Allan Hanson, "The Making of the Maori: Culture Invention and Its Logic," *American Anthropologist* 91 (1989): 890–902; and Dean MacCannell, *The Tourist: A New Theory of the Leisure Class* (New York: Schocken Books, 1989), especially the chapter on "staged authenticity." For "style" and its relation to traditions, see Anya Peterson Royce, *Ethnic Identity: Strategies of Diversity* (Bloomington: Indiana University Press, 1982), 147; and Stephen Stern and John Allan Cicala, eds., *Creative Ethnicity: Symbols and Strategies of Contemporary Ethnic Life* (Logan: Utah State University Press, 1991), xiv.

6. Simon Bronner, ed., *Creativity and Tradition in Folklore: New Directions* (Logan: Utah State University Press, 1992), 2–3. For "bricolage," see Claude Lévi-Strauss, *The Savage Mind* (Chicago: University of Chicago Press, 1966), 16–36.

7. See Elizabeth Mathias, "The Italian-American Funeral: Persistence through Change," *Western Folklore* 33 (1974): 35–50; Robert Teske, "Living Room Furnishings, Ethnic Identity, and Acculturation among Greek Philadelphians," *New York Folklore* 5 (1979): 21–32; Andrew Cincura, "Slovak and Ruthenian Easter Eggs in America: The Impact of Culture Contact on Immigrant Art and Culture," *Journal of Popular Culture* 4 (1970): 155–93; Jack Santino, "Miles of Smiles, Years of Struggle: The Negotiation of Black Occupational Identity through Personal Experience Narrative," *Journal of American Folklore* 96 (1983): 393–412; and Richard R. Flores, "The *Corrido* and the Emergence of Texas-Mexican Social Identity," *Journal of American Folklore* 105 (1992): 166–82.

8. For food, see Linda Keller Brown and Kay Mussell, eds., *Ethnic and Regional Foodways in the United States: The Performance of Group Identity* (Knoxville: University of Tennessee Press, 1984); Theodore and Lin Humphrey, eds., *"We Gather Together": Food and Festival in American Life* (Ann Arbor: UMI Research Press, 1988); and Charles Camp, *American Foodways: What, When, Why, and How We Eat in America* (Little Rock, Ark.: August House, 1989). For festivals, see Victor Turner, ed., *Celebration: Studies in Festivity and Ritual* (Washington, D.C.: Smithsonian Institution Press, 1982). For regional cultures, see Barbara Allen and Thomas Schlereth, *Sense of Place: American Regional Cultures* (Lexington: University Press of Kentucky, 1990). Ethnic "strategies" are discussed in Stern and Cicala, *Creative Ethnicity*. For "organizational ethnography," see Michael Owen Jones, Michael Dane Moore, and Richard Christopher Snyder, eds., *Inside Organizations: Understanding the Human Dimension* (Newbury Park, Calif.: Sage Publications, 1988). For groups and genres, see Elliot Oring, ed., *Folk Groups and Folklore Genres: An Introduction* (Logan: Utah State University Press, 1986) and the companion volume *Folk Groups and Folklore Genres: A Reader* (Logan: Utah State University Press, 1989).

9. Frederick Barth, ed., *Ethnic Groups and Boundaries: The Social Organization of Culture Difference* (Boston: Little, Brown, 1969). See especially Barth's "Introduction," 9–38. For useful applications of his boundary maintenance thesis, see Richard N. Adams, "Internal and External Ethnicities, with Special Reference to Central America," *Texas Papers on Latin America*, Paper No. 89–03 (University of Texas Institute of Latin American Studies, 1989); Dan R. Aronson, "Ethnicity as a Cultural System: An Introductory Essay," in *Ethnicity*

in the Americas, ed. Frances Henry (The Hague/Paris: Mouton, 1976), 9–19; Daniel Bell, "Ethnicity and Social Change," in *Ethnicity: Theory and Experience,* ed. Nathan Glazer and Daniel P. Moynihan (Cambridge: Harvard University Press, 1975), 141–75; George De Vos, "Ethnic Pluralism: Conflict and Accommodation," in *Ethnic Identity: Cultural Continuities and Change,* ed. George De Vos and Lola Romanucci-Ross (Palo Alto, Calif.: Mayfield Publishing Company, 1975), 5–41; and Edward Spicer, "Persistent Cultural Systems," *Science* 174 (1971): 795–800. The phrase "conversation of images" is from Milton Singer, *When a Great Tradition Modernizes* (New York: Praeger, 1972), 12. See also Stern and Cicala, *Creative Ethnicity,* xii.

10. Américo Paredes and Richard Bauman, ed., *Toward New Perspectives in Folklore* (Austin: University of Texas Press, 1972). In this volume, and in much of the performance-oriented folklorists' subsequent work, the general influence of Américo Paredes is inestimable. Bauman, crediting his coeditor with "foundational importance," has recently cited Paredes's 1964 essay "Some Aspects of Folk Poetry" as "a pioneering work linking form explicitly to performance." See Américo Paredes, *Folklore and Culture on the Texas-Mexican Border* (Austin: Center for Mexican American Studies, 1993), xx. The anthology includes the "Folk Poetry" paper as well as Bauman's appreciative and insightful introduction. Barre Toelken's popular textbook is *The Dynamics of Folklore* (Boston: Houghton Mifflin, 1979). For an excellent essay on the historical context of performance-oriented studies, see Simon J. Bronner, *American Folklore Studies: An Intellectual History* (Lawrence: University Press of Kansas, 1986), chapter 4, "Folklore in an Era of Communication," 94–129. The "young Turks" tag appeared in Richard Dorson, *Folklore and Folklife: An Introduction* (Chicago: Chicago University Press, 1972).

11. Stern and Cicala, *Creative Ethnicity,* xiv; Hobsbawm, "Introduction," 11.

12. Max Weber, "Ethnic Groups," in *Economy and Society: An Outline of Interpretive Society,* ed. Guenther Roth and Claus Wittich (Berkeley: University of California Press, 1978), 388.

13. Ibid., 390.

14. Hobsbawm, "Mass-Producing Traditions," 287–90.

15. Emile Durkheim, *The Elementary Forms of the Religious Life* (New York: Free Press, 1965), 262–65.

16. Barth, "Introduction," 29.

17. Steven Feld, "From Schizophonia to Schismogenesis," in *Music Grooves,* by Steven Feld and Charles Keil (Chicago: University of Chicago Press, 1992).

18. For a discussion of "producerly" consumer behavior, see John Fiske, *Understanding Popular Culture* (Boston: Unwin Hyman, 1989).

19. See Royce, *Ethnic Identity,* 151; Américo Paredes, "On Ethnographic Work among Minority Groups: A Folklorist's Perspective," *New Scholar* 6 (1977): 1–32; and J. D. A. Widdowson, "Language, Tradition, and Social Control: Blason Populaire and Social Control," in *Language, Culture, and Tradition,* ed. A. E. Green and J. D. A. Widdowson (Sheffield: Centre for English Cultural Traditions and Language, 1981).

20. For the classic definition of differential identity, see Richard Bauman, "Differential Identity and the Social Base of Folklore," in *New Perspectives,* ed. Paredes and Bauman, 31–41.

21. Sir Hubert Parry, Editor's address, *Journal of the Folk Song Society* 1 (1899): 1.

22. Handler and Linnekin, "Tradition, Genuine or Spurious," 273–90.

23. The American battle over fakelore began in 1950, when Richard Dorson and James Stevens, author of a Paul Bunyan book, locked horns in the pages of the *American Mercury.* For Dorson's view of the case, and of Botkin, see Richard Dorson, "Folklore, Academe, and the Marketplace," in *Folklore and Fakelore: Essays toward a Discipline of Folk Studies* (Cambridge: Harvard University Press, 1976), 4–8. For an excellent report from the European front, see Bendix, "Folklorism."

24. For folklore's status as the problem child of literature and anthropology, see Rosemary Zumwalt, *American Folklore Scholarship: A Dialogue of Dissent* (Bloomington: Indiana University Press, 1988).

25. See MacCannell, *The Tourist,* and Bendix, "Tourism and Cultural Displays."

26. Linnekin, "Defining Tradition," 245.

27. See Kathleen Stewart, "Nostalgia—A Polemic," *Cultural Anthropology* 3 (1988): 227–41; Richard Dorson, "We All Need the Folk," *Journal of the Folklore Institute* 15 (1978): 267–69; Charles Keil, "Who Needs the Folk?," *Journal of the Folklore Institute* 15 (1978): 263–66; and Keil's rejoinder to Dorson's rejoinder, "Comment: The Concept of the Folk," *Journal of the Folklore Institute* 16 (1979): 209–10.

28. Richard Tapper, "Ethnic Identities and Social Categories in Iran and Afghanistan," in *History and Ethnicity,* ed. Elizabeth Tonkin, Maryon McDonald, and Malcolm Chapman (London: Routledge, 1989),

232–46; Ana Maria Alonso, "The Effects of Truth: Re-Presentations of the Past and the Imagining of Community," *Journal of Historical Sociology* 1 (1988): 33–57; Ted Swedenburg, "The Palestinian Peasant as Signifier," *Anthropological Quarterly* 63 (1990): 18–30; Barre Toelken, "Folklore and Reality in the American West," in *Sense of Place*, by Allen and Schlereth, 14–27; George Lipsitz, "Mardi Gras Indians: Carnival and Counter-Narrative in Black New Orleans," in *Time Passages: Collective Memory and American Popular Culture* (Minneapolis: University of Minnesota Press, 1990), 233–56.

29. Alan Dundes, "The Fabrication of Fakelore," in *Folklore Matters* (Knoxville: University of Tennessee Press, 1989), 50–51.

30. Richard Maxwell Brown, "The New Regionalism in America, 1970–1981," in *Regionalism and the Pacific Northwest*, ed. William Robbins, Robert Frank, and Richard Ross (Corvallis: Oregon State University Press, 1983), 61.

31. George Lipsitz, "History, Myth, and Counter-Memory: Narrative and Desire in Popular Novels," in *Time Passages*, 211–31.

32. David Thelen, "Memory and American History," *Journal of American History* 75 (1989): 1123.

Part I

Marking the "Tribal"

The people whose expressive practices are examined in this section are what conventional sociology refers to as "ethnics." Given the original meaning of *ethnos* as "tribe" or "nation"—meaning those beyond the pale of the Greek city-states—the term should be viewed as inherently marginalizing. It conveys the sense of ethnicity as an alienating characteristic, a colorful trait that applies to *other* people—especially those of a quaint or clannish nature.

In spite of, or perhaps because of, this marginalizing tendency, "ethnic" is a common label in pluralistic North America. Quite in line with the Greek usage, it applies most forcefully to those recent immigrants who have yet to be acculturated into the mainstream and whose practices still reflect their "tribal" conventions. In using the label, one risks both imprecision and the bias that is ironically known as ethnocentrism. Yet its heuristic value as a sociological marker is undeniable. Contemporary "ethnics" themselves recognize this readily. The slang of hyphenated America provides ample evidence that the imperfectly assimilated are not clamoring to be melted down. Proof of that is abundant in self-ascriptions. Consider only African American "brother" and "sister," Chicano *raza*, Italian American *paesano*, Jewish *Landsmann* and "member of the tribe."

Nancy Peake's analysis of a Navajo weaving tradition shows how, in the establishment of "tribal" markers, personal and even idiosyncratic creativity can radically modify a group aesthetic. Her discussion

21

of the relatively little-known "pictorial" style shows weavers practicing their art not hermetically but in active exchange with other peoples, including Anglo traders. The study forces us to reconsider the depiction of Native American art—and for that matter Native American culture—as the self-absorbed productions of "tribals in a bottle." It is an excellent example of how expressive traditions are manipulated by people whose identities are continually remade at cultural borders.

An actual physical, as well as a cultural, border informs Mario Montaño's study of Chicano foodways. Montaño's analysis of the "Anglified" *fajita* is a telling example of what Marcus Raskin once called the "packaging of marginality"—the sanitization and adoption by a mainstream culture of what started out as symbolic opposition. It is important to note that once this process has begun, the original "owners" of the symbol typically reinscribe the field. In this case Mexican Americans of the Rio Grande Valley, having seen a "junk" food reinvented as an upscale delicacy, turn to culinary variants that are less amenable to sanitization—the blood and organ meats that Anglos find unpalatable.

There is class as well as border politics involved in this dynamic, and for that reason it is useful to compare Montaño's essay with George Lewis's study of the lobster in Part III. In both instances, a despised food category becomes a register of prestige—both "straight" prestige and what sociolinguists call "covert" prestige—as social competitors contest the valence of tradition. Thus "tribal" markers, no less than regional ones, are inevitably engaged with the processes of outside hegemony. This point, which provides the thread of Montaño's argument, is revisited in the nation-level essays that close this volume.

In Deborah Silverman's assessment of Dyngus Day activities, we see "tribal" traditions cast in a somewhat different light. By comparing a very personalized and a more public reinvention of this old Polish celebration, Silverman highlights the flexibility of cultural pluralism and reveals the potential saliency of *internal* struggles over expressive forms that an outsider may see as "fixed." The line between "them" and "us," in other words, is not the only border that revivers of usable pasts must negotiate. As this essay makes clear, insiders who deride a revived tradition may invest as much in its meaning as those who defend it. I make a related point in my chapter on yellow ribbons.

The interplay between outside and inside is also relevant in the essays by Jerrilyn McGregory and Joel Saxe. Here the members of self-organized "friendship societies" gather periodically to avow community. United as much by shared histories as by ethnicity, the African American women of McGregory's Lucky Ten club and the Yiddish-speaking elders of Saxe's Ocean Drive circle sustain their sense of continuity through expressive forms that, in McGregory's phrase, "reconcile the present with the past." While these forms are traditional in the narrow sense—the passed down practices of testimony and song-sharing—they are also reactive responses to the societal pressures of straightened economic circumstances and advancing age.

Both groups, as a result, utilize expression as a way of asserting not only text, but context, that is, sociability. They recall Durkheim's often noted observation that the original "object" of worship may have been community itself, that primordial reverence for the social that becomes religion. Given the recent troubled history of black-Jewish relations, it is heartening to consider these essays together. They hint at a remarkable parity in the modalities of communion— a parity that may remind us, in these ethnically charged times, that traditional pariahs may have more in common than they suppose.

CHAPTER I

Through Navajo Eyes: Pictorial Weavings from Spider Woman's Loom

Nancy Peake

What kind of artistic tradition would produce a textile that pictured headless cows with "heartlines," cows with exploding heads, and cows sporting mysterious elongated bars in the center of their bodies? (See Figure 1.) What kind of person would spend hours sitting at an upright loom carefully weaving such a puzzling, nontraditional design? What was happening in the weaver's world that would make these half dozen isolated, strange looking cows meaningful to the woman who created them?

This blanket has none of the diagnostic traits that have come to be associated with Navajo weaving. It does not display the classic bold stripes of the blankets worn by Indian chiefs in the paintings of George Catlin and Karl Bodmer. It bears no resemblance to the familiar "Indian" rug style introduced by Arizona trader Juan Lorenzo Hubbell at the turn of the century, with its central design neatly framed by a double border, all woven in black, grey, white, and Ganado red. Nor does it include any of the Orient-inspired "Indian" motifs popularized by trader J. B. Moore in the early 1900s. This weaving is a far cry from the stereotypical icon that has come to symbolize the Navajo culture for outsiders and Navajos alike. In fact,

Figure 1. *Navajo pictorial.* This weaving of six cows was produced by a Navajo woman in the 1870s, shortly after her people had endured the rigors of the Long Walk. Steven Cleves Weber Collection. Photo courtesy of David Cook/ Fine American Art.

when two young Navajo weavers examined it about a century after it was produced, their immediate reaction was disbelief: "That isn't Navajo."[1]

These weavers, however, were mistaken. This unusual textile was created by a Navajo woman in the 1870s—a particularly traumatic decade for her people. In the winter of 1864, after a relentless pursuit by the U.S. Army, the beleaguered Navajos were driven from their ancestral homeland to the Bosque Redondo reservation in eastern New Mexico. After a four-year incarceration under deplorable, near starving conditions, the Navajos signed a treaty and were allowed to make the Long Walk "home" to a newly created reservation, only one-tenth the size of their former lands. The weaver of this unusual artifact would have been one of those survivors who returned to find burned out hogans and ravaged fields and a world that was forever changed. Her weaving bears the imprint of that time. But who, other than her contemporaries, experiencing the same painful cultural upheavals, could possibly understand its woven message?

These early paintings in wool are in fact cultural tapestries reflecting the reactions and transformation of a people in the face of confrontation and contact. The subject matter of these strange woven pictures is derived from elements in the artists' everyday lives, as is the custom with "folk" art the world over. Hence, these old representational weavings—though far removed from the stereotypical prototypes fostered by the early cultural historians—are true examples of a Native American folk form. They embody a tradition that has evolved over the years into what the trade now identifies as "pictorials." This essay will focus on pre-1940s representative weavings in an attempt to discover the cultural roots of the pictorial and to determine its place within the Navajo weaving tradition as it is perceived today.[2]

Descriptive labels pinned on the "creative curiosities" and "quaint cartoons" called pictorials have run the gamut from "magic," "primitive," "documentary," and "maverick" to "hilarious." Loaded with "personality" and "extremely eccentric and unique," the problematic pictorials have been praised for their "absence of predictability" and their "experimentation with realism" while at the same time being damned as "the stepchild of Navajo weaving."[3] Yet the difficulties in placing these old weavings into neat categories may lie not in the pictorials themselves, but in the need to define and classify all manifestations of Indian art in terms understandable to Anglo eyes. Clifford Geertz cautions about the almost universal tendency of the European world to "respond to exotic arts with an ethnocentric sentimentalism in the absence of the knowledge of what those arts are about or an understanding of the culture out of which they come."[4]

The proliferation of ambiguous and conflicting reactions to the Navajo pictorial has placed it in the center of an ongoing debate between merchants, art historians, and the consumer/collector: Folk art? Or tourist art? Is the Navajo pictorial of today representative of an evolving tradition, periodically adapting to changing social circumstances and the individual needs of the weaver? Or is it the product of a tradition reinvented by the white man to satisfy the demands of myth-conscious consumers?

My argument here is that the older figurative weavings—so personal and so distinct from the universally recognized, traditional "Navajo rug"—may best be understood as examples of what Nelson Graburn refers to as an "art of acculturation."[5] These early pictorials provide what Gary Witherspoon calls "an objective representation, though obtuse [*sic*], of what other people guarding other sheep in other valleys have said about the world."[6] The pictorials were cross-cultural communiqués or woven documentaries—glimpses of the world as seen through Navajo eyes or, in other words, stories that the People told about themselves. They were in no way less "authentic" than the familiar geometrics. Joe Ben Wheat, a renowned scholar of Navajo textiles, suggests that "pictorial weavers have merely ventured beyond the standard designs to depict something that intrigued or amused them, or to create a picture expressive of the life around them."[7]

Pictorials: Inventing a Tradition

Just when did the first such picture take form in the wefts of the Navajo tapestry? Wheat is the first to say, "No one knows . . . but it was long ago."[8] He is right to acknowledge the uncertainty. Museum curators, anthropologists, art historians, and Indian traders all express varying opinions as to the time and circumstance of the earliest pictorials.

Kit Carson claims he saw a Navajo blanket "woven in flowers with much taste" on a trading expedition as early as 1837.[9] Marian Rodee, curator of New Mexico's Maxwell Museum of Anthropology and author of several works on Navajo weaving, is skeptical of the mountain man's report, wondering if he was "even aware of the differences between geometric and pictorial rugs, or if he would even know if it were a Navajo blanket or some other kind.'"[10] Charles Amsden, author of the first definitive study of Navajo weaving, thinks it "doubtful if any weaver ever attempted to draw a picture or tell a story upon her loom until after the American conquest [in 1846]."[11] That same year an American soldier visited a priest at Santo Domingo Pueblo and wrote about "a couch in his reverence's parlor covered with a white Navajo blanket worked in richly colored flowers."[12] But this account is challenged by U.S. Hollister, who suggests in a 1903 study that these flowers "had been embroidered . . . by Mexican women."[13] A post-conquest U.S. cavalryman writes about a blanket purchased in 1865 that had a horse in each corner and a man with a spear in the center.[14] And Walter Kennedy, an Indian trader for fifty-three years who actively encouraged pictorial weaving at his Dennehotso Trading Post in Arizona, insists that pictorials were "definitely not the white man's idea; they've been Navajo from the beginning of time."[15]

But if the historical evidence regarding the earliest pictorials is debatable, there is no argument about the provenience of the oldest pictorial weaving in collection. It is a so-called chief blanket (the common label for the striped blankets depicted in nineteenth-century paintings of Plains Indians) last worn by the Cheyenne chief White Antelope. In 1864, as co-leader of an official peace party summoned by the Colorado governor, White Antelope had the misfortune to be camped with his people at Sand Creek when the Reverend John M. Chivington, colonel of the Colorado volunteers, led his troops in a vicious attack upon the unsuspecting Cheyennes. Witnesses recalled, "White Antelope refused to run. He stood in front of his lodge, folded his arms, and sang his death song . . . until he was cut down by bullets and died."[16] The blanket they took from his body after the massacre was Navajo—not surprising as Navajo blankets were prized trade items, proudly worn by Plains Indians who could "afford" them. What *was* surprising was that this particular blanket was a riot of color, showing a combination of geometric and serrate patterning, with a central Saltillo-like diamond enclosing a cross motif, and—almost hidden amongst the details of the patterned tapestry—*four tiny red ducks*. This tragic souvenir is now the property of the School of American Research in Santa Fe. The historic weaving has been beautifully restored, which is unfortunate considering the story it has to tell.[17]

Although it is difficult to find evidence that figurative weavings were created much before the middle of the nineteenth century, the roots of the Navajo pictorial tradition are deep. Naturalistic forms of animals and plants appeared on Navajo painted pottery as early as the late seventeenth century. Navajo rock art from the same period and on through the early nineteenth century depicts everything from cosmic symbols and supernatural beings to Spanish soldiers on horseback.[18] The Navajos also began ritualistic sandpainting in the seventeenth century apparently influenced by practices of their Pueblo neighbors,[19] and the animals depicted therein bear an amazing similarity to animals in pictorial weavings of later years. Another possible influence was Plains Indian art. On their many forays into Plains Indian territory on trading expeditions, the acquisitive Navajo would certainly have been exposed to, and quite possibly influenced by, the representational hide paintings, tipis, and shields of Plains warriors, examples of their long-standing tradition of recording events, symbols, and visionary impressions on *their* cultural canvas, the buffalo skin.

The Navajos, in the latter half of the nineteenth century, suffered personal, tribal, and cultural tragedies at the hand of the white man. Rebuilding their lives after the destructive incarceration at Bosque Redondo, weavers once again were drawn to the social and economic security of the loom. Rebelling against the loss of political and economic independence, but with an inner confidence and "the freedom to see with their own eyes," they began to interpret the barrage of foreign images that flooded their newborn world.[20] Perhaps the women were also responding to a private need to invent a new tradition that would accommodate the traumatic upheavals of the times.

Using her loom and the trader's Germantown yarns and bright new aniline dyes,[21] the Navajo weaver depicted an incredible variety of naturalistic motifs, from scenes of daily activities around her family's hogan, to bird-bedecked celebrations of corn, to patriotic themes dear to the hearts of the invading white man. Subject matter inspired by her forced contact with the Americans included red, white, and blue "flags" of various shapes and descriptions, cartoon-like railroad trains, and labels from canned goods found on the shelves of the nearest trading post. By demonstrating the People's proclivity for transforming borrowed ideas into distinctly Navajo creations, a new generation of weavers in the late 1880s began turning out some of the "wildest blankets ever made."[22] The "tradition" of pictorial weaving flowered on the newly created reservation, years before the invasion of curio-conscious tourists.

Perhaps then, this expressive period of Navajo weaving, a time of extreme social upheaval and readjustment, was in fact a search for and exploration of cultural roots, rather than what has been referred to as the "dark age of weaving."[23] The old market, the wealthy Plains Indians, had dried up (with the majority relocated onto reservations after the Indian Wars of the 1860s and 1870s); and the Navajos themselves were now wearing the factory-made Pendleton blankets garnered in trade from Anglo merchants.[24] The invention of an identifiable pictorial tradition in such turbulent times was quite natural, given the circumstances, and the development clearly supports Eric Hobsbawm's premise that tradition invention occurs most frequently "when a rapid transformation of society weakens or destroys the social patterns for which 'old' traditions had been designed, producing new ones to which they were not applicable, or when such old traditions and their institutional carriers and promulgators no longer prove sufficiently adaptable and flexible, or are otherwise eliminated. In short, when there are sufficiently large and rapid changes on the demand or the supply side."[25]

The need of the weaver to embed individual interpretations of her changing world into the multicolored fibers of her blanket/rug may best be understood through the expressive, multidimensional boundaries of the world of folk art—a community's endeavors in response to a challenge to its traditional way of life, or what folklorist Henry

Glassie refers to as "rooted creativity."[26] These pre-1900s "folkloric" pictorials are, in fact, a collective communication born out of the experience of life. The artists were undoubtedly women in small Navajo communities that could fit folklorist John Michael Vlach's description of societies "where expressive traditions [were] taught informally . . . by example and perpetuated from generation to generation with some accommodations to changes that arise from either personal desires or influence of externally introduced fashions. The representative art of such societies is not created by deviants, but by normal, intelligent, well-adjusted citizens who care deeply about their history and identity."[27] It should have come as no surprise, then, that the noisy, smoke-spewing, black locomotive, barreling its way across the silent Navajo grazing lands, began to appear in the same weavings with sheep and birds or that the orderly bands of the classic chief blankets began to give way to more chaotic, incongruous visual images—to representations of the alien world that was beginning to bombard the once predictable Navajoland. The new weavings then, produced on the same looms by the same weavers' hands, not only constituted a new tradition, but "despite their novel features, reinforced the familiar local traditions."[28] As a result, these early transitional, yet traditional, pictorials often seem to "transcend Navajo-ness."[29]

Yet, rather than diminish the characteristic honesty and directness of a long-standing tribal tradition, this stylistic evolution of the blanket at the end of the nineteenth century emphasized the potential versatility of a tradition that "possessed a force beyond that customary for a single piece of apparel. . . . Blankets represented both the tribe and the individual in a special way—not in a simple one-to-one symbolic relationship—but rather as a dynamic expression of the self."[30]

Anglo Traders Redefine "Indian Tradition"

The commercial realities of the marketplace often dictate that the artists in any given folk society are "honored more for the roles they play than for their personal inventiveness."[31] This was certainly the case with Navajo weavers. Despite their remote locations on the vast

Navajo reservation at the turn of the century, traders on their isolated posts soon realized the profit potential in selling their customers' traditional native arts to outsiders—traditional arts, in their opinion, being those that existed as a part of the cultural complex *before* the disruptive influences of prolonged outside contact.[32] Hence, they actively discouraged the new pictorial expressions and favored "old style" weavings, which they felt recreated the "true" Indian blanket; at the same time, they introduced new designs that seemed to enhance the mythical view of the red man. Disregarding the important dimension of tradition as an "art that still performs the same functions and has the same meanings for the people who created it as it had had in past generations,"[33] these traders catered to the demands of the buying public by instigating a major change in *function* and thereby meaning. Weavers no longer produced "wearing blankets." Instead, they wove "rugs" to decorate the parlor floors of Anglos back East. And their weavings now expressed "the Indian's idea of the trader's idea of what the White Man thought was Indian design!"[34]

The trader, while offering the Indians alien goods in exchange for prescribed items of their material culture, was at the same time reinventing a tradition to sell to the image-conscious white man, thus setting the stage for a new era in Navajo-Anglo relations—one of cross-cultural consumption. Receptive weavers, with their traditional craft becoming more and more the mainstay of their family's livelihood, began responding to the powerful agent of change, customer preference. The late Kate Peck Kent, an expert on Native American textiles, pointed out that this response was nothing new. "There has never been a time in the long history of Navajo weaving when the artists were not aware of the needs of the marketplace nor failed to modify their work to some extent to suit the tastes of potential buyers. . . . This flexibility inevitably changed the appearance of Navajo textiles."[35]

The flexibility was also in a sense inherent in Navajo weaving practice. Because weaving was not an ancient art among the Navajo (as it was, for example, among the Pueblo Indians), their weavers were not bound by traditional constraints. Thus, receptive to new ideas presented through cultural contact and yet following her own aesthetic, the creative Navajo commonly drew upon and developed designs that appealed to her, including pictorial images she found pleasing—whether she found them decorating canned goods on the trader's shelves or chugging along newly laid railroad tracks across her native homeland.

In an apparent lack of understanding of such artistic independence, purists John Sloan and Oliver LaFarge later described the resulting "barbarian market" in their catalog for the 1931 Exposition of American Indian Tribal Art as one comprised of "curio-minded White Men . . . who viewed the Indian himself as a curio." They expressed extreme displeasure with the "deteriorating pressures" which were then "forcing the traditional Indian artists to produce wretched souvenirs."[36] Although they acknowledged the "versatile, progressive" Navajo as a people who have "always borrowed freely" and professed that the blanket "which results from this assemblage is not only Indian, but deeply expressive of Navajo character," Sloan and LaFarge left no room for innovation or further borrowing on the part of the so-called progressive weaver. Apparently they preferred that the Navajo blanket freeze in time as "the arrangement and repetition of a few elements either in stripes or around a centre . . . with that extraordinary sense of spacing which is innate in the American Indian." They allowed no room for the weaver's personal expressions: "No blankets portraying arrows, bows, thunderbirds, swastikas, animals or whatnot are really Navajo, no matter who wove them."[37]

Fifty years later, Edwin L. Wade and Rennard Strickland, respected scholars of Native American art, would have chided Sloan and LaFarge for failing to see that such innovations were merely part of a natural growth process, examples of "historic evolution consistent with the evolving world of the American Indian." They firmly believe that to demand contemporary artists to depict "ancient" themes or duplicate prescribed traditions not only fails to perpetuate Indian art, "but encourages mass production of caricature and illustration devoid of personal commitment, strength and understanding."[38]

Never a static art form, Navajo weaving loses none of its "traditionality" just because it ceases to live in the past. Henry Glassie explored the development of figurative representation in folk art as a response to outside contact. His work with Pueblo pottery and Hopi kachinas has prompted this conclusion: "There is a pattern in the reaction. When a tradition is figurative, it becomes more naturalistic upon contact. When a tradition lacks figures, they are added . . . and when a tradition's figurative dimension is slight, it is expanded."[39] He might just as well have been tracing the life story of the Navajo pictorial. Indeed, the weaver who denies the urge to express herself while seated at her grandmother's loom fails to make a statement, falls short of the buyer's quest for true authenticity, and produces consumer-oriented stereotypes instead of traditional Navajo "folk" art.

This importance of personal expression was noted several decades ago by Navajo weaver Francisco Mucho, who, after she admitted to an anthropologist that she wove primarily to make a living, added, "Once you get interested in it, I don't know why it is, you just get the most fun out of weaving."[40] Pictorial weavings *are* fun. They are unpredictable. And depending upon the technical skills of the individual weaver, anything is possible. The very process of their creation, in the truest expression of folk art performance, revolves around cultural and personal meanings. The artist's personality is the dominant force behind the human document emerging on her loom. Despite the cold shoulder given these dynamic expressions by the early twentieth-century traders, some women, driven to redefine their world upon their looms, continued to weave pictorials—amounting to about one percent of the total Navajo textile production from the 1880s to today.[41]

That minuscule proportion did not go totally unrecognized. As early as the turn of the century, some collectors sensed the unusual qualities of the pictorials and sought out these "unsalable" blankets. William Randolph Hearst, for example, was an avid Navajo rug collector, buying the bulk of his weavings from Herman Schweizer, manager for the Fred Harvey Company Indian Department. In 1915, when the Harvey/Hubbell-style Navajo rug had virtually become the nationally accepted image, Hearst wrote the following to Schweizer: "Of course, you know I have so many Indian things now that I only want the finest and rarest pieces. I do not mean that that is always the most expensive pieces, but those that have some unique character. . . . In addition to sending me some fine blankets you might send me some quaint and curious ones with odd designs or figures of men or animals. These add variety to a collection although they may not be of themselves particularly valuable."[42]

Somewhat ironic is the fact that some of the major collectors of the spurned pictorials over the years have been the traders themselves. Hardened to the demands of the image-conscious marketplace, these profit-oriented businessmen must have read something between the wefts of the occasional pictorials that crossed their countertops or found in them something "that tickled their fancy."[43] In recent years there have been traders in particular parts of the reservation who, perhaps recognizing the growing acceptance of "individualism" in Native American arts, actively encourage their weavers to bring them pictorial tapestries—representations other than the "symbolic" yei, yeibichai, and sandpainting rugs developed around 1930—and are willing to pay top dollar for them.[44]

Inspiration for the pictorials is as diverse as the weavings themselves—from the angelic iconography of an Arbuckle coffee can to Squaw Dance scenes to strange "birds" flying high over the hogan and emerging from the wool as early twentieth-century biplanes to a trader's request for a customized business advertisement. Trader Gilbert Maxwell tells of ordering one such ad for his business in New Mexico. When he asked the weaver why the completed rug said "Framington" instead of "Farmington," she responded, "What's the difference? It's all the same." The artist knew that "the *real* Farmington was *Totah*, 'where the waters meet,' and that is what counts. The other was just another white man's word."[45] Such a contemporary made-for-sale pictorial, totally devoid of personal meaning for the weaver herself, might typify the evolving trend from the early "folk-inspired" pictorial to those produced for the commercial market today.

Hidden Cultural Messages in the Old Pictorials

Representing all the ambiguities inherent in a traditional folk art produced *by* the people and *for* the people is a "birthing blanket," dated around 1880–1890, that was purchased from a Santo

Domingo medicine man nearly a century after its creation. (See Figure 2.) Cryptic black figures woven within a white field include a "half man," two pregnant women, one with an empty rectangle in her belly, four animals (a cow, a horse, a lion, and a bird, all full-bellied and apparently pregnant), "storm motifs," and a woman with arms upraised in "pain or ecstasy." All the figures are grouped in orderly fashion around a center "storm" symbol.

Viewing this esoteric weaving as "an early anchor to some other reality," Andrew Nagen, a prominent collector/dealer of old Navajo textiles, reports that the medicine man who sold him the rug said it would have been tied over the hogan door when the woman inside was having difficulty during childbirth.[46] But, given its obvious obscurities, the enigmatic weaving could clearly have other interpretations. Marian Rodee, Maxwell Museum curator, is emphatic that there was "no such thing as a birthing blanket," citing the Navajo belief that it is "bad luck for a pregnant woman to see a horned animal" (such as the cow on the blanket); but she does acknowledge that the woman with the short skirt is "how the Navajos traditionally depict Changing Woman," the mythic figure who created the first four Navajo clans from her own skin.[47] Mark Winter, also a dealer/collector of early Navajo textiles, tells of seeing a similar blanket in an institution and asserts that it was not used during difficult births, but when women were having trouble *getting* pregnant. "The blanket was placed between the man and woman to separate the lovers for a while, creating a tension and excitement" to enhance the possibility of conception.[48] What was the unknown weaver's intent? We will never know. The meaning will forever remain locked within the hand-spun warp and weft, well inside the boundaries of the Navajo world and safe from the inquisitive eyes of the white man.

These puzzling woven pictures often reflect the weaver's adeptness at cultural borrowing. Navajo fascination with the idiosyncrasies of their Native American neighbors has often manifested itself in the pictorial, and as unlikely a group of subjects as Zuni mudheads (Pueblo Indian clowns) have been seen climbing out of kivas woven on the Navajo loom. (See Figure 3.) Although none of its figurative elements can be traced to Navajo roots, this eclectic weaving possesses all the necessary characteristics of the multifaceted, traditional

Figure 2. *Blanket* (ca. 1880-1900). Because it contains several images of pregnancy, some authorities see this pictorial as a "birthing blanket." There is no consensus, however, on its use or meaning. Steven Cleves Weber Collection. Photo courtesy of David Cook/ Fine American Art.

pictorial. The images may be borrowed, but the *synthesis* is wholly and perfectly Navajo.

Yet another pervasive characteristic of Navajo pictorial weaving, and one held in common with traditional folk art throughout the world, is the profound sense of humor, sometimes blatant and sometimes abstruse, that is woven into representational rugs. Hardly subtle is the expressive, doormat-sized weaving, "Go TO hELL." Often seemingly woven with tongue in cheek, these rugs prove that the Navajos are just as apt to poke fun at themselves as at the outside world through a masterful manipulation of Indian stereotypes. Consider the message intended by the graphic weaving, "God Bless Cowboys and Indians." There is no lack of warbonnetted warriors, some aptly labeled "chief," or depictions of Indian paraphernalia including feathers, thunderbirds, bows, and arrows—even an arrow and arrow point with the words "ARROW + HEAD."[49] There may be both personal and cultural symbolism present, as with the weaver who included a bow and arrow in her rug "because she was thinking about her brothers going hunting—although of course they were using modern weapons."[50] But there may also be a more serious and purposeful aspect to the humor, one rooted in the Navajo's reactions to forced cultural contact. Ethnologist Keith Basso believes that laughter should be regarded as "the denial of cultural automation and the affirmation of a complex human freedom to follow, change, or create culture. . . . There may be no highly conscious intellectual or emotional processes in laughter. But [they] are present and represent positive and creative human qualities."[51] This special kind of humor belongs to the phenomenon of boundary maintenance, "the process by which a system limits participation in its culture . . . in order to protect its identity . . . [using] devices by which knowledge of customs and values is restricted to the group and shielded from any alien influence."[52]

Arts reflecting this characteristic frequently perform dual functions for the society they represent: they both protect and reinforce cultural identity. By presenting erroneous stereotypes or deliberately misplacing the emphasis within the visual images it chooses to expose to the outside world (for example, the feathered Indian blatantly labeled "chief"), a cultural group is able to protect its true values from

Figure 3. *Zuni mudheads* (ca. 1915-25). An example of Navajo creative adaptation, this textile depicts a pair of Pueblo clowns. Although the motif is borrowed, the weaving and the synthesis are undeniably Navajo. Bert and Brenda Lazar Collection. Photo by Martha Lochert.

further encroachment by outsiders. On the other hand, because "all groups need symbols of their external and internal boundaries," the weavers, through an art made for an external, dominant world, try to depict "an ethnic image that must be maintained and projected as a part of the all-important boundary-defining system."[53] It is very possible that the weavers of these old, mysterious, and culturally rich pictorials were consciously practicing an effective distancing strategy with their "simple," yet deceptive, woven cartoons.

Folk Art versus Tourist Art

Perhaps it is within this realm of boundary maintenance that tourist art has served its greatest purpose. It is ironic that with the increasing role of the pictorial as a vehicle for personal, cultural expression, there has developed in the past few decades an increased awareness of and appreciation for this "new" kind of Navajo weaving by the outside world. Because of its impressionistic "folk art appeal," the traditional pictorial is now fully accepted and desired by the commercial marketplace.

As stated before, weaving for "sale" was not a new concept introduced by the Anglo-American community, for Navajo blankets had been "commercial art" since their initial adoption from outsiders and their subsequent integration into the Navajo way of life. They were "sold" to Puebloans and various Plains tribes in exchange for foodstuffs, buffalo products, horses, and turquoise; and to the Spanish who mentioned the Navajos' "woolen blankets, many of which they used in trade" in early reports from the 1700s.[54] Nor was the idea of making a product specifically for a targeted market new. Social anthropologist W. W. Hill wrote about the "so-called 'chief blanket' . . . not ordinarily used by the Navaho but manufactured almost entirely for commercial purposes and almost exclusively for the Ute."[55] The difference, however, between early woven commercial art and "tourist art" of today is the change in *function* from the wearing blanket to the "souvenir," a tangible image sought by the alien visitor in search of authentic ethnic experiences. Nelson Graburn points out that "once fully functional . . . these did not become tourist arts until the Anglo started to buy them."[56]

The transformation from folk or traditional art to the tourist art of today need not be degenerative. By their very nature, traditional arts are dynamic expressions of a living culture; and the market-place—as "the most powerful source of formal and aesthetic innovation"[57]—may in fact serve to preserve those vital qualities of the art form while providing a means of expression for the artisan bombarded by culture-threatening forces from another world.

Despite the fears of U. S. Hollister in 1903 that "as soon as they are influenced by the White Man's taste, to the extent of changing their patterns and colors, the beauty of the Navajo blanket will be doomed," such has not been the case.[58] Even the maverick pictorials, first spurned by the entrepreneurial traders, have been given new life in recent years through the impetus of the marketplace. Weaving to meet the expectations of "image junkies," some Navajos have become artistically adept at "transforming historically specific and culturally unique experiences of indigenous people into stereotyped images that can be marketed as commodities."[59] Beginning with the early "train rugs," woven by "gals sitting next to the tracks in Gallup to sell to tourists for twenty-five to fifty cents,"[60] to depictions of the physical features of Navajoland, these woven stereotypes often serve to "illustrate all the objects a tourist would see driving through the . . . Reservation," from Shiprock and Monument Valley to women weaving and cooking mutton.[61] Subsequently, these technically difficult and complex "reservation scenes" have become sought after by collectors who are willing to pay a great deal of money for them as classic examples of Native American folk art. Even though these everyday scenes from an idyllic past may be only the artist's "recreation of past values and ideals that she believes will appeal to the nostalgic inclinations" of commercial buyers,[62] they still represent a picture of the Navajo world as seen by the Navajo.

The Anglo trader, as middleman and long-time interpreter of the white man's desires, has always had a great deal of influence on the kinds of pictorials "his" weavers produce or market through his post. As early as 1911, J. B. Moore was selling through his mail-order catalog a "new design," reflecting Moore's typical Persian-style border-and-floral motifs created specifically for eastern tastes, but also including two small birds. Dorothy Boyd, in her master's thesis on pictorial weaving, suggests that the birds, similar to those she found in an 1880s rug, "may have been a native motif which Moore incorporated to give the rug an 'Indian' character."[63] Walter Kennedy, a modern-day trader in Dennehotso, purposefully built up a pictorial business with his weavers, paying more money—"always cash, that makes a difference"—for the representational rugs. He said he "bought magazines by the tons, tore out and passed out the pictures, and told them to come back with whatever." But at the same time he told the women that "anything the Navajo had done was fine [as subject matter] but what the White Man had done, I didn't want." Describing the pictorial as a "fad," Kennedy recalled that "sometimes you couldn't sell them; and sometimes you didn't have enough."[64]

Noting that "Navajos have a thing against snakes, and some even say a woman went blind after weaving a yei rug with snakes," Kennedy nevertheless offered to pay his weavers $150 for each snake woven into a rug. His personal collection of pictorials includes a few "patriotic eagles" holding snakes in their claws and one good-sized rug with four yei dancers holding a snake in each hand. "She got a bunch of money for that one!" (See Figure 4.) The pictorials were Kennedy's personal favorites, and the most unusual and most expertly woven, no matter what the subject, form the basis for his extensive private collection. The 9' x 12' rug on the floor of his "collection room vault" was still on the loom and half-finished when Kennedy first saw it. He asked the weaver to "add a few animals" to her traditionally geometric design. The finished rug has, in addition to the requested animals in the upper left, some men on horseback and an Arabian sheik on the right. The sheik is no more incongruous than the bicycle-riding tiger that was woven into the center of another room-sized rug created for Kennedy by the same Navajo weaver. Just what do these anomalistic figures mean to the weaver? Kennedy, her prime customer, grinned: "Well, whatever fits her story."[65]

The Pictorial History of an Artistic Tradition

The stories and the traditional ways of the loom as passed down by Navajo women through generations have kept Navajo pictorial weaving alive. Representative weavings have from their very beginning

Figure 4. *Folk art or tourist art?* The history of pictorials shows a constant exchange between native aesthetics and commercial concerns. The rug admired here by trader Walter Kennedy includes images of snakes that were included at his request. Walter Kennedy Collection. Photo by Nancy Peake.

indicated that change—sometimes accidental, sometimes perpetuated by uninvited outside influences, and sometimes self-generated—stimulated experimentation and innovation, creating an open-ended, evolving "style" that "faithfully mirror[ed] the social, economic, and political history of the Navajo people."[66] In many ways (similar to other Native American art traditions of the Southwest), "the survival of the craft symbolizes the survival of the people."[67]

Perhaps more than any other type of Navajo weaving, the pictorial, as a visual historical document, demonstrates the ability of an artistic tradition to serve the aesthetic, cultural, and economic needs of a people through time. Gary Witherspoon suggests that "this ability to synthesize aesthetics with pragmatics, internal cultural expression with external market influence, individual creativity with universal cultural themes, is at the very heart of [the Navajo's] vigor, vitality and adaptability as a human society. Their transformations were culturally inspired and facilitated, not materially determined."[68] The continued production of pictorial weaving, "in organic relationship with the whole of society,"[69] links the Navajo past to the present, even though its form and function have been redefined by the consumer. The very distinctions between folk art and tourist art may be stereotypes themselves because the artist may at once "sell to tourists, exhibit nationally, and express primordial themes."[70] The inevitable transformation from a traditional folk art to commercial tourist art may have, in fact, come full circle, the inherent values of one enhancing the significant worth of the other.

To say, then, that this indigenous, individualized, yet traditional art form was exploited, or reinvented, by the trader and subsequent middlemen would be untrue. For if the commercial marketplace were truly so dictatorial, why did traders interpret the desires of their customers so differently? If the tourist's demand for ethnic authenticity was so great, how did the eclectic pictorial survive for at least a century and a half amid the demand for regional, "Indian-patterned" Navajo rugs?

The inherent ambiguities of the enigmatic pictorial, while contributing to its charm, may also produce internal conflicts on the part of weaver and consumer alike. Weaver Tiana Bighorse, daughter of a

Navajo warrior who fought Kit Carson's troops and avoided capture and imprisonment at Bosque Redondo, once wove her impression of the Painted Desert into a commissioned piece for customers who asked for a rug depicting the landscape of her homeland. Rocks and mesas in all their natural colors wander in and around valleys from the bottom of her finished weaving to the top. But in the middle of this landscape is a row of traditional diamonds. Asked about the ironic reintroduction of the geometric into her pictorial landscape, the weaver explained: "I wanted everyone to know. It's a Navajo rug."[71]

To appreciate the traditions and creative imagination behind the woven pictures of this Native American folk art is to perceive the strength of the connections between peoples and events, both past and present. To listen for the cultural messages hidden between the wefts of these story-telling textiles is to better comprehend who the weavers were, why they chose to weave what they did, and why they felt the need to invent a new tradition. For when the weaver feels compelled to reproduce her world in wool, her finished product forces the viewer to confront the human being behind the creation. Herein lies the power and the spirit of the Navajo pictorial.

Notes

1. Andrew Nagen, dealer/appraiser of Navajo textiles (interview, February 4, 1989) explains that many of today's Navajos have never seen any of the old blankets "because they were traded away when they were new, or people were often buried in them."

2. After World War II all southwestern Indian artifacts, including blankets and rugs, began to gradually make the subtle transition from "curios" or "collectibles" to "Native American art" made specifically for tourists and the fine arts market; hence these more recent weavings are not viable examples for this discussion.

3. All descriptive attributes were accumulated over two years of research, including discussions with a great many traders, dealers, and collectors.

4. Clifford Geertz, "Art as a Cultural System," in his *Local Knowledge* (New York: Basic Books, 1983), 119.

5. See Nelson H. H. Graburn, "The Arts of the Fourth World," *Ethnic and Tourist Arts: Cultural Expressions from the Fourth World* (Berkeley: University of California Press, 1976).

6. Gary Witherspoon, "Navajo Weaving: Art in Its Cultural Context," *MNA Research Paper* 36 (Flagstaff: Museum of Northern Arizona, 1987), 5.

7. Joe Ben Wheat, "Early Navajo Weaving," *Plateau Magazine* 52, no. 4 (1985): 3.

8. Ibid.

9. Joe Ben Wheat, "Three Centuries of Navajo Weaving," *Arizona Highways* 50, no. 7 (July 1974): 13.

10. Marian Rodee, interview, February 8, 1989.

11. Charles Avery Amsden, *Navaho Weaving: Its Technique and History* (Glorieta, N.Mex.: Rio Grande Press, 1934), 213. In August of 1846, General Stephen W. Kearny marched his troops into the Santa Fe plaza and, meeting no resistance from the local Mexican government, announced the annexation of New Mexico to the United States. His action became law under the Treaty of Guadalupe Hidalgo two years later.

12. Uriah S. Hollister, *The Navajo and His Blanket* (Glorieta, N.Mex.: Rio Grande Press, 1972), 95.

13. Ibid.

14. Wheat, "Early Navajo Weaving," 3.

15. Walter M. Kennedy, interview, March 21, 1989.

16. William Brandon, *The American Heritage Book of Indians* (New York: Bonanza Books, 1988), 345.

17. For more details and description, see Kate Peck Kent, *Navajo Weaving: Three Centuries of Change* (Santa Fe: School of American Research Press, 1985), 120.

18. Dorothy Elizabeth Boyd, "Navajo Pictorial Weaving. Its Past and Its Present Condition" (master's thesis, University of New Mexico, 1970), 18–26.

19. Nancy J. Parezo, *Navajo Sandpainting: From Religious to Commercial Art* (Tucson: University of Arizona Press, 1983), 9.

20. Jacob Jerome Brody, *Between Traditions: Navajo Weaving toward the End of the 19th Century* (University of Iowa Museum of Art, 1976), n.p.

21. While the Navajos were still imprisoned at Bosque Redondo, they were issued commercially spun, three-ply yarn from Germantown, Pennsylvania. In the mid-1870s, the traders began carrying four-ply Germantown yarn for their weavers. Synthetic aniline dyes also

became popular with the weavers to dye both the traders' commercially spun yarns and their own hand-spun yarn. Needless to say, considerable time was gained in the overall production of a blanket when the weaver no longer had to wash, card, and spin her own wool as well as gather ingredients for natural dyes.

22. Ruth Underhill, *Here Come the Navaho* (Tucson, Ariz.: Treasure Chest Publications, 1953), 210.
23. Bertha P. Dutton, *American Indians of the Southwest* (Albuquerque: University of New Mexico Press, 1983), 233.
24. Founded in Oregon in 1895, the Pendleton Woolen Mills made their reputation through the manufacture of their "Indian pattern" blankets, which quickly became popular with Indians and whites alike. At this time, the Navajo could obtain a Pendleton blanket from their local traders for the equivalent of five dollars, while the trade value of a good Navajo blanket was about fifty dollars. Andrew Nagen, interview, October 15, 1986.
25. Eric Hobsbawn and Terence Ranger, *The Invention of Tradition* (New York: Cambridge University Press, 1983), 4–5.
26. Henry Glassie, KLSK radio interview at New Mexico Museum of International Folk Art, 1987.
27. Simon Bronner and John Michael Vlach, eds., *Folk Art and Art Worlds* (Ann Arbor: UMI Research Press, 1986), 16.
28. Ibid.
29. Nagen, interview, February 4, 1989.
30. Anthony Berlant and Mary Hunt Kahlenberg, *The Navajo Blanket* (Los Angeles: Praeger, 1972), 15.
31. Ibid.
32. Paul S. Wingert, *Primitive Art: Its Tradition and Styles* (New York: World Publishing, 1970), vi.
33. Ibid.
34. Alice Kaufman and Christopher Selser, *The Navajo Weaving Tradition: 1950 to the Present* (New York: E. P. Dutton, 1985), 2.
35. Kent, *Navajo Weaving*, 3.
36. Oliver LaFarge and John Sloan, *Introduction to American Indian Art,* Exhibition Catalog for the Exposition of Indian Tribal Arts (New York: Diamond Press, 1931), 5–7, 17–21.
37. Ibid, 17–21.
38. Edwin L. Wade and Rennard Strickland, *Magic Images: Contemporary Native American Art*, Exhibition Catalog for Philbrook Art Center (Norman: University of Oklahoma Press, 1981), 5.

39. Henry Glassie, *The Spirit of Folk Art* (New York: Harry N. Abrams, 1989), 45.

40. George Mills, *Navaho Art and Culture* (Colorado Springs: Taylor Museum, 1959), 63.

41. Charlene Cerny, *Navajo Pictorial Weaving* (Santa Fe: Museum of New Mexico Foundation, 1975), 6.

42. Nancy J. Blomberg, *Navajo Textiles: The William Randolph Hearst Collection* (Tucson: University of Arizona Press, 1988), 12.

43. Cerny, interview, February 24, 1989.

44. Jackson H. Clark Sr., "Navajo Pictorial Weaving," *Oriental Rug Review* 8, no. 6 (August/September 1988): 24.

45. Ibid.

46. Nagen, interview, February 4, 1989.

47. Rodee, interview, February 8, 1989.

48. Winter's conversation with Nagen, related in Nagen, interview, February 21, 1989.

49. Boyd, "Navajo Pictorial Weaving," 94.

50. Marion Rodee, *Weaving of the Southwest* (West Chester, Pa.: Schiffer, 1987), 142.

51. Keith Basso, *Portraits of "The Whiteman"* (Cambridge: Cambridge University Press, 1988), 105.

52. Janet Fairbanks Thomas, "Navajo Weaving and Silverwork: Change and Continuity in Response to Contact" (master's thesis, University of Arizona, 1969), 87.

53. Nelson H. H. Graburn, *Ethnic and Tourist Arts: Cultural Expressions from the Fourth World* (Berkeley: University of California Press, 1976), 5.

54. Kent, *Navajo Weaving*, 9.

55. W. W. Hill, "Navaho Trading and Trading Ritual: A Study of Cultural Dynamics," *Southwestern Journal of Anthropology* 4, no. 4 (Winter 1948): 380.

56. Graburn, "The Evolution of Tourist Arts," *Annals of Tourism Research* 11 (1984): 397.

57. Graburn, *Ethnic and Tourist Arts*, 15.

58. Hollister, *The Navajo and His Blanket*, 91.

59. Patricia C. Albers and William R. James, "Tourism and the Changing Photographic Image of the Great Lakes Indians," *Annals of Tourism Research* 10 (1983): 145.

60. Nagen, interview, February 4, 1989.

61. Rodee, *Weaving of the Southwest*, 142.

62. Bennetta Jules-Rosette, *The Messages of Tourist Art* (New York: Plenum Press, 1984), 41.

63. Boyd, "Navajo Pictorial Weaving," 51–52.

64. Kennedy, interview, March 21, 1989.

65. Ibid.

66. Kent, *Navajo Weaving*, 2.

67. Brody, *Between Traditions*, 76.

68. Witherspoon, "Navajo Weaving," 4.

69. Brody, "The Creative Consumer: Survival, Revival, and Invention in Southwest Indian Arts," in *Ethnic and Tourist Arts,* ed. Nelson Graburn (Berkeley: University of California Press, 1976), 83.

70. Jules-Rosette, *The Messages of Tourist Art,* viii.

71. Noel Bennett, "Painted Desert/Woven Desert," *Oriental Rug Review* 8, no. 6 (August/September 1988): 15.

CHAPTER 2

Appropriation and Counterhegemony in South Texas: Food Slurs, Offal Meats, and Blood

Mario Montaño

The literature of foodways includes numerous examples of how people use food to stigmatize social and cultural groups. Typically, after a "dominant" culture conquers a "subordinate" one, the victor labels the defeated group as biologically, morally, and gastronomically defective. Such was the case during the period 1836–1950, when Anglos militarily and politically conquered the Mexican people of South Texas. Texas Anglos considered the Mexicans inferior in many ways and communicated this belief through a vast array of behaviors, ranging from outright violence to racist attitudes symbolically dispersed in food slurs. This essay addresses the social and cultural history of Mexican folk foodways in the lower Rio Grande border region. In doing so, it provides an understanding of how the dominant culture appropriated and redefined the local foodways and imposed a selective Mexican cuisine in the United States.[1]

Greaser, Chili, and Frijole Guzzler: Mexican Food Slurs

Since the beginning of their contact, Anglo Texans viewed Mexicans as biologically, culturally, and morally defective. Their racist attitudes have been traced to a mental framework imported from England, to negative reports of Mexicans in newspapers, and to the outcome of warfare.[2] Anglo losses during the Texas Revolution helped to justify their bitter emotions toward Mexicans. According to Américo Paredes, "The truth seems to be that the old war propaganda concerning the Alamo, Goliad, and Mier later provided a convenient justification for outrages committed on the Border by Texans of certain types, so convenient an excuse that it was artificially prolonged for a century."[3] In the 1860s, an Anglo writer provided a view of Mexicans' alleged racial impurity: "They are of the mongrel blood the Aztec predominating. . . . These degraded creatures are mere pilferers, scavengers, and vagabonds, downright barbarians but a single remove above the Digger Indians, hanging like vermin on the skirts of civilization—a complete pest to humanity."[4] In sum, Mexicans were perceived as a detestable human race, untouchable and repulsive.

In considering Mexicans a contaminated race, Texas Anglos noted particularly that their food was flavored with strong spices and that their diet consisted of poor quality ingredients. Mexican food was considered unhealthy and unfit for human consumption. Because it was unpalatable, very spicy, and irritating to the Anglo stomach, said Anglo Texans, coyotes and buzzards passed up the dead bodies of Mexicans to feed instead on the bodies of horses and Texans. According to one account, wild animals passed over Mexican corpses during the Mexican War because they were full of red pepper. The scavengers' disdain was "attributed to the nature of their food, it being antiseptic."[5]

In general, Mexican food symbolized everything that was degenerate and despicable about the conquered Mexican population. The red pepper, or chile, in particular, was used extensively to refer to Mexicans in a derogatory manner. For example, a nineteenth-century farmer, in trying to convey his feelings about Mexicans, said, "The chilis are Creatures somewhere in between a burro and a human being."[6] Mexican food was thought to be not only dirty, but also greasy. As a result, Mexicans were referred to as "greasers." The ethnic slur "greaser" has also been associated with what was thought to be the dirty appearance of Mexicans, but the food connotation was a common one.[7] Américo Paredes, in addressing the use of food slurs among Texas Anglos, wrote that "the Mexican diet has been a much richer source of derogatory names, among them 'pepper belly,' 'taco choker,' 'frijole guzzler,' 'chili picker,' and (of a woman) 'hot tamale.' Aside from diet, no other aspect of Mexican culture seems to have caught the fancy of the Anglo coiner of derogatory terms for Mexicans."[8]

The psychological function of slurs, according to José Limón, is to "reduce, dehumanize, and shape our conduct toward the object of the slur."[9] Without a doubt, then, Texas Anglos viewed both Mexicans and their food as dirty, contaminated, and unhygienic. Food, which conveniently encoded their racist attitudes, was employed symbolically to denigrate the entire group and its culture. Sidney Mintz summarizes this particular role of food by saying that it can serve to encode racial and class relations. As a result, says Mintz, we sometimes think of people who eat different foods or eat them differently as being less than human.[10]

In recent years, however, Mexican food has been enjoying such popularity that it is considered by many food writers to be the most popular ethnic food in the United States. This is, to say the least, ironic. How can a food considered repulsive, unfit for human consumption, and associated with the working-class poor reach such a level of acceptance by the dominant culture? The answer lies not in the alleged enlightenment of the dominant culture in appreciating the exotic, but in the concept of cultural hegemony, especially as it has been defined by Raymond Williams.[11]

The American food industry, enacting the principles of cultural hegemony, has effectively incorporated and reinterpreted the food practices of Mexicans in the lower Rio Grande border region, relabeling them "Tex Mex" and further using that term to describe any Mexican or Spanish food that is consumed by Anglos. Although Mexicans in this region do not refer to their food as Tex Mex, and indeed often consider the term derogatory, the dominant culture has redefined the local cuisine as "earthy food, festive food, happy food, celebration. It is peasant food raised to the level of high and sophisticated art."[12]

The identification with celebration is not entirely off the mark, for what Anglos now call Tex Mex food was indeed associated with festive occasions in its original communities. The typical community of South Texas in the late nineteenth century, according to Américo Paredes, was the "ranch or ranching village" populated by "small, tightly knit groups whose social structure was the family or the clan."[13] Mexican settlers in these *ranchos* relied extensively on a sufficiency economy based on fruits, vegetables, and livestock. Among the meals that animals provided, special significance was given to those prepared from offal meats and blood. Organ meats, intestines, and glands were part of a food system typically associated with festive occasions.

Along the lower Rio Grande, many of these meats continue to be associated with celebration. During the Christmas season, for example, people along the border still slaughter animals, or have them slaughtered, to prepare *morcilla* (pig's blood sausage), *tamales, chicharrones* (pork rinds), *chorizo, menudo* (tripe stew), *patagordilla* (organ meats and blood stew), *mollejas* (thymus glands), *barbacoa de cabeza* (cow's head barbecue), and *fajitas* (beef skirts). All of these special foods evoke strong images of animal slaughtering and of the festive food events of working-class families.

But at least two of them, menudo and fajita, have also been appropriated by Anglo culture and infused with different meanings. These two folk foods comprise the focus of the following discussion.

Menudo: From Offal to Cook-Off Food

Menudo is a tripe stew: the name refers to the use of calf's stomach, the honeycomb beef tripe.[14] It is prepared with aromatic herbs (oregano, cilantro, marjoram) and spices (ground dried chiles, black pepper, salt, and garlic). Cut into squares or wedges, the tripe is usually braised or boiled, simmered for several hours, and then served in bowls garnished with lime wedges, chopped onions, chopped chile serrano, and chopped cilantro. This is the basic method of preparation, although many other versions of menudo exist throughout the border region and Mexico. Local variations, such as menudo that includes hominy, pork, or calf's feet, or menudo spiced with red or green chile, reflect regional influences such as the availability of ingredients and local cultural rules. Whatever the variations, however, menudo is embedded with a rich history and folklore. In addition, it is widely viewed as an "acceptable" Mexican folk food by the dominant culture throughout the Southwest.

In South Texas, Mexicans prefer their menudo to be fresh, preferably from a recently slaughtered cow. When I interviewed Don Perfecto Mancha, a folk food specialist from Maverick County, he told me that as a child, working at the local slaughterhouse in the barrio de San Lusito, he would go from house to house selling livers, esophagi, lungs, hearts, and stomachs for menudo.[15] However, today it is very difficult to find fresh menudo because sanitation laws prohibit slaughtering animals in one's backyard. As a result, most of the menudo is bought frozen at border grocery stores. According to some vendors, the meat packing and freezing process significantly reduces the quality of the meat. Don Salome, a third-generation Laredo food vendor, complained about the quality of today's menudo: "Well, before, we made menudo during the week and all that. But it was less expensive, the merchandise. Today it is more expensive. You can find it because sometimes the menudo sold today, well, the menudo coming out of the packing company is not that good. . . . Because when you cook it and it ends up, imagine an onion skin, paper thin. Well, twenty-five pounds, well, I believe that in a small pan, all of it fits in. Nothing left of it."[16] Although he has never met Don Salome, "Chaco" Rodriguez, a second-generation butcher from my home town of Eagle Pass, agrees with this assessment. In one of our conversations, Chaco provided a glimpse of how tripe used to be processed at the Uvalde, Texas, slaughterhouse where he worked for several years: "Well, back then, the menudo was given away with the feet until it went up in price a lot, and left a lot of profit. . . . It is cleaned with water and calcium or with some kind of chemical that is used so it will clean faster. But the drawback is that the menudo that they kill today, then it is frozen in a freezer for tomorrow, instead of selling it right away, hanging fresh. They put it in boxes and freeze it for three or four months until it reaches the store and until they sell it to you."[17] Don Salome and Chaco, like many others in this region, agree that the quality of tripe has declined due to the health laws and packing companies' processing procedures. To them, much menudo is not worth selling, and Don

Salome himself has actually stopped selling it because of its high cost and low quality.

The preparation and consumption of menudo embody strong elements of folklore and social practice. As a specialty dish of the border region, it continues to be prepared in households, restaurants, and by street food vendors. In some border towns and urban centers with large Mexican populations, it is a weekend food prepared and sold in neighborhood stores. Although it is consumed at all times of the day and night, it retains strong associations with festive events and is often a party food. For example, it is the custom after a wedding reception to assemble at an in-law's house for the *torna boda* (postwedding party) to eat menudo. After a drinking binge, it is customary to have a hot bowl of menudo in the belief that it will soften the effects of the hangover. Menudo, in short, is still a celebratory folk food.

It is also a food, however, that has gained wide acceptance among Anglos, is sold in Mexican restaurants throughout the border region, and has even made its way into the popular culture of South Texas. It is sold in cans in grocery stores and commemorated on t-shirts with the inscription MENUDO, THE BREAKFAST OF CHAMPIONS. Almost every Mexican cookbook produced in the United States has at least one menudo recipe as though to lend credibility and authenticity to the volume. Menudo has also been incorporated into corporate and business sponsored Mexican cook-off festivals. As early as 1970, these festivals began to proliferate in South Texas in much the same way as chili cook-offs glut the nation today.[18]

These menudo cook-off contests, like the chili cook-offs, have stirred extensive joking and mockery among Mexicans in the border region. I asked a respected folk cookery specialist in Maverick County why he did not participate in these contests. He responded, "Bueno, Mario, para comenzar, tienes que estar panzon, barbon, vigoton, y tienes que ser un 'redneck' para poder ganar." (Well, Mario, to start off, you have to be fat, bearded, mustached, and you have to be a redneck in order to win.)[19] The results of these contests bear him out. Many menudo cook-off champions are indeed members of the dominant culture, leading even some working-class Mexicans to believe that Texas Anglos now know how to cook

Mexican food better than the Mexicans. In addition, women, who traditionally prepare menudo in border households, are usually excluded from participating in the contests—providing a gender as well as a racial bias. Thus, even though menudo continues to occupy a special position in the popular culture and folk food system of Mexicans in South Texas, its appropriation by Anglo entrepreneurs has also invested it with a culturally dominating effect.

Fajitas: The Appropriation Process of a Folk Food

Fajita is the folk name Mexicans in the lower Rio Grande border region give to the cut of meat known as skirt steak; the cut itself is actually the cow's diaphragm muscle. There are two parts to the skirt steak. The inside part is the less desirable because it is tougher and leaner. The outside steak is preferred by fajita cooks because it is thicker and marbled with fat. Since the early 1970s, this cut of meat has been enjoying national popularity, making its way from humble beginnings to some of the most distinguished restaurants in the country. Along the way it has become surrounded with culinary legends. To distinguish them from the facts, it is necessary to provide some historical background.

Among Mexicans in the lower Rio Grande border region, fajitas are typically served with tortillas (either flour or corn) as well as guacamole, beans, and rice. In preparing the dish, the meat is first grilled and sliced in strips. Then the strips are placed into a folded tortilla and garnished with the guacamole and *salsa fresca* (ground fresh chile sauce of tomatoes, garlic, onions, and cilantro) or *pico de gallo* (a relish of fresh diced chile serrano, scallions, tomatoes, cilantro, olive oil, and beer).

Other terms used along the border also refer to fajitas. When I was a boy in Eagle Pass, my parents referred to this cut of meat as *arracherras.* This term appeared in a 1944 cookbook written by Elena Zelayeta, one of the persons responsible for making Mexican food popular in California, and it is still used today in conversations and on restaurant menus.[20] However, this term, although it refers to the same cut of meat, has a slightly different connotation, evoking a different preparation process. In my house, as in other houses in this region, arracherras were broiled or steam-baked in the kitchen oven along with onions, tomatoes, and chile serrano.[21] Today, in many restaurants along the Rio Grande, arracherras are sold by weight as *arracherras asadas* (grilled arracherras), not as fajitas. Another word that often gets confused with fajitas and arracherras is *aldilla*, which means "flank steak." Yet, fajita remains the most common term used to refer to the cut of meat known as skirt steak.

Along with the different words used, correctly or incorrectly, for fajitas, there are culinary legends that proliferate in news stories attempting to define the dish, locate its origin, and describe its history. Most of these legends describe the same supposedly typical social pattern. First, the lowly and despised food is thrown away by members of the upper class and picked up by hungry poor people. Then, the upper class reappropriates and "improves" it so that it becomes "civilized" and socially acceptable. Finally, the food enjoys the status of a delicacy that is legitimized and enjoyed by members of the upper class.

In trying to account for the origin of fajitas, newspaper food writers usually attribute the dish to South Texas Anglo cowboys. One story quotes a Texan from the Rio Grande Valley: "They used to be dirt cheap. They used to almost throw them away, like junk."[22] In another story, fajitas are associated with vaqueros. "Fajitas actually originated in South Texas along the border. They were first used by Mexican cowboys along the border in the 1900s. . . . For a long time . . . fajitas remained a secret among Mexican cowboys in San Antonio and South Texas."[23] In a third article, fajitas are associated with the more general class of ranch hands. "According to legend, it was once the thrown away cut of meat that South Texas ranchers gave to their hands when they slaughtered a carcass."[24]

The folk term fajitas in these newspaper legends takes on the role of different characters or personas. In one, the meat acquires a fairytale persona: "This is a Cinderella story for the skirt steak, a cut of meat once as neglected as the fairytale heroine."[25] In another, the fajita becomes an undocumented worker: "Fajitas crept across the border about a decade ago and in the past three years have swept through the state."[26] All of these newspaper legends rely on non-Mexicans to legitimate the origin of fajitas, associating it with the general culture of South Texas.

Some native Mexicans of this region agree on South Texas as the dish's first home. However, they usually localize it to a certain town or region. Many of the people with whom I discussed fajitas said that they started in the Rio Grande Valley. Some of my friends from Eagle Pass who attended Texas A&I University in Kingsville told me that it was there they were first exposed to the term. My brother, who lives in Mission, Texas, introduced them to our household in 1970, having discovered fajitas himself at a *carne asada* (cook-out) in Madero, which is close to the Rio Grande River. Chaco Rodriguez, a fellow native of Eagle Pass, describes the origin of fajitas in this way: "The fajita is a border name. Started like in the seventies, started over by Laredo, Brownsville, and Harlingen. Started over by the valley, fajitas this and fajitas that. That was not the name used here. The Mexican name is arracherras and the old name that was around was aldilla."[27] Hence, the origin of fajitas has been well documented to have been somewhere in the South Texas border region. However, the cultural meaning of the word has been a source of conflict between the dominant United States culture and Mexicans of South Texas.

Initially an offal meat consumed by working-class Mexicans, the fajita has become a delicacy associated with almost *any* kind of grilled meat consumed by upwardly mobile urban dwellers. In most restaurants, the term refers to any grilled beef served with the side dishes that define the Mexican meal: frijoles, rice, pico de gallo, guacamole, and tortillas. Many restaurants do not use the traditional skirt steak but instead serve chuck, T-bone, round, or flank steak.[28] Some restaurants, moreover, do not even use beef. "Fajita" is now often used to signify the grilling of any kind of meat, from "chicken fajitas" to "shrimp fajitas." One self-styled "Fajita King," Sonny Falcon, reacts adamantly against such innovations, stating that "only the fajita cut makes a fajita. . . . If you put anything else in a flour tortilla, you have a taco al carbon or maybe carne asada, but not a fajita."[29] But this traditional definition is widely ignored by Anglo restaurant owners.

Through these examples, we see that the meaning of the folk food fajita has been changed to signify the grilling process and not the cut of meat—a change that effectively obscures the fajita's origin as an offal meat. To further "sanitize" the dish, restaurants provide menus where the term is spelled phonetically (fah-HEAT-uhs) and where instructions are provided on how to eat a "fajita taco." Restaurants have also altered the traditional presentation of the dish, bringing it to the table sizzling hot in a pancake griddle or iron skillet. This style of presentation, according to one writer, lends "authenticity" to the folk dish: "If they do not come to the table sizzling from the grill, they are not fit to be called fajitas."[30]

This is a particularly vivid example of class appropriation and distortion, for the original eaters of fajitas had no such "tradition." In the border region, fajitas are still served, both in backyards and in restaurants, without any fanfare or theatrics. Mexicans recognize the sizzling griddle as a promotional gimmick that bears no relation to the original culinary frame.

As the level of consumer income rises, the preparation of fajitas becomes more sophisticated and is accompanied by highly charged status ingredients. In a national newspaper column, two food writers state that fajitas are "the ideal food for yuppie grazers. They are packed with flavor and are easy and fun to eat. The meat—chicken, beef, or pork—is first marinated, then grilled and served with guacamole and pico de gallo." The writers continue by presenting an innovative fajita recipe to cater to yuppie taste. "We've used an avocado relish in place of guacamole because the raw green flavor of mashed avocado can be a problem with wine. To counteract this, we used a Chardonnay in the relish and added the drained juices from the tomato salsa." As an accompaniment, they recommend that the best wine matches are a 1983 Pouilly Fumé and a 1983 Beaujolais Village.[31] At this level, the preparation of what was once seen as a "junk" meal assumes a radically altered social significance. It is unlikely that many Mexicans of the border region would take eagerly to an avocado "relish" made with Chardonnay.

Nor, of course, would they be able to afford it, and here we see most blatantly the class distinction that separates the backyard fajita from its upscale cousins. One of the unwelcome, but entirely predictable, side effects to the cultural appropriation of this folk food is that its price has risen dramatically—so dramatically, in fact, that it is now beyond the means of its Mexican originators. The process that George Lewis documents later in this volume with regard to the Maine lobster is just as clearly evident in the case of fajitas. In Manhattan, for example, skirt steak was going for $3.50 a pound in 1984 and over three times that—$10.98 a pound—in 1989. Expensive restaurants buy huge quantities of the meat, and fajita parties have proliferated in urban centers, many of them catered by fajita "specialists." In annual newspaper ratings of Austin, Texas, restaurants, the "Best Fajita" award routinely goes not to any of the city's many Mexican restaurants, but to the sizzling griddle productions of the Hyatt Regency Hotel.[32]

In view of this upscaling of a once working-class food item, many Mexican people in South Texas have reacted by modifying the traditional fare. So intense has been the appropriation process that they have in a sense redefined the fajita according to their own economic needs. In backyard "carne asada" events, many now avoid the high-priced fajita cut entirely and have turned to using the more affordable seven-bone chuck steak known as "El Siete."[33]

Resistance and the Unincorporable

This switch to a less expensive meat, moreover, is only one example of how the appropriation process has encountered resistance. As Williams understood, hegemony is never complete or all encompassing. Its dominance is constantly challenged by oppositional cultural forms. This has clearly been the case in South Texas, where folk foods other than menudo and fajitas have signalled resistance to the upscaling process, being almost totally ignored or consciously excluded from Anglo tables. This is true of *morcilla* (pork blood sausage), *fritada* (goat blood stew), *machitos* (offal meat and marrow), *cabezitas* (goat's head), *tripas* (chitlins), and *barbacoa de cabeza* (cow's head barbecue). These folk foods involve using freshly killed animals, and they rely on organ meats, innards, or blood. As a result, they possess what might be called counterhegemonic qualities, which make them unusually resistant to incorporation. Let me explain with some ethnographic detail from Eagle Pass.

In the case of morcilla and fritada, the main ingredient is fresh blood from a recently slaughtered pig or goat. So, slaughtering is part of the production process—a part that violates the dominant culture's laws. The use of blood for cooking has been outlawed by various legislatures, since blood is considered an "unsanitary" or "uncivilized" element of cuisine. Despite legal restrictions, however, in the confines of their own backyards, Mexicans still slaughter their own animals, keeping the blood to be used in the preparation process. In other cases, they get the blood from the local butcher. When I interviewed Chaco Rodriguez, the son of an Eagle Pass butcher, he recalled, "We slaughtered a lot there in the home for ourselves, and friends would say, 'Ah, we want some blood or something else. Well, just don't tell anybody.' We only did this because it was not sold. Only to relatives and some family members. Mom would give it to them, always to close friends."[34] Today in Eagle Pass, these outlawed folk foods are prepared by vendors who avoid peddling them in the streets because of the health and tax restrictions. These underground food vendors do not sell to the general public, only to select customers. For example, Doña Noemi Herrera recalled her occasional business with a morcilla seller. "This man does it often," she told me. "He comes by and tells me he is going to have morcilla or he comes looking for the ingredients to make morcilla. And I ask him, 'Are you going to make morcilla?' And he says, 'Yes, and I will sell you some.'"[35]

Underground food vendors are not limited to Eagle Pass. Throughout the lower Rio Grande border region I have met food vendors operating without a license and without health certificates. Many of them sell these folk foods to supplement their incomes. They use local plants and animals to prepare items such as *ceviche de matalote* (carp cooked in lime) and *miel de mesquite* (mesquite syrup); they use mesquite wood as fuel in the cooking process; and they make imaginative use of recycled or discarded items such as utensils, cooking pots, and mayonnaise jars. In some cases, this semiclandestine activity involves several families and neighbors who have known each other for generations.

Thus the production process itself, along with the finished products, are intimately linked to nonalienated labor and the rejection of commodity fetishism.[36] At the same time, the production of these foods is an aesthetic and symbolic political act—a subversive act that brings friends and relatives together to express who they are, where they come from, and where they stand in relation to the larger world. The production of unappropriated food items becomes a significant expression of Mexican border identity—an expression that confirms Limón's observation that in the "very aesthetic act of performance may be found the inherent oppositional quality of all folklore."[37]

Conclusion

The concept of cultural hegemony provides insight into the process of appropriation with regard to the food practices of Mexicans in the lower Rio Grande border region. In incorporating folk foods, the dominant culture can succeed in neutralizing, reinterpreting, and setting boundaries that separate "acceptable" foods from those perceived as disreputable or threatening. Many Mexican foods have been appropriated successfully with such strategies. Restauranteurs and food promoters have labeled their versions of Mexican food "Tex Mex," resulting in some of the most alien and adulterated Mexican food forms imaginable; among some natives of the Rio Grande region, these are considered merely another form of ethnic slur.

After twenty years of "Tex Mex" (and "Nouveau Hispano") food popularity, some restauranteurs have recently gone even further, distancing themselves from the cuisine of northern Mexico in favor of more "exotic" cuisines further south. In search of status and of the elusive and ambiguous concept of authenticity, many owners have begun to explore the gastronomy of central Mexico, adding new twists to *its* traditional cuisine. In many urban restaurants, the food is consciously classified as "ethnic," providing customers another opportunity of experiencing a foreign culture without having to deal with its people. These restaurants have become commercialized centers of "staged authenticity" and "internal tourism."[38] So rapid and fierce is the competition to present the latest fashionable "tradition" that what some people consider traditional Mexican food has in fact been around for only a couple of years.

In contrast to these yuppified enclaves of invented tradition, border Mexicans themselves, like the people of other rural cultures, do not consider their cuisine to be exotically "ethnic." Working-class Mexicans eat carne asada because it is what they have eaten for generations, not—as is the case with many middle-class, urban Mexicans—because it is a way to stress their "Mexicanness." Their relation to culinary tradition, in other words, is one of natural, rather than manufactured, group identity. Within this relationship, food can be viewed not only as a source of nourishment, but as what Baudrillard refers to as a "witness object," that is, as a social text embedded with cultural meaning.[39] That meaning is inevitably defined not by the dominant culture, but by the people whose social identity the cuisine encapsulates.

As I hope this case study has shown, the study of folk food preparation and consumption can enable us to go beyond mere description to address issues of cultural outlook and symbolic ethnicity. Oral texts in particular can reveal counterhegemonic discourses surrounding foods that contest the values and beliefs of the dominant culture. Thus the study of folk cuisine can provide concrete evidence of durable social realities that the "official" record ignores. In particular, native discourse about culinary events can expand our understanding of food as expression and its vital link to the "performance of group identity."[40]

Notes

For their help in the preparation of this essay, I would like to thank Richard Flores, José Limón, Victor Nelson-Cisneros, Olga Rubio, Tad Tuleja, and Bill Westerman.

1. The *Handbook of Middle American Indians,* vol. 12 (Austin: University of Texas Press, 1972) identifies four culture areas of northern Mexico: Baja California; the northwest from Sonora south to Nayarit; the north central area including Chihuaha, Durango, and parts of Coahuila; and the border area from Acuña to Del Rio. My research focusses on this last area, which Américo Paredes calls "the lower Rio Grande border" and which falls between the Nueces and Rio Grande Rivers. Also known as South Texas, it is the area where I was born and grew up.

2. Arnoldo De León, *They Called Them Greasers: Anglo Attitudes toward Mexicans in Texas, 1821–1900* (Austin: University of Texas Press, 1983), 10.

3. Américo Paredes, "The Problem of Identity in a Changing Culture: Popular Expressions of Culture Conflict along the Lower Rio Grande Border," in *Views across the Border: The U.S. and Mexico*, ed. Stanley Ross (Albuquerque: University of New Mexico Press, 1978), 19.

4. Cited in De León, *They Called Them Greasers*, 5.

5. Ibid., 67–68.

6. Cited in David Montejano, *Anglos and Mexicans in the Making of Texas, 1886–1986* (Austin: University of Texas Press, 1987), 187.

7. For discussion of the word "greaser," see Américo Paredes, "On Gringo, 'Greaser,' and Other Neighborly Names," in *Singers and Storytellers*, ed. Mody Moatright et al. (Dallas: Southern Methodist University Press, 1961); Paredes, "The Problem of Identity," 79; and De León, *They Called Them Greasers*, 16.

8. Paredes, "The Problem of Identity," 79.

9. José Limón, "Folklore, Social Conflict, and the United States–Mexico Border," in *Handbook of American Folklore*, ed. Richard Dorson (Bloomington: Indiana University Press, 1986), 218.

10. Sidney W. Mintz, *Sweetness and Power: The Place of Sugar in Modern History* (New York: Penguin, 1985), 3.

11. My views on hegemony are based on Raymond Williams, *Marxism and Literature* (Oxford: Oxford University Press, 1977). For a good discussion of the historical development of the concept of hegemony, see M. J. Weismantel, *Food, Gender, and Poverty in the Ecuadorian Andes* (Philadelphia: University of Pennsylvania, 1988), 34–37.

12. This description, by food critic Craig Claiborne, can be found on the back cover of Diana Kennedy, *Cuisines of Mexico* (New York: Harper & Row, 1978).

13. For good descriptions of the typical ranching community, see Jovita Gonzalez, "Social Life in Cameron, Star, and Zapata Counties" (master's thesis, University of Texas, 1930), and Fermina Guerra, "Mexicans and Spanish Folklore Incidents in Southwest Texas" (master's thesis, University of Texas, 1941).

14. The ultimate authority on French cuisine, the *Larousse Gastronomique* (New York: Crown, 1988), refers to tripe as the stomach of ruminants (especially ox, calf, and sheep) used as food. The volume provides a history of tripe as prepared in the *haute cuisine* of French regions.

15. My interview with Don Perfecto took place at his home on July 22, 1982.
16. I interviewed Don Salome in Laredo on June 3, 1983.
17. Rodriguez is a butcher with twenty-five years' experience. I interviewed him on July 7, 1982, in San Antonio.
18. For useful questions about the role of Mexican cook-offs in Anglo society, see Limón, "Folklore and Social Conflict," 219.
19. Jacinto Ramirez, an Eagle Pass native, made this statement in the summer of 1983. Ramirez is what might be called a folk caterer. He sometimes provides free barbecue to wedding parties as a gift to the bride and groom.
20. Elena Zelayeta is mentioned in Barbara Hansen, "The Hot New Sensation from Texas," *Philadelphia Inquirer*, June 14, 1985.
21. Doña Consuela Escontrias, a resident of Eagle Pass and a native of the Coahuila village of Jimenez, told me that as a child she remembers preparing arracherras in the oven and not on the grill.
22. Hansen, "Hot New Sensation." Compare George Lewis's discussion in this volume of the original "junk" character of Maine lobster.
23. Jacque Crouse, "Feasting on San Antonio History," *San Antonio Express*, March 13, 1986, Dl.
24. Kitty Crider, "Austin Fajita Chefs Skirt Issue on Meat That Meets Taste Test," *Austin American-Statesman*, June 8, 1989, p. El.
25. Hansen, "Hot New Sensation."
26. Carol Sugarman, "Fajita Fad Drives up Skirt Steak Price," *Boston Globe*, June 27, 1986.
27. From my interview with Rodriguez on July 7, 1982, at his home outside of San Antonio.
28. Several top-rated restaurants in Austin, Texas, admit that they do not use the beef skirt for their fajitas. Rich Cortese, food and beverage director of the Hyatt Hotel, says of his establishment's fajitas, "It's a corporate secret, but it is not skirt. It is a high quality meat and it is not marinated." Mike Ravago, owner of Fonda San Miguel, uses pork. Bobbie Covey, owner of the Salsa Mexican Restaurant, uses beef flap, the institutional cut of meat that comes from the end of a T-bone steak. See Crider, "Fajita Chefs Skirt Issue," El.
29. Ibid.
30. Hansen, "Hot New Sensation."
31. The yuppie fajitas are described in Anne Linsey Greer and Michael Bauer, "With Tex-Mex, Try a Pouilly Fumé," *Philadelphia Inquirer*, October 30, 1985.

32. Restaurant ratings appear in the *Austin Chronicle.*

33. During "carne asadas" in Eagle Pass, most men in their forties and above seem to prefer the "El Siete" steaks over fajitas. It was common to see these men grilling "siete steaks" behind the Sunset Inn and El Tropico Inn. The hotels' customers would often eat the steaks with beer while they were watching the game of the week on television. For an ethnography of eating fajitas and other organ meats, see José Limón, "Carne, Carnales, and the Carnivalesque: Bakhtinian Batos, Disorder, and Narrative Discourse," *American Ethnologist* 16 (August 1989): 471–86.

34. From an interview at his San Antonio home, July 15, 1982.

35. From an interview at her Eagle Pass store, El Barrio Loma Bonita, June 28, 1981.

36. For the importance of the production process and its link to the oppositional qualities of folklore, see José Limón, "Western Marxism and Folklore: A Critical Introduction," *Journal of American Folklore* 96 (1983): 34–52.

37. Ibid., 50.

38. See Pierre Van den Berghe, "Ethnic Cuisine: Culture in Nature," *Ethnic and Racial Studies* 7 (July 1984): 387–97.

39. Jean Baudrillard, *For a Critique of the Political Economy of the Sign,* trans. Charles Levin (St. Louis: Telos Press, 1981), 37. Other articles that approach food as a medium of communication include Mary Douglas, "Food as a System of Communication," in *In the Active Voice* (London: Routledge, Kegan, Paul, 1982); Arjun Appadurai, "Gastro-Politics: In Hindu South Asia," *American Ethnoloqy* 8 (1981): 494–511; and B. S. Turner, "The Discourse of Diet," *Theory and Culture and Society* 1 (1982): 23–32.

40. Linda Keller Brown and Kay Mussell, eds., *Ethnic and Regional Foodways in the United States: The Performance of Group Identity* (Knoxville: University of Tennessee Press, 1984). Other books that address the relationship of cuisine to cultural outlook include Michael Owen Jones, Bruce Giuliano, and Roberta Krell, eds., *Foodways and Eating Habits: Direction for Research* (California Folklore Society, 1981); Theodore C. Humphrey and Lin T. Humphrey, eds., *"We Gather Together": Food and Festival in American Life* (Ann Arbor: UMI Research Press, 1988); and Charles Camp, *American Foodways: What, When, Why, and How We Eat in America* (Little Rock, Ark.: August House, 1989). See also Yvonne R. Lockwood and William G. Lockwood, "Pasties in Michigan's Upper Peninsula: Foodways,

Interethnic Relations, and Regionalism," in *Creative Ethnicity: Symbols and Strategies of Contemporary Ethnic Life*, ed. Stephen Stern and John Allan Cicala (Logan: Utah State University Press, 1991), 3–20.

CHAPTER 3

Creative Ethnics: Dyngus Day in Polish American Communities

Deborah Anders Silverman

In a small town in upstate New York, a 66-year-old politician, pussywillow whip in hand, dons a special clown costume every Easter Monday to observe an ancient Polish fertility rite, Dyngus Day. On that same day fifty miles away, in Buffalo, New York, thousands of Polish Americans and their non-Polish friends take part in a public variant of the celebration, Dyngus Day parties, which are held in social clubs, taverns, and church halls throughout the metropolitan area.

Although the politician's private rite and the public parties differ in some respects, the two Dyngus Day celebrations contain similarities. Both promote an awareness of the Polish heritage to outsiders and help Polish Americans define their identity as individuals through their ethnic group's folklore, an idea articulated by Alan Dundes.[1] This essay, utilizing Stern and Cicala's concept of "creative ethnicity" and Hobsbawm and Ranger's idea of "the invention of tradition," will explore how Polish Americans have revived the Dyngus Day tradition as a creative, personal expression of their ethnicity at both the individual and communal levels.[2]

Historical Background

Dyngus Day has been observed as a springtime fertility rite in Poland and other eastern European countries for over a thousand years. In this rite, one of many related to the agricultural cycle of Poland, boys carrying containers of water broke into girls' homes at daybreak on Easter Monday to surprise the girls while still in bed, soaking them thoroughly. Often, after all the buckets were emptied, the girls were dragged, screaming, to the nearest river for another soaking. In some localities, the girls were able to buy immunity from the drenching by giving the boys a few colored eggs, believed by Poles since the Middle Ages to be magical charms ensuring success in childbirth, sexual relationships, and harvests.[3] The following day, the girls would soak the boys.

Although the practice was intended as good-natured horseplay, occasionally someone would get hurt, which prompted the Bishop of Pozna in 1420 to issue a "Dingus Prohibetur" in which it was "forbidden on the second day [Easter Monday] and third day [Tuesday] of Easter to pester or plague others in what is universally called Dingus."[4] Despite the edict, the custom thrived among the peasants, although the nobility, and in later years city dwellers, considered themselves too refined for such rough-and-tumble nonsense; they chose to sprinkle others lightly with perfume or water from a small flask.

Peasants in Hungary and Czechoslovakia also participated in the water dousings. In Hungary, Easter Monday was known as *Vizbeveto*, or Water Plunge Monday, when young men splashed unmarried girls with water, sometimes receiving red Easter eggs from the girls.[5] Pirkova-Jakobson notes that the sprinkling custom was carried from Czechoslovakia to America, where it was practiced among Slovaks in Manhattan.[6]

A variant of the custom, practiced both in eastern Europe and in America, involved the use of pussywillow whips in addition to, or in place of, water. Knab suggests that pussywillows were used during the Easter season because Poles lacked the palms indigenous to Jerusalem. These branches were blessed by the priest in church on Palm Sunday. After Mass, parishioners struck one another with pussywillow branches, saying "*Nie ja biję, wierzba bije, za tydzień, wielki dzień, za sześć noc, Wielkanoc,*" meaning, "I don't strike, the willow strikes, in one week, the great day, in six nights, the great night, Easter."[7] Returning home, the people placed the blessed pussywillows in the rafters of buildings or behind holy pictures to protect against lightning, in beehives to encourage honey production, or near animals to protect them against harm. The pussywillow branch was believed to bring good luck to humans as well; according to one Polish American informant, a girl who swallowed one of the pussywillow buds on Easter Monday would enjoy good luck in the year to come. In Poland, each family member swallowed three pussywillow buds on Palm Sunday to prevent health problems involving the throat, teeth, and stomach.[8]

On Easter Monday in some eastern European and American communities, boys chased girls with the whips, attempting to strike their legs; the girls reversed roles the following day.[9] As in the water dousing version, girls sometimes could buy immunity from the whipping by offering colored eggs to the boys. A male Slovak American informant stressed the ceremonial nature of the whipping: "It is nothing. It is in name only. It is to commemorate that in our country we used to whip the Christ. It is not real."[10] The reference to the scourging of Christ also appears in some accounts of Dyngus Day as observed in nineteenth-century Poland, where the whipping was done either on Palm Sunday or Good Friday.[11]

Another aspect of Dyngus Day both in America and Poland was a procession by younger boys through the town, known as *po dyngusie*, or "going on the dyngus." *Po dyngusie* can be placed within the context of European solicitation customs extending from Christmastime to the summer solstice, many of them associated with fertility rites.[12] One version of *po dyngusie* in rural Poland was known as *kogutek* ("rooster"), focussing on the rooster, which symbolized the onset of spring and assured fertility.[13] Boys placed a rooster on a small, two-wheeled red wagon decorated with ribbons and flowers, then hauled the little cart from house to house, crowing like roosters, singing, and in general trying to amuse the inhabitants in order to receive food from the festive Easter tables, especially decorated hardboiled Easter eggs, ham, or sausage.[14] The Dyngus songs generally contained good wishes, requests for gifts and food, or threats, as in the following popular song:

> Your duck has told me
> That you've baked a cake
> Your hen has told me that
> She's laid you a basket and a half of eggs
> Your sow has told me that you've killed her son
> If not her son then her little daughter
> Give me something if only a bit of her fat
> Who will not be generous today
> Let him not count on heaven.[15]

In another version of *po dyngusie*, the boys proceeded through the village accompanied by a comrade wearing a bell on his head and dressed as a bear, either in a real bearskin or one made of pea vines. The bear was the most important animal to Indo-Europeans, believed to have the power to prevent evil, bring good crops, and cure diseases.[16] The *po dyngusie* group went door to door, collecting food gifts from each home, before proceeding to a nearby stream to "drown" the bear. Polish folklorist Oskar Kolberg has recorded another variant of *po dyngusie* in Mazowsze and Malopolska, where boys wearing bear skins chased girls. Often the "bears" were invited into homes for food, since they were believed to ensure a good harvest.[17]

In some regions, the girls also made their rounds on Easter Monday, going cottage to cottage with a *gaik*, a freshly cut green branch. Like the boys, they too sang traditional songs in return for holiday food or small gifts. Songs such as the following welcomed the new year:

> Our green little tree, beautifully decked
> Goes everywhere
> For it is proper that it should
> We go with it to the manor house
> Wishing good fortune, good health
> For this new year
> Which God has given us.[18]

In addition to the processions, families often called on one another on Dyngus Day, bringing gifts of Easter eggs or rolls. They were welcomed with greetings of the season and food from the Easter table.

Origins and Etymology

Both the meaning of *Dyngus* and the holiday's origins are shrouded in mystery. One possible source of *dyngus* is the German word *dingeier*, meaning "the eggs that are owed," a reference to the aforementioned custom of going out to ask for eggs at Eastertime;[19] another possibility is the German word *dingnis*, meaning "ransom," referring to the girl's ability to buy immunity from the ritual punishment intended for her. A Polish-English dictionary suggests that *dyngus* is synonymous with *śmigus*, which means "a water dousing on Easter Monday."[20] The most widely used definition, however, is from informants in the Buffalo, New York, area, who say *dyngus* means "a switch" or "a reed used in whipping."[21] In addition to Dyngus Day and Śmigus Day, the day is less often referred to as *Swęity Lej*, literally, "holy rein" (for whipping); *dzien swiętego Lejka*, "day of the holy whipping"; or *oblejor lany poniedzałek*, "the Monday to pour from a container."

Most sources agree that the Dyngus Day holiday predates Poland's conversion to Christianity in A.D. 966, but beyond that, there is much speculation. Knab asserts that it dates back either to the time of the early Christians in Jerusalem, when Jews used water to disperse the Christians who had gathered together to talk of the risen Christ, or to the immersion of early Christians in water as a means of baptism.[22] Another source claims that the drenching originated with the baptism of Poland's ruler Prince Mieszko in 966 and that the beating with pussywillows commemorates the scourging of Christ by Roman soldiers.[23] Since literacy did not emerge in Poland until well after the establishment of Christianity, verification of such claims is virtually impossible.

László Lukács notes that written sources trace the dyngus switching custom back to the Middle Ages, women whipping their husbands on Easter Monday and men lashing their wives the next day as a reminder of the prohibition on marital sex during the period of Easter Communion.[24]

The similarity of Dyngus Day to such ancient pagan Roman festivals as the Lupercalia—with its emphasis on the ritual whipping of women to make the crops grow—cannot be overlooked. Scholars have long noted the similarities between ancient Roman and Slavic customs.[25] Lupercalia occurred during the month of Februarius, the last month of the year in the early Roman calendar, which was dedicated to acts of purification in preparation for the new year. During the feast of Lupercalia on February 15, men wearing only a loincloth ritually struck women with strips of skin from sacrificial goats. This ceremony honored the god Faunus and was thought to ensure fertility and an easy delivery.[26] The Lupercalia and Dyngus Day whippings exemplify the principle of homeopathic or imitative magic as described by Frazer: People personified the powers of vegetation as male and female "to quicken the growth of trees and plants by representing the marriage of sylvan deities as a King and Queen of May."[27]

The pagan Slavs who lived in what is now Poland in the period A.D. 500–900 worshipped trees, which were believed to make rain fall, sun shine, flocks and herds multiply, and women bear children easily.[28] Groves of oak trees were the sites where the pagans worshipped the thunder god Perun, the deity of fertility. It is possible that the ancient Slavs' Dyngus Day rite was a symbolic reenactment of the battle between Perun and the death god, Iarilo, which resulted in Perun's victory over Iarilo.[29] It is probable that Slavic goddesses also played a role in the dyngus rites, since all were associated with fertility. The most likely candidate is the Corn Mother, who made crops grow. In pagan times, a Corn Mother doll or wreath was symbolically drenched with water and kept until the following spring, when its grain was mixed with new seed grain at planting time to ensure a successful harvest.[30]

With the arrival of Christianity in Poland, the worship of Iarilo, Perun, and the other pagan gods did not disappear immediately. Early records of the Catholic Church contain reports about pagan temples, practices, and idols, some of which were fused with Christian figures to produce a "double faith."[31] The Church's Easter cycle was superimposed upon the old pagan springtime fertility rites such as Dyngus Day. This may explain why some informants in this study referred to Dyngus Day as a rite of spring, but others demurred, giving the holiday Catholic attributes:

> [It was] a very joyous day after the dullness of Easter, the long sessions in church, because you had to get up at 4:30 to make a five o'clock sunrise Mass, which was traditional in Polish churches. And of course, the Lenten season was stringently enforced food-wise. You never had meat on Friday, and you only had meat once a day on the other days. Then, your two lighter meals were not to exceed the last meal.
>
> And then, everyone also gave up candies, particularly children, and all kinds of goodies as a show of personal discipline. So consequently, you really looked forward to an unabashed explosion of hijinks and good spirits, which is Dyngus Day. Everyone wants to have some very deep explanation of the event, but that's about it.[32]

Going on the Dyngus: A Personal Expression

Such an "unabashed explosion of hijinks and good spirits" is at the heart of the Dyngus Day ritual performed by county legislator Chester Tarnowski of Dunkirk, New York. Dyngus Day is an opportunity for him to express his ethnicity in a highly idiosyncratic, creative manner as his response to social problems that have largely undermined the Polish American community in which he was raised. Like so many of the ethnic Americans studied by Stern and Cicala in their book *Creative Ethnicity*, Tarnowski has adapted a traditional genre, the Dyngus Day rite, to a new setting:

> For Dyngus Day, I take a personal day from my job. It's been a tradition, back when I was a kid, when my dad and I used to go out for Dyngus Day, and he always taught me, you dress up as a clown or whatever it is, and you go out there and make people happy. That's the most important thing. If you can't make people happy, you might as well stay home. Like I said, I go out and I whip the girls, no matter where, down to the *Observer*

[newspaper], I make some stops. They know I'm coming. On Tuesday, the girls are supposed to whip the boys. But you don't see that tradition any more. But I keep this tradition going. Maybe I'm the only one. I don't know.[33]

When he was a young boy, Tarnowski not only accompanied his father, whose rounds were unique at that time in town, but observed his own Dyngus Day routine with other boys: "Sometimes, when we had the Polish school here at St. Hedwig's, while we were on Easter vacation when we were kids, we used to go chase the girls around on Easter Monday with our whips. But the girls very seldom chased us around on Tuesday."[34]

Tarnowski's father's custom follows the lines of the eastern European solicitation customs previously cited, in which entertainers sing, dance, or recite verses in exchange for gifts of food or drink. In keeping with his late father's practice, Tarnowski, accompanied by a friend,[35] makes the rounds of family, friends, and business acquaintances during his early morning "dyngusing," carrying a pussywillow whip and dressed in a funny costume: an old, oversized suit; ancient, worn-out shoes; and a top hat. It is different from his father's costume, which was calculated to win guffaws from the Polish immigrants in the neighborhood: a big, old-fashioned hat; patched, old clothes; and an old scarf—"like he was just off the boat from Poland, but not as a clown."

In the fifties and sixties, when the generation of original Polish immigrants who appreciated the "boat" humor died and Tarnowski's father retired from dyngusing, Tarnowski decided to update his Dyngus costume for a new generation, which, like Tarnowski himself, appreciated the Marx Brothers. He added a Harpo Marx wig, a Harpo-style horn, and Harpo's distinctive whistle. "The reason for that is, I'm like a Harpo, you know. I get more laughs out of it, I guess. The younger people enjoy that more than if I did it like my dad. But I still go out for the Dyngus, though. I don't color my face or anything, but I put the old pants on and the suspenders and the wig and the hat."

The Dyngus Day clown costume is just one of many outfits that Tarnowski dons for various community celebrations such as

Figure 1. *Po dyngusie: a personal expression*. Wearing a Harpo Marx wig, Chet Tarnowski of Dunkirk, New York (at right) pauses for a beer with friend Alex Uszacki, his driver, on Dyngus Day. Photo by Deborah Anders Silverman.

Halloween parades, Fourth of July street dances, or firemen's parades. On these occasions, Tarnowski dresses in a clown suit or long johns and an old derby, pretending to play a saxophone along-side the musicians in the band. But he stresses the uniqueness of his Dyngus Day costume, which he has adapted to his generation's tastes much like the British "invented traditions" of 1870–1914.[36]

At about the same time that Tarnowski selected the Harpo Marx concept for Dyngus Day, he also switched from the Polish to the English language during his rounds because Polish was no longer the primary language spoken in the neighborhood. There also were other changes by the mid-sixties: People no longer offered him the foods that he and his father had collected in earlier years, such as oranges, apples, coffeecakes, sausages, cakes, "whatever they had handy." He only receives these foods when he stops at his brother's house.

The foods were no longer offered because of another change that occurred around 1970 in the Polish American neighborhood. A microcosm of American society, Tarnowski's neighborhood at that time began to reflect the economic realities that impelled large num-bers of women into the paid workforce. This forced Tarnowski to follow his intended victims to their new locations, the businesses, "because I couldn't find nobody on the streets any more." Therefore, after a few early morning visits to relatives, Tarnowski drives down-town and hops out of his car. He moves with lightning speed through businesses, greeting women with a breezy, "Hi, honey, happy Dyngus Day!" lightly switching each one with a pussywillow branch. Although he enjoys disrupting office routines as much as his beloved Marx Brothers did, Tarnowski realizes there are limits: "You want to just go right in and right out, because you don't want to cause hard feelings. They've got their jobs."

Despite the speed with which he goes *po dyngusie* through the local newspaper office (which once publicized his run), a bank, a travel agency, a nursing home, city hall, and the county office build-ing, Tarnowski manages to squeeze in a few minutes along the way to conduct some business, an example of an esoteric folklore form that has become exoteric, crossing ethnic boundaries.[37] Tarnowski's approach is illustrated in the following exchange with a male bank officer who was holding a staff meeting: "Look, Wednesday night the Legislative Board's got a meeting in the county building and we're recognizing all the sports teams. I see you're the sponsors from Lake Shore Bank. Could anybody be there to accept a little certificate? Wednesday night at 7:30, in Mayville. You can send any one of these girls. You can send them all!" (Everyone laughs.)[38]

After his whipping ritual is finished downtown at mid-morning, Tarnowski returns to his brother's house for a beer, some light-hearted banter with other relatives and friends, and Polish Easter fare cooked by his brother from recipes orally transmitted from their father: kielbasa, Easter *barszcz* (soup), and homemade horseradish served with hard-boiled eggs. It is a morning for socializing, networking with business associates, and, from Tarnowski's perspective, for educating his female victims about Dyngus Day, since they are of all ages and ethnic backgrounds, unlike the young Polish girls who were the targets a generation ago. His fear that his message would be lost for future generations surfaced repeatedly when he urged me, "Get everything down for your book." He was convinced of the importance of his mission despite the possibility of looking undignified: "Me being a politician, you'd think I wouldn't bother, you know? That's crazy. You stay with your tradition. I don't give a damn how big a politician you are or whatever. You just go out and do your thing. I think the people enjoy it more when they see you like this than with a freaking regular suit on."

Tarnowski insists that his victims "love" the routine, a claim that is somewhat exaggerated according to one informant, a newspaper reporter of Polish descent: "It's the day we most dread because we know what's coming. It's the same routine every year. Most of the women here are not Polish, or if they are, they don't practice the Dyngus Day custom. Once I knew that's what he [Tarnowski] does every year, I decided to head for the bathroom as soon as he comes through the front door."[39]

The newspaper's British receptionist has similar thoughts: "I want to run and hide. [She laughs.] Because he's so up when he comes in and he usually comes in and says, 'Go-o-o-d morning! Happy Dyngus Day!' And he hits you with the switch, that switch, and then off he goes into the newsroom as fast as can be. I didn't know what

Dyngus Day was until I came to work here, then Leo Kaleta explained it. I didn't know any Polish customs. But Chet's a harmless type."[40]

Tarnowski's wife of thirty-five years, Joyce, was also a newcomer to Dyngus Day because her family is of Swedish descent. When they were dating, he came to her house in a nearby village to administer the Dyngus Day whipping; after they got married, he continued the tradition, which she "went along with," either amused by or annoyed with her husband, depending on her mood on a particular Dyngus Day.[41]

It is doubtful whether future generations will comprehend the meaning of Dyngus Day as practiced by Tarnowski. For Tarnowski, the ritual functions both as an expression of his personality and a link to his past, a heritage that seems to be vanishing since the dwindling ranks of young Polish Americans in town are not interested in maintaining his Dyngus Day rite. Even Tarnowski's two sons, who accompanied him on his rounds when they were children, have shown no interest in the family custom. Tarnowski's explanation for the lack of interest is that the city's shaky economic base has forced many young adults to move to other communities lacking a Polish American culture, where they forget about their ethnic heritage. As for those who remain, Tarnowski believes their interests have been influenced by contact with non-Polish Americans.

A more plausible explanation, however, focusses on the meaning of the Tarnowski Dyngus Day ritual for its victims. A generation ago, they were Polish women who were participants in an ongoing ritual in their culture. They had a well-defined role on Dyngus Day, in some cases giving eggs to the boys who whipped or drenched them, with the promise of retaliation the next day. Today, most of the women are passive recipients from other ethnic and racial backgrounds for whom Dyngus Day is meaningless. Furthermore, given the fact that they are seated behind office desks conducting business when Tarnowski visits them, they have little opportunity to respond to Tarnowski's Dyngus Day ritual.

However, in Poland and other Polish neighborhoods in North America, the Dyngus Day water sprinkling ritual has retained its vitality. In the Detroit suburb of Hamtramck, for example, Polish

Americans of all ages participate in the custom.[42] In southern Ontario, pussywillows and buckets of water are utilized as weapons by Polish Canadians of both sexes in good-natured horseplay. One woman in her mid-thirties climbed up to a friend's window at six o'clock on a recent Dyngus Day morning to soak her when she opened her window.[43] Another Ontario resident reported that when she visited her grandmother in Poland in 1991, she sat on the landing of a stairwell to soak her male cousin with a bucket of water when he came to visit on Dyngus Day.[44]

This tomfoolery continues in an increasingly popular folkway, which is, to borrow Hobsbawm and Ranger's phrase, an "invented tradition," the Dyngus Day party, which attracts several thousand tourists and Buffalo residents each year.

Going on the Dyngus: Community Expressions

Buffalo's Dyngus Day parties were created in the sixties, a period when the traditional East Side Polish community was on the decline. David Franczyk, the city councilman who now represents that district, recalls the community as it had existed for many years before: "This neighborhood was built like a village. You had the neighborhood tavern in between each block, dance halls, churches, a Dom Polski community center, the Polish Union insurance hall. The city also had other ethnic groups interacting and a mixing of classes as well."[45]

Novelist Verlyn Klinkenborg, chronicling the demise of his father-in-law's East Side tavern during the sixties, believes the neighborhood began to decay as early as 1947, the year his father-in-law returned from World War II to run the family business: "Here in Buffalo, as in Europe, the neighborhood as they have constituted it is beginning to be over—over, at least, for the Poles whom the East Side has sustained for half a century, as it did the Irish and Germans and Jews before them. No one sees it coming, though it surrounds them, in small ways as yet."[46] Klinkenborg points to the arrival of blacks in the neighborhood, increasing numbers of restaurant patrons commuting from other suburban Buffalo neighborhoods, and the out-migration of Polish Americans from the city to the suburbs as signs of change apparent well before 1950.[47]

Census figures indicate that many foreign-born Poles and second-generation Polish Americans moved from the city to suburbs such as Cheektowaga, where housing values were higher, between 1960 and 1970. In 1960, Buffalo's total population of 532,759 included 47,589 of Polish foreign stock; ten years later, Buffalo's total population declined to 462,781, including 31,699 of Polish stock. In contrast, the ranks of Poles increased in nearby Cheektowaga during that decade. Cheektowaga's total population of 52,362 in 1960 included 5,519 of Polish stock; in 1970, its total population grew to 58,778, including 5,648 of Polish stock.[48]

Thus, by the 1960s, those who remained in Buffalo's East Side Polish community were anxious about its future. They turned to their ethnic past for some solutions, among them the Dyngus Day party. A more public, updated version of the old neighborhood Dyngus Day, the party is an example of a folk group's holiday custom that offers an outlet for temporary identity change, since "everybody is Polish on Dyngus Day," as proclaimed by the Buffalo news media.[49] The colorful parties at dozens of bars, restaurants, churches, and social clubs originated in 1962 at the clubrooms of the Chopin Singing Society in Buffalo with club members Ted and Ann Mikoll and Ted's brother James:

> He [Ted] said, "Wouldn't it be great to sort of bring back the spirit of fun and getting together the day after the holy day, and have a grand old party?"
>
> So we began. To begin with, the entire event was free. You were admitted, the Chopin Society played host to this, and we had huge buffet tables and a lot of the businessmen donated hams and sausages, and bakeries gave us baked goods, and we baked ourselves, because the Poles are very famous for wonderful baked goods. The only thing that cost money was if you bought drinks, then you bought them on your own. But the food was there for everyone to partake of.[50]

In later years, as Chopin's party began to attract upward of 3,000 people, tickets were sold for the buffet meal. Other social clubs, churches, and taverns, some of them *not* run by Polish Americans,

soon followed Chopin's lead, selling tickets to what one major organizer calls, in disgust, merely a "moneymaker" by tavernkeepers
unconcerned about the holiday's ethnic origins.[51] According to one
estimate, there were twenty different parties in Buffalo and its suburbs on Dyngus Day in 1993, most starting early in the afternoon
and lasting until the wee hours of the following morning.[52]

The Chopin Singing Society is both a social club and a semi-pro-
fessional choir. Founded in 1899 by the organist of a nearby Polish
Catholic parish, the society has performed with the local
Philharmonic Orchestra, in national singing competitions, and on
concert tour in the United States and Poland. Promoting an awareness of the Polish heritage is one of the society's stated goals. The
Dyngus Day party was among the first of the Chopin Society's
recreations, coming at a time when membership was at its nadir, a
reflection of the city's demographic changes cited earlier.[53] Only fifteen men remained in the choir; they were passing the hat to pay the
club's bills. A new series of concerts emphasizing Polish folksongs
and dances and the Dyngus Day party were viewed as a way to revi-
talize the society both culturally and financially. More recently, in the
seventies, the organization hired a choreographer who led the chorus
through a series of twenty-six television programs that recreated
Polish traditions, including "Dozynski" (Harvest Festival), the
"Polish wedding," and "Jaselka" (Christmas Pageant). In 1984, the
society presented a "Noc Swiętojanska" (Night of St. John) Festival
marking the summer solstice for five thousand viewers at Delaware
Park Lake in Buffalo.

Chopin's Singing Society, which sets itself apart from later imita-
tors by selling buttons reminding all that it was the originator of the
Dyngus Day party, presents a carefully crafted expression of Polish
American identity on Dyngus Day. It offers an opportunity for in-
group bonding and for outsiders, as Olivia Cadaval has noted in discussing Latino festivals, a chance to experiment with another
culture.[54] Chopin's party features a number of elements, including
local dignitaries such as the Irish American mayor and the Polish
American county executive who officially sanction the event by giving short opening remarks at noon.[55] During the lunch hour, many
community leaders, judges, and aspiring politicians of all ethnic

backgrounds find their way to Chopin's to socialize, a feature not found at the other Dyngus Day parties and a reflection of the Chopin Society membership's leading role in Buffalo's political life. However, not all politicians appear there willingly; one retired Polish American judge told me his family considered the traditional Dyngus Day whipping barbaric, and he appeared at the Dyngus Day party only in the days when he was campaigning for office.[56]

Other elements of Chopin's party include the presence of a leading Polish American priest who performs, in Polish, a traditional Easter blessing called the *święconka* before the food is consumed; spring flowers and pussywillows for sale at a flower stall reminiscent of the market in Warsaw, another link to the old country; and young costumed folk dancers who do not dance during the party but instead mingle with the crowd and pose for photos.[57] Chopin's party also features Polish folksongs (sung in Polish) and American patriotic songs (in English), performed by the Chopin Singers on cue from the television reporters covering the event. The variety of elements offers entertainment for all ages.

Polka music, reflective of the *Polish American* rather than *Polish* heritage, is the central element at Chopin's and the other Dyngus Day parties.[58] Generally, the parties feature at least two polka bands, one of them a nationally known band. Tickets usually cost about five dollars, which includes food and admission to the dance floor; drinks are extra. One organizer believes that the key to a successful Dyngus Day party is picking the right entertainment: polka bands that people want to dance to and lyrics sung in English rather than Polish.[59] This will appeal to polka music's wide audience, which includes people not only of Polish descent, but Italians, Germans, Irish, and others.[60]

Unlike the traditional neighborhood Dyngus Day of a generation ago when Polish was spoken, today's Dyngus Day party participants converse in English, and nearly sixty percent of the polka lyrics are in English as well.[61] Both the polka musicians and the audience acknowledge their limited facility in the Polish language, although those who are middle-aged or older may have studied Polish in the parochial elementary schools, and younger adults may have taken a formal Polish language course in college. When songs at polka

Figure 2. *Dyngus Day: community expressions.* Garbed in traditional Polish folk costumes, Chris Krawczyk, Katarzyna Kumor, and Michael Zachowicz pose for photographers at the Chopin Singing Society's Dyngus Day party in Buffalo. Photo by Deborah Anders Silverman.

dances or Catholic Masses are sung in Polish, most often they are sung phonetically.[62]

Another important element is traditional food, which, as Susan Kalčik has noted, is a significant and emotional way of celebrating one's ethnicity and group identity.[63] Chopin's Dyngus Day party features the widest array of Polish Easter foods, offering a buffet with ham, Polish sausage, hard-boiled colored eggs, lazy pierogi (a noodle casserole), salads, breads and Polish coffeecakes, cakes, and cheesecakes. Other parties offer a more limited menu, generally featuring Polish sausage or drinks only.

In addition to the traditional foods, special clothing and other visual elements make a statement about ethnic identity. Occasionally, one will see men with pussywillows or squirt guns loaded with water or perfume, aiming for their favorite ladies (although the women rarely reciprocate). Partygoers often wear clothing in the Polish colors red and white, Dyngus Day buttons and t-shirts or "Polka Maniac" headbands sold by the various party sponsors, and red and white bow ties or hats. Other visual elements include banners saying *witamy*, meaning "welcome" in Polish; red and white balloons; "Happy Dyngus Day" signs in English; and the flags of Poland, America, Canada, or the sponsoring organization. All of these promote group identity. As one organizer noted, "That's our logo: 'Polka Pals' with the eagle, the crown, and 'Buffalo, New York' on it. Anybody that sees that flag or the shirts that we wear, they know they're in for a good time."[64]

As in peasant Poland's *po dyngusie* celebration, today's American Dyngus Day revelers travel from party to party. Polka musicians who have the day off join local residents and busloads of tourists from other cities in the northeastern United States and Canada. Unlike the planners of the Chopin party, who are intent upon maintaining their Polish heritage, these tourists are seeking something else, according to the editor of a national Polish American newspaper: "They're not looking at this as cultural anthropologists. They get on those buses, and the vodka's open by nine o'clock in the morning. I'm not saying they're rabble-rousers, but they party!"[65]

The editor's comments point to a class division within the Polish American community, centering around the issue of authenticity, most commonly reflected in the members' attitudes toward polka music. As a Buffalo city councilman remarked, "You will find ethnic music [the polka] created in an art form that might be looked down upon by certain people that like 'High C' culture: Chopin music, Adam Mickiewicz lectures. You know where you find good 'Low C' culture? Polka music. But some consider it low class, blue collar. Those people have aristocratic pretensions, although most of them are sons and daughters of peasants."[66] Nonetheless, polka music prevails at the Dyngus Day parties.

The immediate future for this invented tradition looks promising. In 1993, Buffalo's major parties each drew upward of 700 people of all ages, drawn by the polka bands' promotional flyers, newspaper announcements, or the New York State Tourist Guide's listing of the Chopin Dyngus Day party as one of the state's unique folk festivals. Syracuse, New York, held its first Dyngus Day party weekend in 1993 with 650 people in attendance; Chicago, home of the largest Polish American population, began a similar party in 1990, hosted by polka musician Eddie Blazonczyk; and South Bend, Indiana, for many years has held Dyngus Day parties similar to Chopin's.[67]

Conclusions

The Dyngus Day party is an example of an invented tradition that serves two purposes: to establish social cohesion within a group and to offer, as Hobsbawm and Ranger noted in discussing British invented traditions, an occasion for socialization and the inculcation of beliefs, value systems, and conventions of behavior.[68] The party was founded by Chopin's to promote an awareness of the Polish heritage and to encourage local residents to socialize at the clubrooms, although admittedly to make a profit for the club as well.

Whether the parties and the Tarnowski ritual will be maintained for any length of time is open for debate. Tarnowski vows to continue dyngusing, even if only for five minutes, as long as he remains in good health: "To me it means a lot because it's a Polish tradition. Sometimes you have to have a gift. And the people laugh. And while you're doing that, you're keeping up the Polish tradition."

The proliferation of Dyngus Day parties in Buffalo, when considered in tandem with the upsurge of interest in other Polish holiday folkways, genealogical societies, and Polish culture "hobby clubs" on computer networks, suggests that many ethnic Americans are returning to their roots in a quest for meaning.[69] As one informant put it, "The yuppie thing is sort of burned out, as [sociologist] Eugene Obidinski has pointed out. We've all got enough money now, and we're saturated. We've got every CD player that we need, every VCR, and we're going, 'Yeah, I've got twelve computers and I can run them. So what else is there?' They're looking for something."[70]

This is not to imply that one's ethnic identity is primary; it is just one of many identities available to Polish Americans. Nor am I suggesting that *most* Polish Americans are transmitting their folklore to the next generation. The future of Dyngus Day parties largely depends on individuals that Wsevolod Isajiw calls "ethnic rediscoverers," people socialized into the general society's culture who have developed a symbolic relation to the culture of their ancestors.[71]

Their quest for an ethnic identity has led them to invent a tradition, which, as Eric Hobsbawm has observed, occurs most frequently when a rapid transformation of society weakens or destroys the social patterns for which the "old" traditions had been designed.[72] Polish American communities have participated in such a rapid transformation during the twentieth century, a period that saw the disappearance of a number of folklore genres and their reemergence in altered forms.[73] The folk celebration of Dyngus Day, as indicated in this study, has been creatively reenacted at both the individual and group levels as a response to these rapid societal changes.

Notes

1. Alan Dundes, *Folklore Matters* (Knoxville: University of Tennessee Press, 1989), 2.

2. Stephen Stern and John Allan Cicala, eds., *Creative Ethnicity: Symbols and Strategies of Contemporary Ethnic Life* (Logen: Utah State University Press, 1991); Eric Hobsbawm and Terence Ranger, eds.

The Invention of Tradition (Cambridge: Cambridge University Press, 1983).

3. In the mid-thirteenth century, a monk living in Poland, known as Frater Rudolfus, published a "Catalogue of Magic Behavior," which mentioned eggs among the food products necessary for magical performances in connection with childbirth, relationships between the sexes, and for achieving happiness and an abundant harvest. The "Catalogue" is described by Maria Dembińska, "Some Symbolic Aspects of Food Products in the Light of a Thirteenth Century Polish Historical Source," in *Food in Perspective*, ed. Alexander Fenton and Trefor M. Owen (Edinburgh: John Donald, 1981), 69–76.

    Girls in Poland often gave red eggs to their boyfriends on Dyngus Day, the red symbolizing Christ's blood and new life. Until the mid-1800s, decorated eggs called *pisanki* were gifts during courtship; in some districts of Poland, girls would conceal eggs in their bosoms in hopes that their boyfriends would search for them. A girl would allow herself to be searched by the boy she hoped to marry. For details, see Sophie Hodorowicz Knab, *Polish Customs, Traditions, and Folklore* (New York: Hippocrene Books, 1993), 105–6.

    In Germany at that time, boys spanked their girlfriends with canes if they failed to give them red eggs at Eastertime; see Dorothy Gladys Spicer, *Festivals of Western Europe* (New York: H. W. Wilson, 1958), 61. In the former Czechoslovakia and in Slovak American communities, boys received painted eggs after whipping girls, as noted by Svatava Pirkova-Jakobson, "Harvest Festivals among Czechs and Slovaks in America," *Journal of American Folklore* 69 (1956): 275. A detailed explanation of the egg's role in springtime rites is contained in Venetia Newall, "Easter Eggs," *Journal of American Folklore* 80 (1967): 3–32.

4. Knab, *Polish Customs*, 110. For an excellent account of traditional Dyngus Day activities in agricultural Poland, see Knab, *Polish Customs*, 106–15. As Knab notes in the book's introduction, scholarly journals and books in the English language have carried very few articles about eastern European fertility rites such as Dyngus Day. Two notable exceptions are an essay by Polish ethnologist Cezaria Baudouin de Courtenay Jędrzejewicz, "Polish Peasant Rituals and Seasonal Customs," in *Polish Civilization: Essays and Studies*, ed. Mieczysław Giergielewicz (New York: New York University Press, 1979), 1–24; and Lászlo Lukács, "Easter Whipping: A Festive

Custom in Central Europe," *International Folklore Review* 3 (1983): 106–19.

5. Newall, "Easter Eggs," 14.
6. Pirkova-Jakobson, "Harvest Festivals among Czechs and Slovaks in America," 275. In addition to sprinkling girls with water at the beginning of the agricultural season, Czechoslovakian peasants did the same at harvest time, when the farmhands formed a procession to bear the first fruits of the harvest to the landowner. The leading girl in the procession was the victim of the drenching. For details, see Pirkova-Jakobson, 268.
7. Knab, *Polish Customs*, 95.
8. Taped interview with Florence Ruszaj, Eden Polka Festival, Eden, New York, July 21, 1991. The information about the use of pussywillow buds in Poland is contained in Knab, *Polish Customs*, 96.
9. In Germany and Hungary, whipping also took place on December 28, Holy Innocents' Day, the anniversary of King Herod's slaughter of Bethlehem's children. In the German version, boys and girls armed with switches and green branches would go out into the streets, spanking passers-by with their rods and demanding small gifts of money. See Spicer, *Festivals of Western Europe*, 84. Spicer theorizes that the custom originated in pagan times when whipping was an early spring purification rite. In Hungary, girls and young children would be whipped on that date to make them healthy; see Tekla Dömötör, *Hungarian Folk Beliefs* (Bloomington: Indiana University Press, 1982), 195.
10. Pirkova-Jakobson, "Harvest Festivals among Czechs and Slovaks in America," 275.
11. See Helen Stankiewicz Zand, "Polish American Holiday Customs," *Polish American Studies* 15 (1958): 88; and Knab, *Polish Customs*, 100. Knab notes that on Good Friday in the Pomorze region of Poland, boys and girls hit each other with willow branches, calling out "Boże rany, Boże rany, Chrystus byłukrzyjowany," meaning, "God's wounds, God's wounds, Christ was crucified." In another region, Kaszuby, Good Friday was known as "Płaczebóg," or "God crying." That morning, individuals in Kaszuby are awakened by being struck with a green branch; they are told to cry, because God is crying.
12. Knab, *Polish Customs*, 97, notes that on Palm Sunday in Poland, schoolchildren went door to door, reciting verses about the upcoming Easter holiday, for which they received eggs or baked goods. Barbara Bazielichówna reported on door-to-door solicitations during the

Christmas season by groups of adults in southern Poland; see Barbara Bazielichówna and Stefan Deptuszewski, "The Guisers of Koniaków," *Folklore* 68 (December 1957): 497, and Barbara Bazielichówna, "Further Notes on the Polish Guisers," *Folklore* 69 (December 1958): 254–61. Venetia Newall notes that in England, the last Saturday before Lent was Egg Saturday, when children visited homes, begging for gifts of eggs; and Bulgarians celebrated *Lazarovden*, St. Lazarus's Day, eight days before Easter, when groups of six girls would go house to house, singing and dancing about the resurrection of Lazarus. The performers received coins and red eggs from the peasants, who believed the girls brought good luck. See Newall, "Easter Eggs," 17–22. Northern Italy was yet another site where springtime solicitation customs were observed; see Clara Regnoni-Macera, "The Song of May," *Western Folklore* 23 (January 1964): 23–26.

13. Knab, *Polish Customs*, 111.
14. Sula Benet, *Song, Dance, and Customs of Peasant Poland* (New York: Roy Publishers, 1951), 58.
15. Ibid.
16. In Slavic lands, when a person became ill, a tame bear and its keeper were invited to the house. Then the sick person was placed on the floor and the bear would be ordered to step over the person, thus expelling the disease and the devil from the body. The bear also occupies a prominent place in Slavic literature, where metaphors for the bear and descriptions of bear hunts are frequent. See Maria Zagórska Brooks, "The Bear in Slavic and Polish Mythology and Folklore," in *For Wiktor Weintraub: Essays in Polish Literature, Language, and History Presented on the Occasion of His 65th Birthday*, ed. Victor Erlich et al. (The Hague: Mouton, 1975), 107–11.
17. Oskar Kolberg, *Lud* 38 (1948): 242 ff., cited in Brooks, "The Bear in Slavic and Polish Mythology and Folklore," 109.
18. Benet, *Song, Dance, and Customs of Peasant Poland*, 60.
19. Newall, "Easter Eggs," 26.
20. See Benet, *Song, Dance, and Customs of Peasant Poland*, 56–57; Sophie Hodorowicz Knab, "The Spirit of Dyngus," *Polish-American Journal*, April 1990, 9; and the *Kosciuszko Foundation Dictionary*, vol. 2 (New York: Kosciuszko Foundation, 1982), which on page 101 equates *dyngus* with *śmigus* and on page 566 defines *śmigus* as "water dousing on Easter Monday." A variant of the definition of *dyngus* as "water dousing" is offered by a United Press International newswire story, which

claims *dyngus* means "sprinkling." See Dennis O'Shea, "The Party's Not Over Yet," United Press International, April 4, 1983, PM cycle.

21. The definition of *dyngus* as "switch" was provided by informant Chester Tarnowski, taped interview, Dunkirk, New York, April 20, 1992; as "reed used in whipping" by New York State Supreme Court Associate Justice Ann Mikoll, taped interview, Depew, New York, July 13, 1992.

22. Knab, *Polish Customs, Traditions, and Folklore*, 108.

23. Tom Greenwood, "Smigus Dyngus! Watch Out for Water and Willows," Gannett News Service, April 1, 1991.

24. Lukács, "Easter Whipping: A Festive Custom in Central Europe," 116.

25. W. Warde Fowler, *The Roman Festivals of the Period of the Republic* (London: Macmillan, 1916), 48. Fowler notes the similarity of the ancient Roman festival of Mamurius Veturius on March 14, in which a man dressed in skins was beaten with long white rods and driven out of Rome, to the Slavic custom of "carrying out Death" in the spring.

26. Laurence Urdang and Christine N. Donohue, eds., *Holidays and Anniversaries of the World*, 1st ed. (Detroit: Gale Research, 1985), 68; and Robert Schilling, "Lupercalia," in *The Encyclopedia of Religion*, vol. 9, ed. Mircea Eliade (New York: Macmillan, 1987), 53.

27. Fowler, *Roman Festivals of the Period of the Republic*, 156.

28. James George Frazer, *The Golden Bough* (New York: Macmillan, 1922; reprinted, New York: Macmillan, 1971), 136.

29. Until the twentieth century, a vestige of this battle could be seen in eastern Europe as the custom of "carrying out Death" at the end of the old year, in which a person representing Iarilo or his female counterpart Marzanna was submerged in water. See Marija Gimbutas, "Slavic Religion," in *The Encyclopedia of Religion*, vol. 13, ed. Mircea Eliade (New York: Macmillan, 1987), 353–61. Sula Benet theorizes that a variant of "carrying out Death" was the custom of "drowning the bear" on Dyngus Day. See Benet, *Song, Dance, and Customs of Peasant Poland*, 59.

30. Gimbutas, "Slavic Religion," 360.

31. Ibid., 354. Also see Jdrzejewicz, "Polish Peasant Rituals and Seasonal Customs," 1–2.

32. Interview with Ann Mikoll previously cited.

33. Taped interview with Chester Tarnowski, Dunkirk, New York, July 7, 1991.

34. Taped interview with Chester Tarnowski and wife, Joyce, Dunkirk, New York, December 22, 1992. Subsequent quotations from Tarnowski, unless otherwise noted, come from the December 22, 1992, or July 7, 1991, interviews.

35. Tarnowski's friend, Alex Uszacki, does not participate in the Dyngus Day ritual. He drives Tarnowski to each location, then accompanies him inside. Tarnowski's father's rounds, in contrast, were made entirely on foot.

36. See Eric Hobsbawm, "Mass-Producing Traditions: Europe, 1870–1914," in *Invention of Tradition*, 263–307, for a discussion of the European traditions created in the four decades before World War I, a period which witnessed profound and rapid social transformations comparable to those in Polish American communities since the 1950s.

37. See Richard Bauman, "Differential Identity and the Social Base of Folklore," in *Toward New Perspectives in Folklore*, ed. Américo Paredes and Richard Bauman (Austin: University of Texas Press, 1972), 31–41. Bauman argues that not all folklore performances are intended for one's own ethnic group; some are directed toward outsiders, which seems to be the case with Tarnowski's Dyngus Day performance in his town's business district.

38. Recording of Chester Tarnowski, Dunkirk, New York, April 20, 1992 (Dyngus Day).

39. Telephone interview with Denise Zaffalon, Dunkirk, New York, January 10, 1993.

40. Taped interview with Joy Edwards, Dunkirk, New York, December 22, 1992.

41. Taped interview with Joyce Tarnowski previously cited.

42. See Greenwood, "Smigus Dyngus," n.p.

43. Taped interview with thirty-six-year-old Dianne Ziosk of Oshawa, Ontario, at a Dyngus Day party in the Buffalo, New York, suburb of Cheektowaga, April 12, 1993.

44. Taped interview with Lynda Waszczuk, age twenty-eight, of Oshawa, Ontario, at a Dyngus Day party in Cheektowaga, New York, April 12, 1993.

45. Taped interview with Buffalo Common Council Member David Franczyk at the Dyngus Day party at Chopin's Singing Society, Buffalo, April 12, 1993.

46. Verlyn Klinkenborg, *The Last Fine Time* (New York: Knopf, 1991), 135.

47. Ibid., 133–36 and 175–80.

48. U.S. Census of Population and Housing, *Census Tracts*, Buffalo, N.Y., 1960, Table P-1; and *Census Tracts*, Buffalo, 1970, Table P-2. This information is also reprinted and analyzed in an excellent article by sociologist Eugene Obidinski, who returned to Buffalo in 1977 to investigate the "alleged disappearance" of the Polish American community. See Obidinski, "Urban Location: A Necessary or Sufficient Basis for Polonian Ethnic Persistence," in *The Polish Presence in Canada and America*, ed. Frank Renkiewicz (Toronto: Multicultural History Society of Ontario, 1982), 243–67.

    It should be noted that the 1960 and 1970 census information probably underrepresents the true size of Buffalo's Polish American community, since it counts only immigrants and their children as Polish ("foreign born" or "native of foreign parentage"). By 1970, many Polish American families had lived in Buffalo for three or four generations.

49. See Dundes, *Folklore Matters*, 20, for a discussion of temporary identity change. In Buffalo, media interest in Dyngus Day has increased in recent years. The nationally distributed *Polish–American Journal*, for example, ran the headline "Everybody is Polish on Easter Monday" in its March 1991 edition, followed by a listing of Dyngus Day parties. Each year, the only daily newspaper, the *Buffalo News*, runs a photo of leading Polish American dignitaries preparing for Dyngus Day parties, and the three local television stations report portions of their newscasts live from these parties.

50. Interview with Ann Mikoll previously cited.

51. Taped interview with Bob Asztemborski at the Polish Falcons Club Dyngus Day party in Depew, New York, a suburb of Buffalo, April 12, 1993.

52. Taped interview with Fred Gordon at Chopin's Singing Society Dyngus Day party, Buffalo, New York, April 12, 1993.

53. Information on the history of the Chopin Singing Society is taken from *History of the Chopin Singing Society*, a typed document given to the author by Ann Mikoll.

54. Olivia Cadaval, "Making a Place Home: The Latino Festival," in *Creative Ethnicity*, ed. Stern and Cicala, 204–22.

55. Speeches by Erie County Executive Dennis Gorski and Buffalo Mayor James Griffin at Chopin's Singing Society Dyngus Day party, Buffalo, New York, April 12, 1993. Both stressed the need to instill in youngsters a love of their ancestors' heritages via such occasions as Dyngus Day.

56. Taped interview with retired Buffalo City Court Judge Alois Mazur, Buffalo, New York, September 14, 1991.

57. The presence of the young dancers—in their teens and early twenties—is significant because nearly all of Chopin's singers are in their fifties and sixties.

58. Information about the polka as a Polish American rather than a Polish phenomenon was provided by two informants: Buffalo native Steve Litwin, a polka musician now living in Binghamton, New York, in a taped telephone interview on January 30, 1993; and Gabrielle Merta, who emigrated to America from Poland in 1976, in a taped personal interview in Derby, New York, July 20, 1991. Charles Keil and Angeliki V. Keil also offer an extensive discussion of the origins of polka music in *Polka Happiness* (Philadelphia: Temple University Press, 1992), 19–35.

59. Taped interview with Tom Warzecha at the Rescue Fire Hall Dyngus Day party in Cheektowaga, New York, April 12, 1993. He was the promoter of the Syracuse, New York, Dyngus Day weekend first held in 1993, which drew over 650 people.

60. Taped interview with Edward Sabloski, president of the United Polka League of Mohawk Valley, at the Knights of St. John's Club Dyngus Day party, Cheektowaga, New York, April 12, 1993.

61. This estimate was provided in a taped interview by polka musician Chris Gawlak at the Polish Falcons Club Dyngus Day party, Depew, New York, April 12, 1993.

62. Gawlak interview previously cited and taped interview with polka band leader Ted Szymanski at the Eden Polka Festival, Eden, New York, July 21, 1991.

63. Susan Kalčik, "Ethnic Foodways in America: Symbol and Performance of Identity," in *Ethnic and Regional Foodways in the United States: The Performance of Group Identity*, ed. Linda Keller Brown and Kay Mussell (Knoxville: University of Tennessee Press, 1985), 38.

64. Taped interview with Ron Polak, leader of the Polka Pals polka booster group at the Eden Polka Festival, Eden, New York, July 21, 1991.

65. Taped interview with Mark Kohan, age 32, a polka musician and editor of the *Polish-American Journal*, in Buffalo, New York, December 29, 1992.

66. Taped interview with Buffalo Common Council member David Franczyk cited previously. Mr. Franczyk's council district includes Chopin's clubrooms.

67. Attendance figures were gathered by the author from each party's organizer; for Chicago, from informant Mark Kohan in a taped interview in Buffalo, New York, December 29, 1992. Regarding South Bend's parties, Democratic politicians of Polish descent independently developed their own Dyngus Day parties at approximately the same time as Buffalo's Chopin Singing Society. But neither city was aware of the other's event until a Buffalo newspaper columnist took note. See Bob Curran, "Buffalo Has Dyngus Day Spirit to Match South Bend's Big Blast," *Buffalo News*, April 12, 1992, B-2.

68. Hobsbawm and Ranger, *Invention of Tradition*, 9.

69. Home computer buffs can access the Polish Club on the Prodigy computer network. The Polish Club, founded in 1991 by retired judge Alois Mazur of Buffalo, has more than 100 members nationwide. Club members turn to one another for information about various aspects of Polish and Polish American culture, including recipes, holiday customs, brief reviews of new books, and translations of Polish proverbs and songs.

70. Interview with Mark Kohan previously cited. Eugene Obidinski, a sociologist at the State University of New York College at Oneonta, has written extensively about Polish American communities and is a frequent contributor to the *Polish-American Journal* edited by Kohan.

71. Wsevelod W. Isajiw, "Definitions of Ethnicity," *Ethnicity* 1 (1974): 111–24.

72. Hobsbawm and Ranger, *Invention of Tradition*, 4.

73. In the 1950s, Helen Stankiewicz Zand noted the disappearance of items in several folklore genres in a series of articles, which appeared in *Polish American Studies*. See, for example, Zand, "Polish Folkways in the United States," *Polish American Studies* 12 (July–December 1955): 65–72; "Polish Family Folkways in the United States," *Polish American Studies* 13 (July–December 1956): 77–88; "Polish American Holiday Customs," *Polish American Studies* 15 (July–December 1958): 81–90, previously cited; "Polish American Folkways: Cures, Burials, Superstitions," *Polish American Studies* 17 (July–December 1960): 100–104; and "Polish American Leisureways," *Polish American Studies* 18 (January–June 1961): 34–36. My own fieldwork since 1991 has confirmed that a new generation of Polish Americans is demonstrating renewed interest in folksongs and dances, crafts such as *pisanki* (decorated Easter eggs), foodways, folk celebrations, and rites of passage, particularly wedding customs.

Chapter 4

"May the Work I've Done Speak for Me": African American Women as Speech Community

Jerrilyn McGregory

This study of Philadelphia's Lucky Ten Social Club points to a phenomenon largely ignored by social scientists: the wide proliferation of voluntary associations among urban African Americans. The sociological commonplace that "organizations and associations of every kind multiply in the city" does not adequately explain the phenomenon.[1] Nor has its richness been properly revealed in a literature that tends to focus on political units to the neglect of those that are more social or aesthetic.

Historically, African Americans have developed voluntary organizations as part of what I would call a survival strategy. Such organizations tended to function as benevolent associations, dispensing mutual aid to their members. Their importance to social life was recognized by St. Clair Drake, who distinguished between African Americans "organized around churches and a welter of voluntary associations of all types" and those deemed "disorganized," whose dysfunctioning could be attributed to the absence of such networks.[2] Other scholars, however, have been slow to acknowledge the positive gains produced by these nonpolitical sodalities.[3] By privileging the political over the social, they have missed the survival imperative implicit in such groups.

Community groups of working-class African American women, moreover, remain virtually unexplored. In discussing women's groups, most scholars have highlighted the elite constituents of the "club movement."[4] The focus has been on the activities of politicized women—those who, under the banner of the National Association of Colored Women (NACW), "eschewed such traditional groups as sewing circles, church clubs, and sisterly orders and organized reform-oriented women's clubs."[5] Yet the "traditional groups," by their sheer numbers, were powerful forces. As valuable as the work of the NACW may have been, the bulk of African American women who empowered their families and communities through the maintenance of core values and traditions belonged to social clubs without a political agenda.

As a corrective to the imbalance in the literature, this study introduces the Lucky Ten Social Club, a group that is representative of a certain type of African American organization that effectively blends the sacred and the secular realms. Such groups tend to be headed by females, perhaps in response to male domination of many churches. The special fusion of realms that characterizes the LTSC, along with its members' attachment to group devotions, make it a unique phenomenon: a sacred/secular performance community.

The Lucky Ten: An Overview

The Lucky Ten Social Club began as a sewing circle over seventy years ago for women who had migrated from York County, Virginia, to Philadelphia. According to its founder and first president, Laura Barbour, the original name of the club was the Needle Guild. Barbour recalls that she first suggested the idea of the club to Irene Williams, whom she knew from Virginia, by saying, "Come on, let's form a club, a sewing club, so that we'll have something to do once a week from house to house."[6] Later, members changed the name to the Lucky Ten Social Club to reflect a sense of their group identity: "There were ten of us, and we thought we were lucky." Flossie Hargraves, who, along with Barbour, is one of the two surviving original members, relates that they once considered naming it the Virginia Club, "but that was too personal."[7] In time, that name perhaps would have hindered the admission of new members from outside their home state.

I base this essay on information gathered from many encounters with the Lucky Ten Social Club between 1987 and 1990. I first learned of the club while conducting research on a guide for the Philadelphia Folklore Project, a model urban folklore program.[8] I was then a doctoral candidate at the University of Pennsylvania in search of a dissertation topic, and I soon decided to focus on nonpolitical social organizations—the kinds of sodalities that supplied the social context for the preservation of many African American cultural traditions, but that folklorists and other researchers seldom mention.[9] Over three years, I attended club meetings, a fiftieth anniversary celebration, a tribute, choir rehearsals, a wedding, and most important, an annual pilgrimage to Virginia. By popular vote, I also gained permanent status as an auxiliary member. Even today, across the miles, members continue to expect me to acknowledge major transitions in their lives and to fulfill other obligations.

As a mainly working-class women's club, the LTSC represents the numerous social clubs that fulfilled a primary, adaptive role for African American migrants in a new social milieu. Announcements in one local African American paper, the *Philadelphia Tribune*, document the existence of hundreds of such social clubs with names like the Ideal Four, the Sophisticated Nine, Club Duo Decimo, the Blue Dahlia, and the Jolly Rovers.[10] Other clubs devoted to needlecraft bore names like the Busy Bee Sewing and Savings Fund Club, the Progressive Sewing Circle, and the Sunshine Sewing Club. Since many members of the LTSC worked outside the home as seamstresses or laundresses, it was fitting, if ironic, that they focussed their recreational activity on a sewing circle. At least sewing was the ostensible purpose of their meetings. Mrs. Hargraves puts things in the proper perspective when she asserts, "We didn't get together to sew. We got together to talk. You'd think we hadn't seen nobody in over ten years."[11] Ultimately, sewing became merely an excuse to bond together through a collective exchange of song, speech, and sociability.

Today the club is multigenerational, with members ranging in age from forty to ninety, and its twenty-two members include many descendants of the original founders. The family links are not incidental. In fact, the LTSC is a community of women formed around an intricate kinship network. Aunt Flossie and Aunt Carrie (Aunt being an honorific title conferred upon these women by their peers) are sisters-in-law, as are Aunt Carrie and Mary Anderson, the child of another of the original ten women. Aunt Flossie is also Mary Anderson's aunt, and both her daughter and granddaughter are club members. Mary Anderson has two daughters who are very active members. They also have nieces and cousins in the club.

Initially, all the members were from the same state, but the circle presently supports many members who did not originate from York County or even from Virginia. The club has also modified the original limit of ten members—"We just kept on accepting members that wanted to come in," says Alice Howard—so that the current membership is more than double that.[12] Even with the expansion, however, the links to Virginia remain strong, and the multiple family connections provide each member from Virginia a variety of conduits through which to acquire news of home. As Alice expressed it, "We call one another. 'You heard from Virginia?' 'You heard from Virginia?' 'So and so and so.' And if you got anything that was juicy, oh, we'd call then and it would go all around."[13]

Spirituality

Spirituality operates as a pervasive quality in the lives of many African Americans, and the LTSC members are no exception.[14] Operating as a sacred/secular performance community, Lucky Ten members uphold the collective values of church, community, and home. What Herskovits observed in general about African American culture is also true specifically about these women: "The essence of their belief is its intimate relation to life."[15] Spiritual fulfillment can be witnessed daily in many social contexts.[16] Because these women understand all daily activities as Christian experiences, they "witness" before the Lord through all that they do; their spirituality constitutes a state of being, not mere "religiosity."

Although there are no denominational requirements, most LTSC members are Baptists who belong to different Philadelphia area churches.[17] Regardless of church membership, however, their spirituality constitutes a common denominator. The club's organizational structure relies heavily on common operational elements from their Christian experience. In conformity with Christian values, their songs, words, and social discourse all revolve around overt forms of religious expression.

One central expression is the group's signature song, "May the Work I've Done Speak For Me," which is Hymn 399 in the New National Baptist Hymnal.[18] The hymn is dear to them because it has travelled with their chorus countless times on their annual pilgrimage back to York County. As Aunt Flossie describes the lyrics: "I think that's [they're] nice because [they're] true."[19] The lyrics suggest that work, good living, and service epitomize the spiritual ethos of all involved.

> May the work I've done speak for me
> May the work I've done speak for me
> When I'm resting in my grave
> There is nothing that can be said
> May the work I've done speak for me.

> *Refrain:* May the work I've done speak for me
> It seems so small
> Sometimes it seems like
> Seems like nothing at all
> But when I stand before my God
> I want to hear Him say, "Well done."
> May the work I've done speak for me.

> May the life I live speak for me
> May the life I live speak for me
> When the best I try to live
> My mistakes He will forgive
> May the work I've done speak for me.

> May the service I give speak for me
> May the service I give speak for me

When I've done the best I can
And my friends don't understand
May the work I've done speak for me.

For these women, then, good living comprises an unnegotiable part of thier daily lives and an extension of a spititualized work ethic.

An emphasis on good living, however, does not mean that members lead the lives of saints. Some even drink and smoke at club meetings—an innovation that one club member considers the biggest change over time. Rather, good living expresses the concern that individuals maintain strong spiritual connections with the Creator. One must work at this proposition, which entails the desire to live a God-centered life without becoming rigidly fundamentalist.[20] As the club's president and choir director, Kathryn Minnis, explains, it is not theological preciseness but "rightly directed" service that is of value:

> "May the Work I've Done Speak for Me" bespeaks not necessarily the Lucky Ten's or the Love & Trust's music, but it bespeaks all music. All those who make up singing groups, who sing for the grace of God, or who sing just to be happy to be singing with one another in terms of the community or for those home in houses. In terms of churchbuilding, whatever work that they have done, be it small, if rightly directed, it will in time be remembered.[21]

About 1932, because members found that they were doing more hymn singing than sewing at their meetings, some members organized an auxiliary group, the Love and Trust Chorus (L&TC), and this chorus has become an important element of their service orientation. When the choir performs at churches, it prides itself on always contributing to the host churches and accepting no pay. They have also made appearances at local nursing homes and hospitals, and they maintain several standing committees to strengthen their own members in sickness and in health through cash awards and more personalized forms of contact. It is very much through these service projects that they function as a spiritual community.

Traditions

While spirituality supplies the LTSC's basic glue, various expressive traditions enhance its sense of community. Three traditions—*esusu*, hospitality, and an annual pilgrimage—are particularly effective in connecting members to a "usable past."

Esusu. Because of the often harsh impact of the natural environment and economic systems upon their lives, black women both in Africa and in the diaspora "have had to rely on their own resources and to be ingenious with the meager resources at their command in order to survive."[22] One example of ingenuity is the West African savings system known as *esusu*, which is preserved in many variations throughout the New World.[23] Usually *esusu* operates as a sort of rotating credit association, with everyone contributing to a central fund and drawing from it in turn. As practiced by the LTSC, the tradition is more complex, since members juggle several funds at once, enumerate their profits, and act as a benevolent association.

Unfortunately, due to the comparatively few real dollars such associations generate, researchers have not granted them the attention they deserve. Some social scientists even deem the activities of these voluntary associations pathological because, considering the low economic return generated, they seem to serve merely a "sociable" or "expressive" function rather than an economic or political one.[24] The experience of the Lucky Ten refutes that reading. *Esusu* here combines expression and fiscal management to support the primary organizational objective of survival.

As a part of a traditional system of collective economics, one of the LTSC founders recalls, "We got together and everybody paid twenty-five cents for savings and twenty-five cents for Christmas."[25] The savings ritual remains the highlight of the monthly meetings. With three treasurers (a miscellaneous, a vacation, and a grand treasurer), suggesting the importance of savings to the group, today's members regularly deposit funds into their rainy day, vacation, and Christmas Club accounts. At the end of the year, each member receives these direct deposits along with a share of the profits from fund-raisers that may range from raffles to fashion shows to Atlantic City bus tours. Not only do they divide the profits from their collective endeavors, but they receive a percentage based on the level of participation from their reciprocal support network (friends whom they similarly assist). Therefore, members who sell the most fund-raising tickets receive the largest return. They realize that this arrangement will not make them wealthy, but it clearly enriches their lives in a nonfinancial way.

Hospitality. Descendants of the original LTSC members strive to sustain principles of hospitality that they learned from their foremothers and to extend them to one another and their coterie of friends. As practiced in many African societies, hospitality constitutes a primary social ritual.[26] Due to the enculturation that they received from their mothers, the LTSC members view hospitality as an essential part of their identity and an emblem of their commitment to tradition. Hospitality becomes the foundation on which collective interaction is built.

It is because of the importance of hospitality that individuals expend much energy on the presentation of food. Each meeting ends with a virtual feast. In the beginning, members attempted to conform to the more formal tradition of a tea social, but according to Aunt Flossie, "As time went by we got greedy, and we started to have full course dinners. . . . Until now we're still in that habit."[27] Following this traditional pattern, few meetings finish without a full complement of entrees (ham, chicken, beef, turkey, chitterlings), side dishes (greens, macaroni, salads), desserts (pies, cakes, ice cream), and beverages. Hosting such a feast can be a financial burden, but members clearly consider it worth the cost to reaffirm their foremothers' values in an urban context.

Pilgrimage. In the eighteenth century, the camp meeting revivals of the Great Awakening served as a primary vehicle for converting enslaved Africans to Christianity. Ever since then, revivals have had a deep spiritual meaning for many African Americans. They were truly "special occasions, when the congregation swelled with prayers for the unbaptized, who sat on the mourner's bench while others prayed and wept for their souls until the spirit came and they 'confessed religion.'"[28] In accordance with agrarian work patterns, August was the appointed month for most Christian revivals, and whole families planned their summers accordingly, arranging for part of their vacation time to be spent in celebration at these outdoor meetings. The LTSC's annual pilgrimage back to York County follows this time-honored pattern of return and renewal.

Their pilgrimage tradition began in the 1930s when, with the formation of the Love and Trust Chorus, they developed a means to reinsert themselves periodically into their community of origin. Indeed, the formation of the choir in the first place may have been largely a subconscious mechanism by which their mothers and grandmothers were able to recontextualize themselves as performers in their old congregations. Ever since, their annual August journey back to perform at Grafton Baptist Church and to "leave something on the table" (make a group donation) has held a paramount and ritualized importance for them.

The ritual return also constitutes an obligation to honor their ancestors and, as is the case with most pilgrimages, "when one starts with obligation, voluntariness comes in; when one begins with voluntariness, obligation tends to enter the scene."[29] In 1989, the Grafton church was rebuilt; and when they marched into the new structure for the first time, the L&TC recentered the church into a tradition that had already outlived one structure and perhaps will survive yet another.

The L&TC members make these trips at some financial cost, which speaks to their need to uphold the traditions of their foremothers along with their own childhood memories. Even for those who come along for conviviality but have no familial ties to the region, it is a weekend to experience vicariously the phenomenon of "going home." For these guests, the pilgrimage provides a symbolic integration into a surrogate community of fictive kin. This integration was described colorfully by the club's youngest member, relating en route to Virginia how she came to be involved with the Lucky Ten:

> I like to come on this trip. The first time I came on this trip, I got conned into coming on this trip. I thought it was going to be a *trip* trip. Next thing I know, I got the room and am in the service. The next thing, I'm sitting up in the choir loft, thinking what the hell am I doing here. You know?
>
> After that big breakfast, they went to the choir loft to rehearse. I was sitting down. My mother had gone out to the

bathroom. I heard Rita in the bathroom. They were peeling paint off the wall already, and she was just doing scales. I said, "I'm absolutely petrified of Rita." Minnis said, "We need another voice. Go get your mother." I said, "Oh, God. This is going to be good."

Mommy came back into the church and everything, and Minnis got her up in the choir loft. They said, "We need another voice. Diane, will you sit right here until the person who's supposed to sit here gets here to fill it out." They conned me, okay? My mother said, "Get on up here." I don't know none of those songs, okay? I don't know none of those songs.

I don't know none of those songs. So, I'm sitting there. And the next thing I know, I'm actually singing. "We're wearing white and black tomorrow." "We're wearing white and black tomorrow? Is that supposed to mean something?" "You'll have to get something. You sound good. You sound good. We can actually hear you."

So, I've been down every time since.[30]

Of course, the speaker was not necessarily as gullible as she pretends here; in reality, a combination of circumstances made her refusal to sing impossible. Her feigned naiveté, however, adds the charm of a congenial personal experience narrative to an already respected tradition.

The Lucky Ten Speaks: The Role of Testimony

bell hooks recalls how the fact that African American women form a social world apart from men implanted in her the desire for "talking back" along with the "craving to speak, to have a voice, and not just any voice but one that could be identified as belonging to me."[31] In the African American speech community, often seemingly dominated by the stylized speech acts of men, social clubs like the LTSC represent an arena where women may claim such a voice, may empower themselves and display their verbal competence.

It is important to make this point because most of the folklore literature on African American verbal artistry has concentrated exclusively on male speech acts.[32] When researchers mention their speech acts at all, women receive credit for their role in socializing the young men-of-words or for providing a female "counterpoint" within male-dominated discourse.[33] In many community contexts, African American women operate as the auxiliary units to male-dominated groups. Because they accept these roles, their public expressions—including their verbal performances—are often deemed more peripheral than those of men.

Exceptions to this general rule may be found, however. For example, in the Baptist denomination, during the devotion period that precedes the Sunday morning worship service, non-clergy can deliver impromptu prayers and testimonies, address personal concerns, and sing hymns; this format has traditionally afforded women a major oratorical role. That role is even more pronounced in club and auxiliary formats that are modelled on the church devotion but that are under the more direct control of women. Settings like that of the Lucky Ten Social Club meetings reflect the religious model by employing the same "formal religious tone and ritual of prayers, songs, and Bible verses prior to the business session and formal program; the collection of dues and a decided emphasis upon money matters."[34] But what unites these various elements is oratorical display—a display whose liberating potential illustrates the observation that "the magical incantation of the word and its transformative power gave sustenance and hope to Afro-Americans even in their darkest hour."[35]

From the club's inception, LTSC members displayed their competency in speech as well as in the conventional "female" areas of needlework, song, and the culinary arts. Today, the LTSC affords many opportunities for a sociolinguistic documentation of the role speech plays within a community of women. Mirroring the sacred performance community of the church, a devotional period traditionally opens each monthly meeting with the singing of hymns interlaced with spoken testimony. The president, Mrs. Minnis, explained that it is an LTSC tradition "to ask God's blessing and share how the Lord has blessed you and a prayer for those who are ill or less fortunate."[36] Such speech events are central to the group's experience.

The chaplain's opening prayer not only sets the spiritual tone, but alerts the group that the devotion is a ritualized, stylized moment when words may triumph. Mrs. Meekins, who has been the club's chaplain "forever and a day," typically opens the proceedings with a prayer like the following:

> Most Holy and everlasting Father,
> we want to thank you for this day.
> Father,
> we want to thank you that when we arose this morning,
> the blood still running warm in our veins.
> Father,
> we just want to thank you for each one of the members
>   who came out to the meeting.
> Father,
> we want to thank those
>   who wanted to come but couldn't,
> Father.
> Father,
> bless those who are in far-off lands.
> Bless them, Father.
> Father, we just want to thank you, Jesus.
> A thousand times.
> We couldn't have gotten here without you, Father.
> And ask you, Father,
> for those who stand by us
> and those who are not well in the body,
> touch them, dear Jesus.
> These and all other blessings I ask
>   in your name,
>   for your sake.
> Amen.[37]

Speaking mainly in the third person plural, Mrs. Meekins acts as the group's intermediary, addressing Jesus, who will deliver their message to God the Father on their behalf. Here, the speaker sets aside personal petitions in the interest of all. In comparison with the testimonies delivered by Pentecostal women, these rely less on the use of personal pronouns and, through multiple voices, create a unity of selves instead of a single introspective focus.[38]

Like many religious testimonies, LTSC testimonies tend to follow formulaic modes of address that include standardized phrasings of personal gratitude, such as, "I want to thank Him and praise Him."[39] LTSC members also direct each other as intercessors or intermediaries, creating a type of "symmetrical mediation" that is also found in West African prayer traditions.[40] The following example is a testimony by a member whose ill health had prevented her from attending many meetings that year.

> Truly I want to give my help to God.
> I want to thank Him and Praise Him
> for another chance
> and another privilege that He's given me
>   to meet with you all again.
> Sometimes I think that last time was the last time,
> but knowing God as I do,
> I know if I trust Him,
>   and I do—
> I put all of my trust in Him—
> And I know whatever you ask Him for—
> And ask honestly from your heart—
> He will give it to you.
> So,
> I'm asking y'all to just pray for me
>   that the Lord will ever keep me humble
> and that I still will be able to go
>   as long as I can
> and, when that time comes that I can't go,
>   don't worry about me
> because, when I leave here,
>   I'm going home to Jesus.
> So, pray much for me.[41]

Spoken in the first person with a sense of assurance that her fellow club members will honor her request for their prayers, the above text signifies not only the ability of a woman to "create for herself a space as the center of attention,"[42] but also the fact that a testimony is not a one-dimensional musing between one's self and God, but a means of addressing and morally engaging the members of the performance community. Petitioning God through prayer is one thing, but petitioning the group regenerates and involves everyone present.

Moreover, members recognize their meetings as the one setting where they come together with like-minded friends whom they can entreat, invoke, or petition. During devotions, members are free to speak expressly to the glory of God and to give Him thanks and praise. The quest is always to obtain the spiritual uplift one needs to deal with the more mundane concerns of life. In the next example, the vice president makes amends for testifying more than once. Sometimes one's fervor to praise God cannot be contained, and members recognize this sincerity.

> I am not going to be a Jumping Jack,
> but we just can't praise the Lord enough.　　[Amen]
> Because speaking for myself
> (I can't speak for you all),
> I have to speak for myself.
> But I just want to tell you that God is good.
> God is good to me
> 　　and my family
> through all of my trials and tribulations.
> You know,
> if you pray the Lord,
> He'll open the door for you.　　[Yes, He will]
> Not when you want it,
> But He'll open that door for you.　　[All the time]
> He'll open that door for you,
> and then those problems
> and trials and tribulations
> make you stronger—
> make you stronger.
> So, I wanted to say to the club,
> let's pray for one another.　　[Amen]
> Let's pray for one another.　　[Yes, Lord]

Let's pray that we will keep halfway good health
because you know that virus is   [going around]
    going around,
    going around.
Let's try to do the best we can
    so that our circle won't be broken
    until the Lord is ready for us to be taken.[43]
                      [Amen]
                      [God Bless you]

Whereas the chaplain has the authority to speak on everyone's behalf, the above speaker does not feel qualified to speak for all. But here the verbal responses of fellow members reinforce the speaker and signal accord. The form of address shifts to the third person singular as God is personified—a moment which is seen as opening doors, making people stronger, and bringing about good health. The final phrasing indicates that the community is fortified by their common spirit and that "the circle won't be broken" as long as they continue their collective response. The words and intent conform to those rendered in more purely sacred performance contexts so that even this secular community derives a kind of "sanctification" by consciously extending their blessings to each other.

Occasionally, when a speaker has too much pain or adulation to express, she becomes overwhelmed and is unable to complete a testimony. LTSC members find these silences acceptable. The devotion, which is strictly voluntary, is not considered an arena in which one *must* speak. However, members are also aware that failure to take part regularly in the devotional format tends to make one overly reflective and prone to self-consciousness. Therefore, those who have remained silent for a long time sometimes deliver testimonies that explain the silence, assuring the others that their spirituality is intact.

I have never been one to speak publicly.
And I pray throughout the day.
So, there are times
    when I do not get up
    and say anything.
I think, uh,

Madeline said it for me a couple of years ago.
I think you were confused,
but I knew what Madeline was talking about.
Just because we don't get up
    doesn't mean that we are not praying
    and we're not thankful.
So, there will be plenty of times
    that I won't get up.
But I thought that I should explain it to you all
because I believe that when the Bible says,
"Go into your closet and pray,"
You don't have to hear me pray.
So, if I don't get up,
    don't look cross-eyed at me.
And I thank God for everything.[44]

The above statement provides affirmation for those members who prefer private prayer to public testimony. It also enables the speaker to receive group approbation. As soon as this discourse ended—as if to demonstrate that a breach had not occurred—the members promptly responded with the song verse, "I just want to thank you/thank you/thank you." Song choices often pick up in this way on the previously spoken words.

The testimonial format also offers a fitting means by which members can share traumatic experiences. Although individual members routinely express their spiritual contentment, divulging personal trials is not unheard of. Sometimes, testimony can serve as a catharsis by allowing a member to openly express the details of a personal conflict. Mrs. Minnis spoke of a personal difficulty in the following way:

I would just like to say—
you'll have to pardon my sitting,
but I want to say
I have to thank God for blessing me.
I have to thank God for the many blessings
    He has shown me.
But I am now

standing in the need of prayer.   [need of prayer]
I have gone through some turbulent times
        in the last ten days.
I just want you to pray for me
        to give me the strength
that I can be a blessing to my family.
I want you to pray for my family . . .

As Mrs. Minnis was overcome by emotion, the words here became inaudible; however, the group's assent enabled her to regain her composure and continue.

I felt God had reached us
        through others praying for us.
And, you know,
        you never know.
Sometimes you're in a situation where it looks
        like everything's going wrong with you.
But I just want to let you know
        that I am a part of this sisterhood.
My husband did it with tears,
        but I did it with prayer.
Thank you again for your support.[45]

This disclosure was a vivid illustration of the emotional bonding that may sometimes be revealed in devotional testimony. That the speaker remained seated itself signified a great deal about her emotional state, since standing is the customary posture for delivering such a speech act. Her acknowledgment of a sisterhood offered an impressive testimony to the power of communal consciousness in helping to reintegrate a spirit in disarray. Since members generally converse by telephone throughout the month, few were unaware of Mrs. Minnis's difficulties. No one expected a public accounting, but fellow members appeared to appreciate as much as Mrs. Minnis herself did that the collective was important enough to function in this capacity.

The business frame of the meeting usually curtails the flow of expressive discourse, since parliamentary procedure and business matters evoke their own discursive styles. At any moment during the business frame, however, a more oratorical form of discourse may resurface as a member attempts to make a point or to persuade. After one fund-raising venture resulted in a debit, for example, the president chastised members for not supporting the effort and proposed that ticket purchases become mandatory. It immediately became apparent that exceptions would have to be made to this proposal based on the physical and economic limitations of some members. Aunt Carrie presented her own case:

> I would like to speak for myself.
> Excuse me for sitting.
> But I won't be able
> to do as I have
> as far as the club's concerned.
> I don't put anything in;
> I don't expect to get anything;
> and I am not expecting y'all to carry me.
> They told me when I was in school,
> "Nothing from nothing leaves nothing."
> But, if there's anything I can do to help,
> I will.
> But, as far as paying for tickets—
> and I'm not there
> and nobody's going with Carrie.
> She with two teeth
> and hope to get the others
> between now and Christmas.
> No way in the world
> I can sit here
> and tell you I can do it
> and don't do it.
> I'm telling you.
> Whatever I put in,
> give it to me.
> That what I don't put in,
> keep it

or whatever you want with it.
It's perfectly all right with me.
First of all,
I cannot get up on the steps
    of any bus
    by myself.
I can only get this leg up but so high
so that's the reason I'm Mrs. Lester now.
And, if I don't get it no higher than that,
I'll still be Mrs. Lester.[46]

Aunt Carrie supports her contention that she is infirm by not rising to speak, but she more than demonstrates that her infirmity does not inhibit her fluency. Without changing her vocal tone, she manages to end on a comically risqué note, which has the effect of neutralizing an otherwise serious and coherent position statement.

Her concluding remarks may also suggest why, among a collective of retirement age women, she has earned the honorific title of "aunt." She demonstrates the type of speech competency that in the African American community allows direction to be achieved through indirection. As Mitchell-Kernan explains it, "In the context of joking behavior, remarks which might ordinarily find a hearer taking umbrage, are taken in good sport in accordance with expectations."[47] The group's pronounced laughter at the conclusion of her remarks exemplified the success of her humorous transgression.

At the same time, her dexterity at verbal indirection suggests that creative inoffensiveness which some sociolinguists have identified as a common component of feminine speech.[48] In this she is typical of the sisterhood. As assertive as LTSC members can be when communicating on the spiritual level, they often handle conflict with more indirect metasocial commentary.

Conclusion

As Christian mothers, the women of the LTSC probably identify first as spiritual beings because of their upbringing; then as nurturers as part of their traditional roles as women; and necessarily as African

Americans, an inescapable part of their lives in a race-conscious society. Drawing on the dynamics of all three domains, the LTSC through its long history has fashioned a sodality that expresses an emotional, multivocal vitalism that perhaps can be compared to that of enslaved women: "The self-reliance and self-sufficiency of slave women, therefore, must not only be viewed in the context of what the individual slave women did for herself, but what slave women as a group were able to do for one another."[49] By so doing, these women assume the role of tradition bearers, passing on to their offspring the values, customs, and sense of identity that they have inherited from previous generations.

The LTSC suggests a domain where African American women affirm themselves by providing self-definition through their spoken words and performed deeds. Despite the constraints of gender and class, the LTSC sustains much more than the mere rudiments of an aging voluntary association. Taking the cultural knowledge bequeathed to them, these women transmit, through the traditions they uphold, the quintessential elements of the life forces that have assured African American survival: reciprocal support, communal interaction, and spirituality. Community-based women's clubs like the Lucky Ten Social Club preserve the core of a culture-specific worldview, enabling them to reconcile the present with the past.

Notes

1. Peter L. Berger and Brigitte Berger, *Sociology: A Biographical Approach* (New York: Basic Books, 1974), 104.
2. St. Clair Drake, "The Social and Economic Status of the Negro in the United States," *Daedalus* 94 (1965): 779.
3. For a classic example, see Gunnar Myrdal, *An American Dilemma* (New York: Harper & Row, 1962).
4. For more details about this movement, see Gerda Lerner, ed., *Black Women in White America* (New York: Random House, 1972); Paula Giddings, *When and Where I Enter: The Impact of Black Women on Race and Sex in America* (New York: Bantam Books, 1984), 94–102; Beverly Guy-Sheftall, *Daughters of Sorrow: Attitudes toward Black*

Women, 1880–1920 (Brooklyn: Carlson, 1990), 26; Beverly Washington Jones, *Quest for Equality: The Life and Writings of Mary Eliza Church Terrell, 1863–1954* (Brooklyn: Carlson, 1990), 17–29; Cynthia Neverdon-Morton, *Afro-American Women of the South and the Advancement of the Race, 1895–1925* (Knoxville: University of Tennessee Press, 1989), 191–201; Dorothy Salem, *To Better Our World: Black Women in Organized Reform, 1890–1920* (Brooklyn: Carlson, 1990), 29–53.

5. Beverly Jones, "Mary Church Terrell and the National Association of Colored Women, 1896–1901," *Journal of Negro History* 67 (1982): 20.

6. Mrs. Laura Barbour, interview, Seaford, Va., June 9, 1990.

7. Mrs. Flossie Hargraves, interview, Philadelphia, Pa., April 2, 1990.

8. Jan Michaels, ed., *Philadelphia Folklife Resources: A Guide to Local Folk Traditions* (Philadelphia: Philadelphia Folklore Project, 1991).

9. Jerrilyn McGregory, "'There Are Other Ways to Get Happy': African American Urban Folklore" (Ph.D. diss., University of Pennsylvania, 1992).

10. Since no extensive documentation exists for the preponderance of working-class African American women's clubs, primary sources such as the African American press must be used to gain insight into these clubs and their activities. For this study, the *Philadelphia Tribune* serves as a primary resource with microfilm dating back to 1912. Moreover, based on data gathered in Chicago, St. Clair Drake and Horace Cayton indicate in *Black Metropolis* (New York: Harcourt, Brace & Co., 1945) that thousands of clubs have existed there. By all indications, these clubs have not disappeared.

11. Hargraves interview.

12. Mrs. Alice Howard, interview, Philadelphia, Pa., June 16, 1990.

13. Ibid.

14. Among numerous references, see especially Henry Mitchell, *Black Belief* (New York: Harper & Row, 1975), 13–57; Margaret Washington Creel, *A Peculiar People: Slave Religion and Community Culture among the Gullahs* (New York: New York University Press, 1988), 59; Geneva Smitherman, *Talkin and Testifyin: The Language of Black America* (Detroit: Wayne State University Press, 1986), 75; Bennetta Jules-Rosette, "Creative Spirituality from Africa to America: Cross-Cultural Influences in Contemporary Religious Forms," *Western Journal of Black Studies* 4 (1980): 273–85; Mechel Sobel, *Trabelin' On* (Westport, Conn.: Greenwood, 1979), 148; James M. Jones, "Conceptual and Strategic Issues in the Relationship of

Black Psychology to American Social Science" in *Research Directions of Black Psychologists* , ed. A. Boykin et al. (New York: Russell Sage Foundation, 1979), 428–30; Naim Akbar, "Africentric Social Sciences for Human Liberation," *Journal of Black Studies* 14 (1984), 395–414; and Alfred Pasteur and Ivory Toldson, *Roots of Soul* (Garden City, N.Y.: Anchor Press, 1982), 68–72.

15. Herskovits, *Myth of the Negro Past* (Boston: Beacon, 1952), 213.

16. See Dona Richards, "Let the Circle Be Unbroken: The Implications of African-American Spirituality," *Présence Africaine* 117/118 (1981): 247–92.

17. Although it has a sacred component, the Lucky Ten Social Club is not a church auxiliary, but an autonomous social organization with each member having her own church affiliation. In this secular context, individual women can perform key roles that might otherwise be closed to them. For insight about women's roles within religious institutions, see Jacquelyn Grant, "Black Women and the Church," in *But Some of Us Are Brave: Black Women's Studies*, ed. Gloria T. Hull, Patricia Bell-Scott, and Barbara Smith (Old Westbury, N.Y.: Feminist Press, 1984), 141–52. See also Catherine L. Peck, "Your Daughters Shall Prophesy: Women in the Afro-American Preaching Tradition," in *Diversities of Gifts*, ed. Reil W. Tyson Jr., James L. Peacock, and Daniel W. Patterson (Urbana: University of Illinois Press, 1988), 143–56.

18. Hymn #399 in *The New National Baptist Hymnal*, 26th edition (Nashville: National Baptist Publishing Board, 1977).

19. Hargraves interview.

20. Christian fundamentalism is not synonymous with the Baptist denomination, especially for African Americans in a modern context. According to *The Encyclopedia of Religion in the South*, ed. Samuel Hill (Macon, Ga.: Mercer University Press, 1984): "Fundamentalists are evangelicals, but not all evangelicals are fundamentalists."

21. Mrs. Katherine Minnis, interview, Philadelphia, Pa., May 30, 1990.

22. Filomina Chioma Steady, "The Black Woman Cross-Culturally: An Overview," in *The Black Woman Cross-Culturally*, ed. Filomina Steady (Cambridge: Schenkman, 1981), 21–22.

23. For other examples of this organizational structure, see Aubrey W. Bonnett, "Voluntarism among West Indian Immigrants" in *The Apple Sliced* (Boston: Bergin & Garvey, 1984); Herskovits, *Myth of the Negro Past*, 150; and Victor Uchendu, *The Igbo of Southeast Nigeria* (New York: Holt, Rinehart and Winston, 1965), 71.

24. Gunnar Myrdal pejoratively described these associations in *American Dilemma*. For other early references to the wealth of African American benevolent associations, see Herskovits, *Myth of the Negro Past*; W. E. B. Du Bois, *The Philadelphia Negro* (Philadelphia: University of Pennsylvania, 1896); and St. Clair Drake and Horace Cayton, *Black Metropolis* (New York: Harcourt, Brace, & Co., 1945).

25. Barbour interview.

26. Uchendu, *The Igbo*, 71.

27. Hargraves interview.

28. Sydney Nathans, "Fortress without Walls: A Black Community after Slavery," in *Holding on the Land and the Lord: Kinship, Ritual, Land Tenure, and Social Policy in the Rural South*, ed. Robert Hall and Carol Stack (Athens: University of Georgia Press, 1982), 60.

29. Victor Turner, *Dramas, Fields and Metaphors: Symbolic Action in Human Society* (Ithaca, N.Y.: Cornell University Press, 1974), 175.

30. Mrs. Diane Rivers Boykins, statement en route to Grafton, Va., May 29, 1989.

31. bell hooks, *Talking Back: Thinking Feminist, Thinking Black* (Boston: South End Press, 1989), 5.

32. See Roger Abrahams, *Talking Black* (Rowley, Mass.: Newbury House, 1976), 59–80; Michael Bell, *The World from Brown's Lounge* (Urbana: University of Illinois Press, 1983); William Labov, *Language in the Inner City* (Philadelphia: University of Pennsylvania, 1968); Bruce Jackson, *Get Your Ass in the Water and Swim Like Me* (Cambridge, Mass.: Harvard University Press, 1974).

33. See Roger Abrahams, "Symbolic Landscape and Expressive Events," in *The Man-of-Words in the West Indies* (Baltimore: Johns Hopkins, 1983), 146–49; Thomas Kochman, *Black and White Styles in Conflict* (Chicago: University of Chicago Press, 1981); and Claudia Mitchell-Kernan, "Signifying," in *Mother Wit from the Laughing Barrel*, ed. Alan Dundes (reprint, Jackson: University Press of Mississippi, 1990), 310–28.

34. Hylan Lewis, "Blackways of Kent: Religion and Salvation," in *The Black Church in America*, ed. Hart Nelson et al. (New York: Basic Books, 1971), 113.

35. Selwyn Cudjoe, "Maya Angelou: The Autobiographical Statement Updated," in *Reading Black. Reading Feminist: A Critical Anthology*, ed. Henry Louis Gates Jr. (New York: Meridian, 1990), 282.

36. Mrs. Katherine Minnis, interview, May 30, 1990.

37. Dorothy Meekins, prayer delivered at Lucky Ten Social Club meeting, September 28, 1988.

38. Similar women's prayers are discussed in Elaine Lawless's standard works, *Handmaidens of the Lord* (Philadelphia: University of Pennsylvania Press, 1988) and *God's Peculiar People* (Lexington: University Press of Kentucky, 1988).

39. Lawless, *God's Peculiar People*, 87–93.

40. The forms of address typically found in these testimonies often seek to make fellow members vehicles for mediating prayers. This pattern may reflect the symmetrical mediation model discussed in Aylward Shorter, *Prayer in the Religious Traditions of Africa* (London: Oxford University Press, 1975), 11.

41. Sally Pringle, prayer delivered at Lucky Ten Social Club meeting, September 28, 1988.

42. Lawless, *God's Peculiar People*, 86.

43. Mrs. Alice Howard, prayer delivered at Lucky Ten Social Club meeting, February 28, 1989.

44. Ms. Anna Johnson, testimony spoken at Lucky Ten Social Club meeting, February 28, 1989.

45. Mrs. Katherine Minnis, testimony spoken at Lucky Ten Social Club meeting, February 28, 1989.

46. Mrs. Carrie Lester, statement spoken at Lucky Ten Social Club meeting, September 28, 1988.

47. Claudia Mitchell-Kernan, "Signifying," 328.

48. See Celia Halas and Roberta Matteson, *I've Done So Well—Why Do I Feel So Bad?* (New York: Macmillan, 1978), 138–59.

49. Deborah Gray White, *Ar'n't I a Woman?: Female Slaves in the Plantation South* (New York: W. W. Norton, 1985), 119–20.

CHAPTER 5

The "Giving" of Yiddish Folksongs as a Cultural Resource

Joel Saxe

> *Joel: Can you tell me where you learned this song?*
> *Hilda: I learned this song from Mendel, Mendel Lieberman. He used to sing*
> *   this song and I loved it and I learned it.*
> *Joel: Did he teach it to you?*
> *Hilda: No, he never wanted anyone to know his songs. But I listened and*
> *   learned it all by myself. Without him even knowing. You want I should sing?*

A warm, effusive lady in her late seventies, Hilda joined her friends almost every day, sitting in a circle under the palms on a grassy strip along Miami Beach. Every afternoon, this public park along South Beach's famed Ocean Drive was filled with similar gatherings of elderly, eastern European-born Jewish immigrants who had been coming here since the 1950s to spend their winters living in nearby hotels. When I became acquainted with them in 1985, they were still meeting almost daily on the beach, one of the last groups of Yiddish-speaking Jews of their generation who still congregated regularly to express their culture, or Yiddishkeit, in stories, memories and, most pointedly, folksongs.

Hilda's account of how she learned Mendel's song on the sly suggests the special, guarded status of these lyrical narratives, and Mendel himself, confined to a nursing home several blocks away, tells a story that corroborates this status. Once, when he was still performing regularly on the oceanside, a man came to his hotel room offering money to learn a particularly favored song. Because of the man's inadequate singing abilities, Mendel refused. It would reflect badly on his character, he felt, if his peers knew he had

120

taught a folksong to someone who couldn't do it justice. The special status of his songs was not for sale.

Though not all leading singers are as guarded with their songs as Mendel, these two stories indicate the extent to which these elderly folksong enthusiasts will go to learn a beloved melody, as well as the special place of honor that musical performance occupies in the cultural experience of this immigrant population.[1] Born between the 1890s and the 1920s, largely in Russia, Poland, Rumania, and Hungary, these Jewish elders grew up around the traditional form of Jewish prayer known as "dovoning," which involves swaying rhythmically while reading and chanting religious texts. As young adults, coming of age in a vibrant European Jewish society, they experienced Yiddish folk music in the home, workplace, and various social gatherings from the theater to cultural and political associations. Now retired, they see that music as a central symbolic resource around which circles a host of both formal and improvised performance events.

For over a decade, I have been documenting the cultural traditions of these Jewish elders. As I interviewed them, filmed their performances, and collected the songs that brought them together as a Jewish people, I became fascinated with the symbolic, almost magical force of the treasured melodies that regularly rekindled memories from their communal past. The power of that process was captured well by a participant who described their meetings as a daily carnival: "There was lots of singing, especially on this place; lots of, lots of, lots of people, they were singing, singing. And this is the whole thing here that people like. Singing. If somebody singing, they gather round, all the people come together and they gather together and dance and sing and play, and play violin, play mandolin. That's the story."

But what exactly *is* the story these Jewish elders tell about the folksong performance? Why do performers such as Hilda and Mendel display such passionate and possessive feelings about the sharing of these lyrical narratives? What is the cultural rationale that provides such resonance to folksong performance?

Following Malinowski and Geertz's call for interpreting cultures from the "native's point of view,"[2] I try to reveal in this essay the patterns that these elderly performers display in relation to the teaching and performance of folksongs. Those patterns illuminate the elevated status of musical performance, communal narrative, and collective memory in the social life of this immigrant population. Geertz centered on the "deep play" of the Balinese cockfight as an emblematic performance through which participants expressed symbolic meanings, codes, and norms of social identity. The performance of Yiddish folksongs on Miami Beach offers a comparable symbolic terrain.[3]

Ritual and Remembering

Both anthropologists and communications scholars have commented on the fundamental role of symbolic expressions—words, images, narratives, myths, rituals, ceremonies, performances, social dramas—in the ongoing affirmation of cultural patterns.[4] Such symbolic expressions create a heightened form of experience in which life is not merely lived but endowed with meaning. Performative ritual in particular helps to make meaning by creating symbolic "frames" in which such heightened experiences may occur. Indeed, Barbara Myerhoff, whose fieldwork among Jewish elders parallels my own, has called the framing function "the most salient characteristic of ritual": "In ritual, a bit of behavior or interaction, an aspect of social life, a moment in time is selected, stopped, remarked upon. . . . The subject has taken the activity out of the ordinary flow of habit and routine. . . . It is this very feature of framing which coincides with Durkheim's conception of the sacred as the set-apart."[5] In her discussion of social life and symbolic activity at a Jewish senior center in Venice, California, Myerhoff stresses the importance of cultural performances that engage "reminiscence activity," that is, activity that assumes a special significance because of this generation's unique historical memory and cultural status.

As Myerhoff indicates and as my own work confirms, one important element of that status is its marginality. Myerhoff writes that many Jewish elders experience a condition of "invisibility" due to being ignored by a mainstream culture that does not value them. The elders of Miami Beach are well aware of this condition. Realizing that they may be among the last carriers of the language and culture of Ashkenazic (European) Jewish life, these elders express an explicit consciousness of their place as a vanishing people. The idea is most palpable as they note the ever-decreasing number of friends with whom they may speak their beloved *mamaloshn* (mother language). The poignancy of this loss is compounded by their inability to speak Yiddish even with their own children, who abandoned the idiom due to the pressures of assimilation.

Another sign of their marginality is the fact that South Beach singers are all on some level witnesses to the Holocaust, the Nazi pogrom that not only slaughtered their families and friends, but also decimated the cultural reality that had defined their youths—that modernist, emancipated secular Jewish identity that had flourished in eastern Europe until the 1930s. They are thus living witnesses to a rich tradition of cultural creativity that will largely pass with them. In the words of one leading performer, "In here [South Beach] that's the remainder of an epoch that has gone. Hopes and aspirations that weren't filled. And a world of Jewish life and tradition. You see, it's losing here its last position. Because these are the last ones."

Meyerhoff elaborates the findings of various researchers who have emphasized the fundamental importance of "life review" as a means by which those facing mortality come to terms with the implications of this final life phase.[6] Reminiscence activity is a reflexive process that returns elders to youthful memories, intuitively guiding them to experiences that were of substantial import and meaning. This return to a remembered past contributes to feelings of wholeness and continuity. When stimulated by cultural performance, Myerhoff suggests, such reminiscence activity imparts greater meaning as memories are evoked through sensory experiences as well as interpretive processes. In such performances, the past becomes "re-membered": "The focused unification provided by re-membering is requisite to sense and ordering. A life is given a shape that extends back in the past and forward into the future. . . . A life, then, is not envisioned as belonging only to the individual who has lived it but it is regarded as belonging to the World, to Progeny who are heirs to the embodied traditions, or to God."[7] Folksong performance suggests just such a re-membering process. From this perspective, the performances of these communal narratives serve a function as symbolic resources, connecting the individual to the social, past to present, personal reminiscences to collective memories.

But it is not only the songs themselves, the musical texts, that perform this function. The behaviors displayed by singers teaching and performing these lyrical narratives also express patterns that reveal cultural norms that instruct, regulate, and set standards for conduct."[8] Evidence of deeply held cultural codes, values, and beliefs is displayed in patterns of social interaction guiding the sharing and performance of these symbolic resources. Both the songs themselves and the manner of their "giving" are governed by norms that define them as cherished objects.

In characterizing the patterns associated with folksong performance, I use the term "give" rather than "sing," for in my time with them, it was one of the words commonly used by performers to signal that they were about to perform: Many performances would be announced with the formula, "Let me give you a song." The term suggests that performers understand folksong as an exchangeable cultural resource or interactional currency: "Giving" occurs only when one party possesses some object—material or symbolic—that is desired, or at least prized, by another. This native valuing of folksongs as cultural currency is confirmed by the accounts of Hilda, Mendel, and other folksingers, who detail specialized and at times restrictive rules for transmitting the currency, that is, teaching the songs. To illustrate these rules, I present excerpts from two stories that are told by, and about, folksong performers.

"Rachelle"

The first is the autobiographical story "Rachelle," written by Jacob Gorelick, a singer well known from Miami Beach to New York. It recounts a scene from the author's youth when he meets a young woman who "has a lot of songs."[9] Akeva, the storyteller, meets Rachelle at a Catskills resort hotel, where he has gone to restore his failing health; the setting thus provides evidence that special patterns related to "giving" folksongs have a history that goes beyond Miami Beach.

Among the many guests he noticed a young women, a very pretty brunette woman. And later on he learned her name is Rachelle. And she has a lot, a lot of songs in many, many languages. Also Hasidic songs and melodies without words. And truly, he heard her later singing many songs which she sung them beautifully, [and] interpreted. . . . Once Akeva asked her, Akeva was very much interested in songs and he asked once Rachelle she should give him one of the songs.

She told him to go up to her room. But before she give him the song, she wants to talk to him. And then she'll give him the song.

The terms that Gorelick uses to characterize Rachelle's folksong knowledge evoke the image of a precious resource, while his use of "give" to characterize the teaching process suggests that this desired resource should be shared—but not indiscriminately. Akeva's interest in Rachelle derives from her extensive repertoire as well as her performance ability, by which he means not merely a "beautiful" musical quality, but an ability to "interpret," meaning to perform with verisimilitude. "Interpretation" suggests one standard guiding singers as they sort out worthy from unworthy recipients. Recall Mendel's refusal to teach his song to someone who was willing to pay for the lesson. The story reflects a widely embraced cultural code that serves to preserve the status of Yiddish folksong by restricting performers to those with interpretive skill.

The conclusion to this narrative elaborates this author-singer's assessment of the qualities that endow the folksong with its celebrated status. When Akeva comes to Rachelle's room, she presents him with a hypothetical question about socialist ethics that relates to her love for a man who loves another woman. She discloses feelings of deep sadness that have already led to a suicide attempt. Akeva responds by declaring that she must overcome such woes by fulfilling a very special mission in life: "Life is a great gift to humanity. And each person has a mission in life, during this life, to fulfill a certain subject. To do something good. Rachelle, you are young. You sing beautifully. You try to revive songs and melodies. But remember, each song has a soul. Each song has a flame. And revive them upon singing that song. So your mission is in life to sing all the songs, to revive all the songs, to give them life again. And certainly you will have in your life also personal happiness."

The passage reveals the special force of the folksong performance within the Yiddishkeit cultural system. In Gorelick's words, the folksinger is accorded an elevated status as the carrier of a precious symbolic object. The elevated nature of the folksong as a symbolic resource is suggested by his use of the metaphors "soul" and "flame," which are associated with spiritual or sacred properties. There is also a sense of timelessness in his characterization, as the folksong is described in terms that suggest it may survive the folksinger—but only if the singer has "revived" it, has served as a channel through which it can be released. It is as if the ego of the individual singer must be respectful and subservient to the "soul" of the song.

This respect brings a personal as well as a collective benefit. Rachelle's skill as a carrier of precious cultural resources is the special quality that she has been assigned in order to satisfy her own spiritual and emotional longing. Through the symbolic performance of a communal identity, this singer finds her personal identity restored.

"The Genius Schnorrer"

From the 1930s to her retirement to Miami Beach in the 1960s, Dora Laker was part of a network of Jewish folk choruses, the Freiheit Gezangs Ferrain (Freedom Singers Association), which elevated Jewish folk music to the status of a proletarian-classical-folk genre. In the literature produced by this movement, folklorists write frequently about the Jewish folksong as a prized resource. One famous singer and collector called his comrades "cultivators . . . who brought it to the public as a folk treasure."[10] A student of Yiddish song calls it "public property, the possession of the entire Jewish people. Every Jew has a share in it. The people itself created it."[11] Such references suggest the wider cultural context that helped shape these lay performances.

This context is implicitly present in Dora's story about a singer who "learned me all those songs," a singer with an ostensibly contradictory identity: he was both a folksong "genius" and a *schnorrer*, or beggar. The Yiddish term has a broadly pejorative connotation, indicating not only outright beggars, but also those who take from others for their personal gain. Dora's fascination with this character highlights the valuing of folksong as a treasure that even the most impoverished may own.

> Dora: A fella, he used to sing on the beach with us. He was a good singer, he was, he made believe he was a schnorrer, a poor guy. And he used to like to beg. . . . People gave him some money, people gave him some clothing. . . . When he died, they found in the mattress of his, I spoke to his aunt, forty thousand dollars. . . . Fanny [a friend] used to take him up and give him a meal in her house. . . . Anybody, me, he used to like to, he didn't like to learn them his songs, what he used to sing, none of them. But me he trusted, that I'll sing his songs. And he learned me all those songs.
>
> Joel: Was he out singing everyday in the park?
>
> Dora: In the park everyday, everyday. And he used to draw a crowd.
>
> Joel: What was his background? Where did he learn to sing? Do you know?
>
> Dora: No, that was his, everything he possessed was songs. Nothing else, just songs. He could sing day and night without a stop. There's so many, so many songs he had. He gotta be a genius to learn all these songs what he was singing. And every, every song was . . . had a meaning. You had to feel like crying. You had to have a pity to listen to those songs.

Dora's relationship with the schnorrer character stems from his willingness to teach her various songs. In her description of his reluctance to give "his songs," this character displays an awareness of their prized nature. Teaching folksongs is seen as a symbolic interaction that endows both giver and receiver, teacher and student, with an elevated status based on their ability to perform effectively. Finally, in the characterization of this singer's musical knowledge as virtually his sole "possession," Dora contrasts material and spiritual wealth, evoking someone without physical possessions who is nonetheless the guardian of a cultural treasure.

That this treasure is symbolically quite different from mere money is clear from the underlying structure of Dora's story. The value of the songs, indeed, seems enhanced by her emphasis on his feigned status as a beggar. In her account, the "schnorrer's" socioeconomic position—including the role of his hidden forty thousand dollars—seems of little consequence. Rather it is one's inner qualities and resources that determine one's status—so much so that this ostensible pauper is elevated to the level of a genius.

The story thus reflects a central paradigm within eastern European Jewish immigrant culture. Suffering centuries of discrimination, "outsiderness," and poverty, Jews developed a cultural code that emphasized learning, mutual aid, spiritual devotion, and expressive cultural forms. Though one may be materially impoverished, heroic status is possible through the development and expression of these nonmaterial resources.

Though Dora's teacher created a public identity normally held in disrepute—that of a schnorrer—his possession and complete devotion to the performance of folksongs gave him a mythic status within this immigrant community. Echoing Gorelick's story in which Rachelle finds her life's mission in "reviving" folksong, Dora's account ties the identity of a "perverse" character to the lifelong performance of communal narratives. His "true" identity was neither beggar nor miser. It was that of performer and collector.

Self and Community

In both of these stories, the symbolic exchange of "giving" links the affirmation of self to the sharing of communal narratives. In both instances, the "giving" interaction results in an affirmation of the giver's position as one who is able to achieve a "truth-in-performance"—a kind of performative verisimilitude—that is very highly prized among these elders. The ability to do justice to the songs is an essential ingredient in a folksinger's status, for it is understood that, without capable performers, the Yiddish folksong tradition would be debased or lost.

The "giving" exchange suggests a "model of personhood"[12] in which the sharing of communal resources is a valued act. This orientation may be contrasted to the more materialist orientation of the contemporary United States, where status is based on class, rank, the accumulation of material possessions, and the primacy of the "self." Within the culture created by these immigrant Jewish elders, the giving interaction suggests a contrary pattern—one in which status is achieved through the perpetuation of symbolic resources that would not exist without the model person of the folk performer.

For Dora, the outcome of performance is judged in terms of its ability to evoke meaning: "And every, every song had a meaning." Dora's use of "meaning" here seems related to Gorelick's use of "interpret." Yet, while he identifies the prized dimensions of performance as the revival of "soul" or "flame," Dora describes meaning in more direct, experiential terms. For her, meaning evokes strong feelings. "You had to feel like crying. You had to have a pity to listen to those songs." Responding with "pity" or empathy comes from a strong identification with the performed narrative. Dora's memories of this singer's performances evidently evoke feelings of pain and sorrow. From her perspective, one effect of the folksong performance is apparently to *release* such feelings, to achieve a form of catharsis that connects one's own emotional experience with the communal narrative, the collective identity, of the Jewish people. This understanding conforms to Myerhoff's notion that ritual provides a double level of continuity. For the individual, ritual provides a sense "of unity as a person, individual-biographical continuity." For the group, ritual creates a sense of unity, of being "One People" having "collective-historical continuity."[13]

Thus, while "Rachelle" portrays the folksong as a symbolic object whose force is connected with a larger communal identity, "The Genius Schnorrer" identifies an individual process related to the "re-membering" of communal narratives. Both stories indicate that whether performed in individual or shared settings, the folksong creates a sensory experience that links past and present, individual and collective memory. Through the folksong performance ritual, Jewish elders reenter a vanished past, re-membering its dimensions through the medium of song.

"Giving" and the Ocean Drive Friendship Circle

Within the wide range of regular, improvised social gatherings and cultural events I recorded, the performance of these beloved lyrical narratives nearly always occupied an elevated space. At Yiddish cultural clubs, political associations, and semireligious Oneg Shabbat (Sabbath) rituals, the performance of Yiddish folksongs was always included; in many cases, it served as the central focus of the gathering. It was during communal performances that the group seemed to reach its highest sense of shared identity as a Jewish people.

The primary arena in which I observed this process was the folksong gathering I term the Ocean Drive Friendship Circle, the scene I describe at the beginning of this paper. Having grown up in Miami, I have strong memories of such afternoon gatherings. I term these associations "friendship circles" because they served vital social needs for this elderly population during the winter months that they resided in this community. As many had lost spouses, were separated from their families, and lived alone, these gatherings provided a space for meeting new friends, maintaining daily contacts, and creating an arena for meaningful social activity. They also generated an informal network of mutual aid, as elders shared information about housing, social services, medical care, and shopping while also helping one another with immediate tasks and burdens. Last but certainly not least, they provided a space in which the speaking of Yiddish was welcomed.

The greatest pleasure at these gatherings was achieved when participants broke into folksong performance. Often accompanied by mandolins, balalaikas, and guitars, leading singers performed songs in Yiddish, Russian, Hebrew, Polish, and English. When appropriate, the rest of the group joined in. The circle I recorded from 1985 to 1992 was the last one where members were drawn together daily by a special desire to perform and hear folksongs. The result was an arena where the sensual, affective pleasures of singing created great feelings of spirituality and community.

On the weekends, when this gathering included a large number of singers and players, the collective "giving" effect of shared performance visibly heightened the sense of purpose and enjoyment. On

Figure 1. Fruma Winter sings a folk song on Ocean Drive, Miami Beach, December 1987. Photo by Joel Saxe.

these occasions, when as many as forty participants joined the circle, the invitational order appeared to be open and supportive. The performer who played the scheduling role, usually one of the leading instrumentalists, urged the next singer to perform after the previous one had finished. As regular performers arrived, their presence was noted and they too were soon urged to contribute a song. Here the "giving" resource became a shared, cooperative process, where the cumulative effects of each performer being invited to center stage made the atmosphere supportive and democratic. I witnessed a number of gatherings where performers whose vocal quality was failing were nonetheless warmly invited to contribute a song. As a rule, each performance was generally applauded. "Giving" here is a process where everyone may contribute.

In friendship circles, these elders created an arena for a heightened form of experience, which affirmed their identity as Yiddish-speaking immigrants. While in sociological terms they represented a marginal population, when gathered for folksong performance, they overcame their cultural isolation and recreated the community of their shared past. I asked one singer to describe what it meant to be able to sing and play on Ocean Drive. She responded:

> When I go to Ocean Drive, it brings back good memories to me. I like it. I enjoy. Why? Because the people are sincere. They're not trying to fool you. You make friends. And when you make a friend, if they are good friends, you keep them. . . . And since I came here, I find a very fine crowd of people. . . . When you sing a Jewish song, it brings back such fine memories, fine thoughts. . . . You still feel that you're among your own kind. You feel close. You feel brotherly. You don't feel strange. You don't feel you're away from everybody. You feel, you want to be in their company at all times. It's something that you . . . you look forward all your life to be among people that they're congenial, they're nice to talk to. And they still speak Yiddish. And I like it.

Similar feelings were expressed by one of the oldest members of the gathering, a woman who served as an emcee at regular Friday night secular-Sabbath performance events that were held in hotel lobbies along Ocean Drive. When I asked her what singing folksongs meant for her, she said: "It means to me . . . I think it's a part of the people, that people have lived it and have done it and have felt it. Because I feel it. So I'm not the only one. . . . And I think it is very beautiful to feel the beauty of it, the way things have happened, the way people lived. . . . When I sing it and I hear it, I know the feeling and I feel it in my heart." To this speaker, folksong performance is the space in which the Jewish people of her generation may reexperience their history. Like Gorelick and Dora, she values folksong as an emotional release as well as a cultural resource.

On a more mundane level, the oceanside performances create a space in which these elders can satisfy their most essential needs for daily human communication, affirmation of self, and friendship. On this level, the gatherings represent a kind of mutual aid—physical and directed to quite worldly concerns—that is as significant to their healthy interaction as the more spiritual resonance that is evoked in the transmission and sharing of Yiddish songs. Like the Lucky Ten Social Club discussed in the previous chapter, then, the Ocean Drive Friendship Circle might accurately be described as a "sacred-secular" performance gathering.

Conclusion

In examining the patterns associated with the teaching and performance of folksongs, I have described a variety of levels in which folksong enthusiasts display a native understanding of folksong and its performance as prized cultural resources. In stories told by two leading singers, the teaching of folksongs is described as the exchange of a valuable cultural currency, and the exchange itself is seen as a prized cultural act. In both stories, the esteem and social identity of the singer-teacher is intimately connected to his or her ability to carry on the symbolic properties that are evoked through the folksong performance. A singer with such ability can achieve an elevated status in the community, regardless of material wealth, while a singer perceived as lacking it can be denied the opportunity. Whether or not a person is permitted or encouraged to sing depends on whether he or she is seen as capable of preserving the quality of the resource.

In considering the "giving" of folksongs in performance, I have described the special place occupied by the folksong as a secular-sacred object at the center of these Jewish elders' social life. As a means of evoking a common identity, folksong performance elicits pleasurable reminiscences about one's past that are integrally linked to a sense of being "One People." Folksong performance also creates a place for sharing, which allows these marginalized elders to meet their own needs without having to rely on outside agencies. In both senses, the autonomous associations formed around folksong performance offer important forms of mutual aid.

What is central here is the tenacity with which an "outsider" population may nourish an internal cultural tradition that sustains and enriches its communal identity. Unobtainable through material wealth, folksong performance is a resource acquired only through a "giving" interaction within the autonomous forms of social life created by these elders. While that resource may not overcome physical frailty, poverty, or sickness, it seems to nourish the community's collective spirit to carry on amidst loneliness and isolation. Its continual reaffirmation by these elders points to the possibilities for diverse communities to celebrate cultural forms that both enrich and emancipate.

Notes

1. Eleanor Mlotek, *Mir Trogn a Gezang* (New York: Workmen's Circle, 1982); Ruth Rubin, *Voices of a People* (Philadelphia: Jewish Publication Society, 1973); Mark Slobin, *Old Jewish Music: The Collections and Writings of Moshe Beregovski* (Philadelphia: University of Pennsylvania Press, 1982); Mark Slobin, *Tenement Songs: The Popular Music of the Jewish Immigrant* (Chicago: University of Illinois Press, 1982); Mordechai Yardeini, *Fifty Years of Yiddish Songs in America* (New York: Jewish Music Alliance, 1964).

2. Clifford Geertz, "'From the Native's Point of View': On the Nature of Anthropological Understanding," in *Meaning in Anthropology*, ed. Keith Basso and Henry Selby (Albuquerque: University of New Mexico Press, 1976), 221–38.

3. Clifford Geertz, "Deep Play: Notes on the Balinese Cockfight," *Daedalus* 101, no. 1 (Winter 1972): 1–37.

4. Victor Turner, *Dramas, Fields, and Metaphors: Symbolic Action in Human Society* (Ithaca, N.Y.: Cornell University Press, 1974); Barbara Myerhoff, "'We Don't Wrap Herring in a Printed Page': Fusion, Fictions, and Continuity in Secular Ritual," in *Secular Ritual*, ed. Sally F. Moore and B. Myerhoff (Amsterdam: Van Gorcum, 1977), 199–224; B. Myerhoff, *Number Our Days* (New York: Simon and Schuster, 1978); B. Myerhoff, "Life History among the Elderly: Performance, Visibility, and Re-membering," in *A Crack in the Mirror: Reflexive Perspectives in Anthropology*, ed. Jay Ruby (Philadelphia: University of Pennsylvania Press, 1982), 99–117; Dell Hymes, "Models of the Interaction of Language and Social Life," in *Directions in Sociolinguistics: The Ethnography of Communication*, ed. John Joseph Gumperz and Dell Hymes (New York: Holt, Rinehard and Winston, 1972), 35–71; D. Hymes, "Breakthrough into Performance," in *Folklore: Performance and Communication*, ed. Dan Ben-Amos and Kenneth S. Goldstein (The Hague: Mouton, 1975), 11–74; Erving Goffman, *The Presentation of*

Self in Everyday Life (New York: Doubleday Anchor Books, 1959); Richard Bauman, *Verbal Art as Performance* (Prospect Heights, Ohio: Waveland Press, 1977); Richard Bauman, *Story, Performance, and Event: Contextual Studies of Oral Narrative* (Cambridge: Cambridge University Press, 1986); Keith Basso, *Portraits of "the Whiteman": Linguistic Play and Cultural Symbols among the Western Apache* (New York: Cambridge University Press, 1979); James Fernandez, *Persuasions and Performances: The Play of Tropes in Culture* (Bloomington: Indiana University Press, 1986); Donal Carbaugh, "Communication Rules in Donahue Discourse," *Research on Language and Social Interaction* 21 (1987): 31–61; Donal Carbaugh, *Talking American: Cultural Discourses on DONAHUE* (Norwood, N.J.: Ablex Publishing, 1988); Barbara Kirshenblatt-Gimblett, "The Concept and Varieties of Narrative Performance in East European Jewish Culture," in *Explorations in the Ethnography of Speaking*, ed. Richard Bauman and Joel Sherzer (London: Cambridge University Press, 1974), 283–308; Barbara Kirshenblatt-Gimblett, "A Parable in Context: A Social Interactional Analysis of Storytelling Performance," in *Folklore: Performance and Communication*, ed. Dan Ben-Amos and Kenneth Goldstein (The Hague: Mouton, 1975), 105–30.

5. Myerhoff, "Herring," 200.
6. Willa Baum, "Therapeutic Value of Oral History," *International Journal of Aging and Human Development* 12 (1980): 49–53; Robert N. Butler, "The Life Review: An Interpretation of Reminiscence in the Aged," *Psychiatry* 26 (1963): 65–76; Robert N. Butler, "The Life Review: An Unrecognized Bonanza," *International Journal of Aging and Human Development* 12 (1980): 35–38.
7. Myerhoff, "Life History," 111.
8. For a discussion of cultural norms and codes see Carbaugh, "Communication Rules."
9. The excerpts from "Rachelle" are from my recording of Gorelick telling the story in Miami Beach.
10. Yardeini, *Fifty Years of Yiddish Songs in America*, 23.
11. Ibid., 9.
12. For a discussion of model of personhood, see Carbaugh, *Talking American*, 15–19.
13. Myerhoff, "Herring," 218.

Part II

Intentional Identities

To a degree all identity is internal. I may choose to identify you as "Slavic," "papist," or "working class," but if you fail to acknowledge the validity of those ascriptions, my mere utterance of them will not make you so. To be Slavic, Roman Catholic, or blue collar—even if you are ostensibly born to those labels—you must still decide to "own" them yourself, to make the conscious choice of assuming those identities, if they are to constitute a force in your social life.

But not all identities are equally dependent on self-ascription. Some social features are relatively fixed; they are what we might call "overdetermined" identity markers. Chief among these are generally immutable physical features such as height, complexion, and gender. If I am a six-foot-tall Chinese woman, I may choose to represent myself as a short Nigerian man, but the self-ascription will be meaningless as a social marker. As the cases of Michael Jackson and others indicate, even such a seemingly overdetermined category as race *may* be subject to personal manipulation, but the exceptionality of such cases only proves the rule.

On the other end of the scale are "underdetermined" identities: those categories whose validity rests almost entirely on choice, on the intentional embrace of a collective social persona. A currently popular bumper sticker announces the distinction when it proclaims its owner "American by Birth, Gun Owner by Choice." One may debate whether "American" is a given or a chosen category; membership in the NRA is undeniably intentional. The case studies in this section explore the traditions of three similarly intentional, although very different, social groups.

In the first study, Jay Mechling shows how a sense of continuity in a Boy Scout troop is enhanced by the periodic refashioning of customs and traditions—what the troop members themselves call "C&Ts." Of particular interest here is the way in which the Scouts incorporate television and other mass-media images into their reconstructions. Responding to the commonly raised complaint that popular culture destroys youthful creativity, Mechling argues that this "intrusive" social fact may actually be a catalyst for enhanced self-expression. His fieldwork gives us reassuring evidence that the invention of expressive behaviors by the ostensibly powerless may be more than a match for the predations of the culture industry.

Tom Green's study of a Texas martial arts community similarly shows the value of collective creativity as a means of nourishing a sense of common identity. Here it is the group's "traditional" past that is ritually evoked and "re-membered." Since that past is orally and communally transmitted, it reveals to a marked degree the narrative variation with which students of oral traditions are familiar. Green, who acts here as a participant observer, highlights the value of selectivity in creating a usable past as well as the value of replication—in this case, the symbolic reenactment of legendary battles—in bringing its consolidating energies into the present. The narrative thread, the link to the past, also assuages the present by giving students a rationale for extraordinary effort. In so doing, it provides group members with that sense of distinction—here it is expressed outright as an *esprit de corps*—that the Barthian model sees as crucial to identity.

The reconstruction of a narrative history also figures in Eric Eliason's essay. Focussing on Mormon understandings of the pioneer, he shows how Brigham Young's 1847 migration to Utah was extolled by nineteenth-century Mormons as a recapitulation of Exodus, then reimagined by the diversified membership of an expanding church. Collective refashioning is again at issue, and reading the Green and Eliason essays back to back suggests a provisional conjecture about its dynamic: in the elite, closely knit unit of the karate *dojo*, variation seems to tend toward consensus, while in the heterogeneous population of Latter-day Saints, the authority of the "official" record appears more contestable. Similar examples of diversity generating ambiguity can be found in Sylvia Grider's essay on the Alamo and in the national-level essays of Part IV.

A comment on the placement of Eliason's essay may be in order. As I mentioned in the Introduction, it is seldom possible to pigeonhole an expressive tradition by calling it simply (and exclusively) "ethnic" or "regional." The point is especially salient with regard to Mormonism, a once sectarian and staunchly localized creed in the process of evolving, evangelically, into a world religion. Since religious beliefs, even for those born into a faith, are ultimately "owned" only through conscious decision, I have grouped this essay with other examples of "intention." But I do not suppose that this should (or could) silence the church's own debate over Mormon "ethnicity"—or over its members' unique relationship to Zion. Indeed, I placed the essay last in this section so that it may provide a bridge to the following section on place.

CHAPTER 6

Newell's Paradox Redux

Jay Mechling

Tom, one of my key informants in my fifteen-year-long study of a Boy Scout troop from California's Central Valley, was in the midst of explaining to me one of the troop's "C&Ts," customs and traditions, when he stopped abruptly and looked mischievously at me. "You know, Jay," he said, "one of our most important C&Ts is always to invent new C&Ts." He smiled broadly at the paradox he had just enunciated, and I smiled back. The paradox no longer surprises the folklorist working in modern settings, where the "invention of tradition" seems a natural dimension of a "postmodern" society seemingly dominated by the narratives and images of the mass-media.[1]

And the sudden "invention of tradition" certainly no longer surprises folklorists of children's lives. The founders of this specialty saw in their work what Gary Alan Fine much later called "Newell's Paradox," that is, the paradox that children's folklore is simultaneously very dynamic and very conservative.[2] That is to say, children cling rather rigidly to the familiar forms of their folklore, but they constantly bring to those conservative forms new content. Long before others, children's folklorists understood the naturalness of "invented traditions," of traditions invented not for political purposes in the broadest sense, but for purposes of ordering experience, of making meaning, and of managing relationships.

Newell's Paradox was my constant companion during my years of summer fieldwork among the eleven- to seventeen-year-olds at Boy Scout camp. The formal organization and its adult leaders brought to camp one agenda, including "traditions" invented by the founders of the Boy Scouts in the 1910 (and later) *Handbook for Boys*, traditions learned by the scoutmaster as a boy growing up in his own troop, and traditions invented by the first generation of boys and men in the troop. The boys themselves brought to camp their own agenda, driven largely by the nature of the folk cultures of preadolescent and adolescent boys, cultures permeated by Newell's Paradox. The dialectic between the formal culture and the informal culture of this Boy Scout troop resulted in the constant invention of new traditions and elaborations of past inventions.

My fieldwork experiences and my continuing study of children's folklore persuade me we have much more to learn about Newell's Paradox and its implications for our adult attitudes toward the lives of children. Children's lives become cultural "texts" over which adults argue heatedly.[3] Americans have been fretting through the 1980s and into the 1990s about the effects of mass-mediated culture (television, music, films) on children's cognitive and emotional powers, for example, without bothering to examine how children actually "consume" the texts of commercial culture.[4] In this essay, I want to continue Fine's exploration of Newell's Paradox by drawing upon ethnographic research, some my own and some by others, to look at a primary sort of invention one finds in children's expressive cultures—namely, the appropriation of mass-mediated, popular culture.

Invention through Appropriation of Popular Culture

Some culture critics worry that mass-mediated, popular culture is the enemy of children's folk cultures. Neil Postman, for example, has spilled much ink over his concern that television has "disappeared" childhood in America, erasing the distinction between adults' and children's knowledge of adult society.[5] Echoing real parents' complaints, Calvin's parents in the popular comic strip *Calvin & Hobbes* are forever urging him to stop watching television and go outside to play in the fresh air. Certainly the most ironic moments in this public rhetoric of worry about kids' television habits occur when television sitcom parents, such as those on *Roseanne*, comment on the mind-numbing effects of television upon the kids.[6]

Folklorists are more sanguine about the purported demise of children's expressive cultures. Folklorists know that there is a dynamic dialectic between American children's folk cultures and mass-mediated, popular culture, that children are resourceful humans who learn early how to read power relationships and who develop their own cultural resources for resisting control.

For the sake of analysis, we might tease apart two "moments" in the dialectic between children's folklore and mass-mediated culture. The first "moment" is *the commodification of children's folklore.* Successful capitalists discovered early in this century how to turn folk art and other genres of folklore into profitable commodities. Folk culture and popular culture are highly formulaic in their structures, satisfying (no doubt) some of the same psychological and social motives. Plastic monster play figures, for example, likely appeal to children not only for the sociality and creativity of the play, but also for the psychological satisfaction of controlling unnamed fears.[7] Similarly, the Teenage Mutant Ninja Turtles have been so successful because their narratives are familiar to the preadolescent boys who are their primary audience.[8] Moreover, the formulaic, repetitive nature of the folk aesthetic also lends itself to mass production.

A folklorist's stroll through any major toy store reveals the results in that realm. Some children's pencil-and-paper games, such as Hangman and Battleship, appeared as commercial games in the 1970s and now are available in electronic form. Some commercial toys, like skateboards, have their origins in folk toys created by kids. The Garbage Pail Kids, enormously popular in the 1980s, demonstrate the relentlessness of commodification. Picking up on children's fascination with "gross" things, the creators of the Garbage Pail cards and stickers provided children with a slick, commercial way to ridicule the Cabbage Patch doll phenomenon and to explore forbidden topics of disorder and bodily mutilation. Some critics even see in children's love of the Garbage Pail Kids an unconscious commentary upon adult discourse about abortion.[9]

Some commercial filmmakers have made their fortunes taking children's traditional oral narratives and turning them into movie scripts. Especially lucrative are film transformations of adolescent legends. Commercial films like the *Friday the Thirteenth* series, the Freddy Krueger *Nightmare on Elm Street* series, and the *Halloween* series, as examples *ad nauseum*, are simply elaborations of well-known contemporary legends, including "The Hooked Hand," "The Boyfriend's Death," "The Roommate's Death," and "The Killer in the Back Seat." The 1992 horror film *The Candyman* features two female graduate students researching urban legends, and the legends (e.g., the legend game "Mary Worth" and the legend of the white boy castrated in a restroom by people of color) become real.[10] Parents in the 1980s need not have fretted (as they did) over their teenagers' appetite for these films. The films are actually very conventional in their morality. Teenagers who have sex die horrible deaths (often pierced by phalluslike knives and spears), so the films meet the same psychological and social needs as the oral legends, simultaneously exciting and warning the audience.[11]

This first "moment" in the dialectic between American children's folklore and mass-mediated culture tells us little about the sources of invention in children's cultures, but it does show us that children of the twentieth century increasingly have seen a familiar folk culture mirrored in the commercial culture aimed at them. Mass-mediated culture, in other words, is a familiar, friendly, comfortable realm for children. The poetics and aesthetics of successful children's television match in many respects the poetics and aesthetics of children's oral cultures.[12]

I suspect it is the familiar feel of mass-mediated culture that leads to the second "moment" in the dialectic between children's folklore and mass-mediated culture, namely, *the children's appropriation of commercial culture*. Children are not the passive recipients of popular culture's narratives and images that Postman and other critics portray. Children are quite adept at appropriating adult-given culture for their own purposes. We see this all the time in children's narratives, play, and games. Sutton-Smith and his colleagues have found plenty of evidence of the influence of television narrative formula and content upon children's folkstories.[13] In one of their studies, children shown Bugs Bunny cartoons later incorporated the structures and elements of the traditional trickster tale in their own stories.[14] The skinwalker stories told to Margaret Brady by bicultural Navajo children likewise show the effects of the form and content of mass-media narratives. Each child drew upon a "repertoire of cultural resources—some Navajo, some Anglo" in fashioning a specific telling of a traditional skinwalker narrative. Sometimes the child drew upon the content of the Anglo world, as in an eleven-year-old's version of a skinwalker that threatened a Navajo family in the Dallas- area hotel they were staying in on a trip to the Six Flags theme park. Sometimes the narrative forms and structures reflected Anglo poetics and aesthetics. The appropriation of popular culture always served the child narrator's purpose of enhancing the believability of the story.[15]

An especially interesting version of children's appropriation of popular culture for their own uses has turned up in ethnographic studies of children's fantasy play. In a study aimed at understanding playfighting among preschool children, Sutton-Smith and his graduate students inquired whether television had any effect upon children's rough-and-tumble playfighting. "The majority of observers," report the authors, "took the position that, while television sometimes contributed to the names of the games and even to the occasional adoption of costumes and props, these were grafted onto the traditional play of the good versus the bad guys."[16] To be sure, television sometimes provided richly textured fantasy frames for the traditional play, as in the school where three boys "played out the theme of Ghostbusters and Slime Baby." But there is an even more interesting example in this study of the children's appropriation of popular culture for their traditional play. Two of the observers

> carefully noted the way in which non-aggressive children used the fantasy of the symbolic content to tone down and contain the physicality of the more aggressive children. Here was a

stage in which they sought to capture violence, if not the con-science of the Kings. Interestingly, when play therapists ration-alize the use of war toys to evoke the violence of their child patients, they apparently are making use of a similar expecta-tion that the "wild beasts within" can be tamed through well-ordered fantasy, which is to say, in our case, "folk games."[17]

Clearly, children borrow fantasy narratives from a number of sources in service of their social and psycho-sexual needs.

Patricia Banez found a similar dynamic in her intensive ethno-graphic study of a play group of five children.[18] The children (ages seven through thirteen) built an ongoing fantasy play scene around the television show *The Simpsons,* calling themselves "The Simpletons." Playing out the roles and scripts from the television show, the children were creating a dramatic text that combined three separate sorts of narratives—the media narrative of a family, the nar-rative realities of the families of the children, and the narrative reali-ty of the social relations in this ongoing play group. The children were appropriating a media narrative and turning it to their own uses. For some children the outline of the script provided by televi-sion permitted them to play roles unavailable to them in their own families or in the play group. For some, the scripted family permitted them a mode for making "safe" commentary on their own families, and so on.

Banez's study helps put into perspective parental concern over the popularity of *The Simpsons,* a concern that has led to parents' forbid-ding their children to watch the program and to school administra-tors' banning Bart Simpson shirts in the schools. These adults see in Bart Simpson only a sassy role model who hates school and con-stantly gets into trouble, as if children's resistance to schools were the product of a cartoon character on a t-shirt and not of the sometimes awful conditions of schooling. Adults might draw very different con-clusions if they looked closely at how the children actually consume and reenact mass-media narratives like *The Simpsons.* Even a cursory look at the show will discover, once again, a rather conventional morality in the show, and Banez's play group reproduced many aspects of that morality.

Syndy Slowikowski describes a "fake Nintendo" game created by her kindergarten-age son and three of his friends, and, as in Banez's study, we discover the unexpected when we actually examine closely children's appropriations of popular culture. Not to be stymied by the lack of a real Nintendo game, the children drew a television screen with a number of Nintendo game sequences and characters and linked two cardboard "control panels" to the "television" with shoelaces. "To the outsider," writes Slowikowski, "the screen was an indecipherable code of stick figures, scribbles and what appeared to be clouds and plants. But, the children remembered each figure, and uninitiated children immediately recognized the figures and story-line."[19] To the author's amazement, the children continued to play with the "fake Nintendo" even though the family finally purchased a "real" Nintendo. In fact, the children even expressed a preference for the "fake" version, their own creation. Slowikowski observes that the "fake Nintendo" makes possible the active participation of several children at the same time, that the children can adjust the pace of the game to suit the players, and that "no one loses, or runs out of time." Children can stop the play at any time to draw new figures, as needed, so the "fake Nintendo" is interactive with the children in a way far more important than the illusory "interaction" between a programmed microchip and a child. The children's responses to Slowikowski's direct question about why they played "fake Nintendo" so much reveal the sense of power and control the folk version gives them:

> "This is better than real Nintendo because it is fake."
> "Yeah, you don't have to die."
> "You don't have to miss any duck birds."
> "I can change into anything."
> "You get to go wherever you want."
> "Things don't have to eat or kill you."
> "Or you can kill what you want. Not like the other Nintendo."
> "And, you can go slow."[20]

We recognize in these comments the sense of control and power the "fake Nintendo" gives the children. Commercial culture's "real Nintendo" provides the basic script for the play, but their control over their fantasy play permits them to make the play serve their own individual and collective needs. Children constantly change the rules of their games to accommodate younger or less able players, so it is natural that they would prefer a version of Nintendo that allows them to adapt the play to individual needs.[21] Fantasy role-playing games appeal to teenagers for the same reasons.[22]

From Appropriation to Parody

I have observed the appropriation of commercial culture in my own fieldwork with a Boy Scout troop summer encampment in the Sierra Nevada. The usual troop campfire program features skits, songs, and some special events that rely heavily upon parody of commercial culture. The troop now specifies one night as "commercial skit" night, warning each of the patrols in the afternoon that they will have to think up and perform a comic television commercial skit at the evening campfire. At the 1989 encampment, for example, two patrols built commercials around garbage disposal (a daily chore for the boys). The third patrol presented a commercial for "Spameos" Cereal, slamming the dreaded meat that shows up on their camp menu. And the fourth presented a commercial for portable latrines—small size (a trowel plus a roll of toilet paper), medium (a foxhole shovel plus toilet paper), and large (a shovel with toilet paper). The skits demonstrated clearly the boys' mastery of the forms and language of television commercials, along with an ability to turn the commercials into humorous comment upon their own bodily concerns about food, waste, and symbolic "dirt."[23]

The troop's Nugget Auction, recounted elsewhere,[24] parodies television's "Let's Make a Deal," as patrols use earned points to bid for items, some known and some unknown, with the ever-present possibility of being "zonked" with a gag prize. And commercial culture appears every so often in the traditional campfire songs sung by this troop, as in this rendition of a familiar "gross" song:

"Gopher Guts"
[Tune of "The Old Gray Mare"]
Great green gobs of greasy, grimy gopher guts

Itty bitty birdy feet,
Mutilated monkey meat,
One-pint portion of all-purpose porpoise pus,
And me without a spoon!
(But here's a straw!)
(Have it your way, have it your way!) [sung to Burger King jingle]
(Take that, McDonald's!)[25]

The most elaborate example of the boys' appropriation of popular, commercial culture began in the summer of 1988. For many years, the troop had included in its summer camp schedule a traditional "Insane Day," a long afternoon of contests on an island in the lake where they camp.[26] In 1988, the Senior Scouts, the over-fourteen scouts who are the camp counselors and who organize Insane Day, decided that they wanted to tie together the day's contests with a unifying theme borrowed from television. By the next summer, 1989, this new dimension of Insane Day had become traditional with the troop. I watched the seniors make elaborate plans around the theme of "Gilligan's Island: The Final (We Hope) Episode."

By the time I arrived on the island by canoe, ahead of the forty scouts, the seniors had already set the stage for their theatrical production. Up from the beach at the edge of the trees, they had erected a cardboard "Minnow" boat wreck, a cardboard chest, and a grass hut, all reminiscent of the television show. One of the fathers had dressed as a menacing native (a cannibal, probably) to add a frightening surprise to the drama. Each senior played a role in costume—Gilligan, the Skipper, the Professor, Ginger, Mary Anne, and Mr. Howell. There was no Mrs. Howell (a running gag throughout the day). Some troop alumni in their twenties played the director and the cameraman, and the director explained to the scouts coming ashore that they were going to participate in the filming of the final episode of *Gilligan's Island*. Each of the afternoon's traditional contests, from the watermelon eating to the tug-of-war and the "Poison Pit" game at the end of the day, was "themed" as an episode in the film. The seniors did not work from fixed scripts but improvised dialogue from a general outline of the "meaning" of each "scene/contest." The scouts clearly appreciated the elaborate frame created by the seniors, and not a little of the fun came from seeing two seniors dressed and behaving as women.

By the summer of 1990, the new C&T clearly had taken hold, as the seniors themed Insane Day around the *Star Trek* television series and theatrical films. Again, the seniors scripted the traditional contests within the *Star Trek* frame and created elaborate props, including a transporter beam. Unfortunately a violent summer hailstorm ended the activities before the scouts even reached the island, but even this disaster has now become the stuff of troop stories and tales of harrowing canoeing as already loaded crafts filled with rain and hail. The 1991 Insane Day was themed around *The Addams Family*, but with the added innovation that characters from the previous two summers (that is, from *Gilligan's Island* and *Star Trek*) would wander occasionally through the day's story line.

What might the folklorist say about this elaborate example of adolescents' appropriation of mass-media texts for their traditional games? First, we note that the evolution of the traditional games is toward greater elaboration, with the mass-media providing the narrative frame that ties the days' games together with a single narrative thread. These teenagers respect and leave untouched the basic formula of the day's activities, and they leave relatively untouched the details of the contests themselves. But the boys apparently feel free to change and play with the usually ordinary framing behavior. So the event carries simultaneously the comfort of the familiar games and the excitement of the new framing ritual.

But let us notice closely the nature of this appropriation of narratives from television. The boys do not simply and faithfully reproduce the television narrative of, say, *Gilligan's Island*. Rather, they produce a wholly new kind of text, a text that amounts to a mixing of the traditional folk text of Insane Day and the mass-media text. And each succeeding year, the composite text adds a new mass-media text without subtracting the old. The result each year is a text full of blurred genres, intertextual references, parody, irony, self-reference, and double coding; in short, each year the text has a structure and aesthetic the culture critic would not hesitate to call postmodern.

There is a minor cottage industry in books and essays debating the meaning of "postmodernism" as the cultural aesthetic of late capitalism, and I shall spare the reader (and myself) a review of this literature.[27] Just as "high modernism" or "late modernism" was having its last gasps in the high art of the 1940s and 1950s, there arose a popular culture aesthetic reflected in everything from commercial architecture to rock 'n' roll music. The postindustrial society that emerged in the United States in the 1950s was a consumer society looking increasingly to the mass-media for its dominant narratives, and television emerged as the queen of the media. The narrative forms and aesthetic of television, therefore, stand as a good example of postmodernism, for in television we find the loss of historical depth, the self-reflexivity, the blurring of genres, the references of texts to each other, and the nostalgia that mark so many postmodern texts.

Returning to the texts our scouts constructed on Insane Day, we can see that they rip references from their usual contexts and combine them in new ways. There is a great deal of self-referential, insiders' humor in the characterizations of the television characters, and the three television narratives (*Gilligan's Island*, *Star Trek* , and *The Addams Family*) get increasingly blurred in a text that mixes all three. It is relevant, too, that the television texts the boys choose are older series in syndication, a suggestion that there is a postmodern nostalgia at work even in these teenagers.

If we were persuaded that the Insane Day events amount to a postmodern text, what of it? Some critics would conclude, no doubt, that the postmodern aesthetic of the day confirms the totalizing influence of television in the lives of children, destroying the authenticity of the traditional play of Insane Day. How sad it is, these critics might say, that Boy Scouts cannot have fun at summer camp in the mountains without bringing television into their traditional games.

But the folklorist would have us put quotation marks around both "authenticity" and "traditional play," reminding us that these are spurious distinctions from the point of view of the boys themselves. Folklore is not a fixed thing but a process, an orientation toward organizing human experiences. Here, then, is Newell's Paradox; these adolescents are engaged in a process of inventing their own traditions, layering new materials on top of the old. As Tom told me in his own way, the *process*, the endless creation of new C&Ts, is what is traditional with the boys; no single "custom" or "tradition" is sacrosanct if it serves the group's sense of itself to change that custom or tradition.

Moreover, one could argue (as I began earlier) that the aesthetic "invasion" works the other way around. If the oral folk cultures of children feature Newell's Paradox, the simultaneity of tradition and innovation, then perhaps television has been adopting the structures and aesthetics of children's folklore. The rise of television with the first wave of Baby Boomers (born 1946–1964) in the 1950s, and the influence of those Boomers now as artists, musicians, directors, producers, and continuing consumers of mass-media, suggest that commercially successful popular culture has appropriated a *postmodern folk aesthetic*. I cannot elaborate this argument here, but I raise the point to show that taking the child's perspective on cultural aesthetics and seeing the complex dialectic between folk and popular cultures can lead to conclusions very different from those touted by critics and worried parents.

Conclusion

The current scholarly interest in the invention of traditions would benefit greatly from considering the dynamics of tradition in the expressive folk cultures of children. As Gary Alan Fine has taught us, Newell's Paradox is fundamental to children's cultures. Sometimes children are actively appropriating popular culture, where they experience the pleasure of finding their own cultures mirrored and transformed. Sometimes children invent ritual traditions out of a more fundamental, developmental dynamic. In any case, the ideologies and "politics" of children's cultures are more basic, perhaps we can say more human, than the politics of adult cultures, where adults invent traditions to serve ideologies of class, race, and gender.

Newell's Paradox tells us that children understand the social construction of reality. Born into a world of existing institutions, roles, rules, and power, children take power where they can, and one way of taking power is by putting their own folk cultures entirely in their own hands, changing and preserving things as they see fit. Children are as capable as adults of invoking "tradition" as a way of imposing one's will upon another, but children also seem quite capable of seeing through this fragile appeal to tradition and of insisting that the rules be changed. In this sense, children seem less prone to "reification," to the process by which people forget the human-madeness of institutions and attribute to institutions a naturalness and a taken-for-grantedness pernicious to human freedom.[28] Part of becoming adult, it appears, consists of losing the child's sense that the world is a great deal more malleable than others would have us believe. To be sure, we should not romanticize children and their lives, but looking at children's cultures helps us bracket all talk of "authenticity" and forces us to find new questions to ask about the ways in which human beings come together to make meaning in their lives.

Notes

1. Richard M. Dorson first railed against "fakelore," or "the spurious and synthetic writings under the claim that they are genuine folklore," in his essay "Folklore and Fake Lore," *American Mercury* 70 (March 1950): 335–43; see also, Richard M. Dorson, "Fakelore," in his *American Folklore and the Historian* (Chicago: University of Chicago Press, 1971), 3–14. Folklorists have also adopted the neologism *folklorismus*, or "folklorism," to describe folk traditions invented and performed in service of a political ideology. For discussions of this idea, see Richard Handler and Jocelyn Linnekin, "Tradition, Genuine or Spurious," *Journal of American Folklore* 97 (1984): 273–90; Deirde Evans-Pritchard, "The Portal Case: Authenticity, Tourism, Traditions, and the Law," *Journal of American Folklore* 100 (1987): 287–96; and Hermann Bausinger, *Folk Culture in a World of Technology*, trans. Elke Dettmer (Bloomington: Indiana University Press, 1990).

2. Gary Alan Fine, "Children and Their Culture: Exploring Newell's Paradox," *Western Folklore* 39 (1980): 170–83. Fine attributes the first recognition of this paradox to William Wells Newell in his classic study *Games and Songs of American Children* (1883). See also Jay Mechling, "Children's Folklore," in *Folk Groups and Folklore Genres*, ed. Elliott Oring (Logan: Utah State University Press, 1986), 91–120.

3. See, for example, Joel Best's *Threatened Children: Rhetoric and Concern About Child-Victims* (Chicago: University of Chicago Press, 1990).

4. Most of the studies of media are formalist exercises in textual criticism, without any fieldwork among the actual consumers of the texts. In response to this narrow approach, some scholars have developed a "reader response" or "audience response" theory, using interviews and other field methods to examine how an audience becomes an active player in negotiating the "meanings" of the media texts. Janice Radway's *Reading the Romance: Women, Patriarchy, and Popular Culture* (Chapel Hill: University of North Carolina Press, 1984) stands as the best example in popular literature. See also Michael Real, "The Challenge of a Culture-Centered Paradigm: Metatheory and Reconciliation in Media Research," in *Communication Yearbook/15*, ed. Stanley A. Deetz (Newbury Park, Calif.: Sage, 1992), 35–46. Most of the "media effects" research on children focusses narrowly upon the effect of media violence, and much of that research is marred by the confounding effects of laboratory settings.

5. Neil Postman, *The Disappearance of Childhood* (New York: Dell, 1982) and *Amusing Ourselves to Death: Public Discourse in an Age of Show Business* (New York: Viking Penguin, 1985).

6. It is interesting, in this regard, to contrast *Roseanne* and *The Simpsons* with *The Cosby Show*. Children and adults in the working-class homes of the Connors and the Simpsons watch a great deal of television, and both shows hint at the social and psychological functions of television-watching in the ecology of a working-class family. Nobody watches television on *The Cosby Show*.

7. Bruno Bettelheim, *The Uses of Enchantment: The Meaning and Importance of Fairy Tales* (New York: Vintage, 1977).

8. Gary Alan Fine, "Those Preadolescent Ninja Turtles," *New York Times*, June 1, 1990, p. 19.

9. John Broughton, "Image of Evil in the Post Modern Child" (paper delivered at the annual meeting of the American Folklore Society, October 1989, in Philadelphia).

10. The game "Mary Worth" (or Bloody Mary or Mary Jane) requires a preadolescent child, usually on a dare and usually at a party, to look into a mirror in a darkened room and repeat Mary Worth's name a specified number of times, at which point Mary appears behind the child, reflected in the mirror and usually bearing a knife to threaten the child. See Mary and Herbert Knapp, *One Potato, Two Potato: The Secret Education of American Children* (New York: Norton, 1976), 242,

and Simon J. Bronner, *American Children's Folklore* (Little Rock, Ark.: August House, 1988), 168–69. Barre Toelken explores the long history of the Child ballad "Sir Hugh, or, The Jew's Daughter" as it works its way forward in time to become the legend of the boy castrated in the men's room. See Toelken's *The Dynamics of Folklore* (Boston: Houghton Mifflin, 1979), 176–79.

11. Alan Dundes, "On the Psychology of Legend," in *American Folk Legend: A Symposium*, ed. Wayland D. Hand (Berkeley: University of California Press, 1971), 21–36; Harold Schechter, *The Bosom Serpent: Folklore and Popular Art* (Iowa City: University of Iowa Press, 1988).

12. Walter J. Ong's *Orality and Literacy: The Technologizing of the Word* (London: Routledge, 1982) is filled with provocative ideas about the relationships between oral, written, and mass-mediated narratives.

13. Brian Sutton-Smith et al., *The Folkstories of Children* (Philadelphia: University of Pennsylvania Press, 1981).

14. David M. Abrams and Brian Sutton-Smith, "The Development of the Trickster in Children's Narrative," *Journal of American Folklore* 90 (1977): 29–47.

15. Margaret K. Brady, *"Some Kind of Power": Navajo Children's Skinwalker Narratives* (Salt Lake City: University of Utah Press, 1984).

16. Brian Sutton-Smith, John Gerstmyer, and Alice Meckley, "Playfighting as Folkplay amongst Preschool Children," *Western Folklore* 47 (1988): 172.

17. Ibid., 174.

18. Patricia D. Banez, "The Simpletons: An Ethnographic Study of Children's Use of Media Narratives" (senior thesis in American Studies, University of California, Davis, April 1991).

19. Syndy Slowikowski, "The Culture of Nintendo: Another Look," *Journal of Play Theory and Research* 1(1993): 8.

20. Ibid., 11.

21. On the ways children change rules to accommodate different players, see Linda A. Hughes, "Foursquare: A Glossary and 'Native' Taxonomy of Game Rules," *Play & Culture* 2 (1989): 102–36.

22. Gary Alan Fine, *Shared Fantasy: Role-Playing Games as Social Worlds* (Chicago: University of Chicago Press, 1983).

23. Jay Mechling, "High Kybo Floater: Food and Feces in the Speech Play at a Boy Scout Camp," *Journal of Psychoanalytic Anthropology* 7 (1984): 256–68.

24. Jay Mechling, "Patois and Paradox in a Boy Scout Treasure Hunt," *Journal of American Folklore* 97 (1984): 24–42.

25. Jay Mechling, "The Magic of the Boy Scout Campfire," *Journal of American Folklore* 93 (1980): 35–56.

26. Jay Mechling, "Male Gender Display at a Boy Scout Camp," in *Children and Their Organizations: Investigations in American Culture*, ed. R. Timothy Sieber and Andrew J. Gordon (Boston: G. K. Hall, 1981), 138–60.

27. I prefer the view of postmodernism first outlined by Fredric Jameson in his essay "Postmodernism and Consumer Society" in *The Anti-Aesthetic: Essays on Postmodern Culture*, ed. Hal Foster (Port Townsend, Wash.: Bay Press, 1983), 111–25. For other, equally interesting formulations, see Charles Jencks, *What Is Post-Modernism?* (New York: St. Martin's, 1986); Andrew Ross, ed., *Universal Abandon? The Politics of Postmodernism* (Minneapolis: University of Minnesota Press, 1988); and Linda Hutcheon, *The Politics of Postmodernism* (London: Routledge, 1989). Especially interesting on the postmodern logic and aesthetics of television is E. Ann Kaplan, *Rocking around the Clock: Music Television, Postmodernism, and Consumer Culture* (New York: Routledge, 1987).

28. This is the language of the sociology of knowledge, laid out most exquisitely by Peter L. Berger and Thomas Luckmann, *The Social Construction of Reality* (Garden City, N.Y.: Doubleday/Anchor, 1966).

CHAPTER 7

Historical Narrative in the Martial Arts: A Case Study

Thomas A. Green

Won Hop Loong Chuan (Coordinated/Combined Dragon's Fist) is a martial art that incorporates a range of striking and grappling techniques common in Okinawan, Japanese, and Chinese fighting systems.[1] The standard curriculum includes basic striking and blocking techniques, combinations of these basics into *waza* (self-defense maneuvers executed against an attacker or attackers), *kata* (choreographed solo exercises lasting from one to fifteen minutes), meditation, and the history of the System (the preferred name for the art among practitioners). Students are also required to learn and use Japanese and Chinese names for techniques, to count cadences and sequences of exercises in Japanese and Chinese, and to observe traditional Asian martial etiquette during class time. Black belts are addressed by titles in Japanese (*sempai* [elder sibling], *sensei* [teacher]) and Chinese (*sifu* [father/master], *sigung* [grandfather/ grandmaster]), which indicate their rank in the hierarchy.

In these respects, Won Hop Loong Chuan does not differ markedly from many other traditional Asian martial arts. Compared to the better known and more heavily enrolled systems taught in the United States, such as Japanese karate or Korean Tae Kwon Do, however, the membership of Won Hop Loong Chuan is minuscule. As I will argue here, this fact is far from irrelevant when considering the relationship between the System's tradition and its members' identity: the smallness of the membership is an important factor in the cadre's appreciation of its special status.

An accurate count of active students of the art is difficult to establish, but a 1991 estimate supplied by Master J. W. McGlade—the second-highest ranking teacher of the art—suggests an enrollment of between 190 and 200. Of this total, there were 18 at the highest rank of black belt, followed by approximately 15 brown belts and 14 green belts, with the remainder of the membership filling the lower ranks of blue, red, and white belts. Compared to other martial arts systems, this is a fairly high percentage of high-ranking belts, and this fact too contributes to the group's identification of itself as a specially trained, elite organization.

From 1984 to 1988 and again from 1990 to 1992, I was a student of Won Hop Loong Chuan under Master McGlade. During this time, I advanced from the rank of white belt to the rank of second-degree brown belt, when my active practice and teaching of the art was terminated by an injury. Master McGlade's *dojo* (training studio) in College Station, Texas, is the largest school dedicated to study of the System, and it operates as a university club under the auspices of Texas A&M University. This has led to two peculiarities of the membership that may not be typical of other martial arts dojos. First, the average member of the System, both at College Station and at the various dojos that have been started by black belts trained by Master McGlade, is relatively young; ages range from seven to fifty years, with an average age of around twenty-four. Second, an overwhelming number of members are well educated; most have undergraduate degrees and many have advanced degrees. As a result most would be characterized sociologically as middle-class and upwardly mobile; this is a fairly atypical configuration for martial arts schools.

The System has schools in a dozen states and Mexico, all of them with relatively small memberships. A single Tae Kwon Do organization, for example, might enroll as many students in a single dojo in the United States as the combined worldwide membership of Won Hop Loong Chuan.[2] Even the largest school, Master McGlade's, maintained (before its demise in 1993) an average stable member-ship of only 70 to 75 students. Master McGlade's continuing involvement with the school best explains its relatively large size. The paucity of numbers overall is largely explained by the fact that the System has been open to the public only since the early 1980s; prior to that, instruction was by invitation only.

But other factors also contribute to keeping the membership down, chief among them the System's rigorous training and the demands made on the time of advanced members, which tend to drive away all but the most determined students. This also explains the preponder-ance of students at the higher ranks. Most students drop out at the lower ranks, and those who stay must maintain a motivation that makes martial arts a major part of their lives. The difficulty of the Won Hop Loong Chuan curriculum eliminates students unwilling to make a major commitment to learning the art. As practitioners at the higher ranks phrase it, "The System weeds them out."

Thus most members regard the previously closed nature of the System, the spartan regime, and the low enrollment as the marks of an elite group. This self-perception, which informs the entire con-sciousness of the group, is consciously and almost ritually reinforced by a detailed narrative folk history of Won Hop Loong Chuan. It is that narrative history that I explore in this study.

Narrative, Esoteric Knowledge, and Transmission

Not only does the narrative history portray the System as available to only a select few and as encompassing the best of many martial arts; in addition, esoteric knowledge is itself highly valued in the System, and although gaining and documenting such knowledge is encour-aged, securing it is not a simple matter. One must learn the proper procedures for asking questions to obtain bits of knowledge from those at the higher ranks, and these bits of knowledge are surren-dered primarily as rewards or when the questioner reveals that he or she has already uncovered clues to the matter through individual effort. Commonly, only the bare outline of the history of the System is conveyed to new members upon joining. Further information must be obtained piecemeal and then put together or "constructed."

The constructed histories developed by individual students, while not really unique, do reflect individual practitioners' training, level of interest, and personalities. While a rough consensus exists about the facts of the narrative and while Master McGlade attempts to create an environment for its maintenance, each history inevitably reflects an individual perspective, and to a degree this means that the official past of the System is the product of dialogue and imagination rather than chronology.

I can illustrate with a personal example. Most oral accounts of the careers of the Ten Tigers (legendary guardians of the System) label the group as a *tong,* or Chinese fraternal organization. On one occasion, however, I had the opportunity to ask Grandmaster A. F. Walker—Master McGlade's immediate superior in the System's lineage—if the Ten Tigers weren't more accurately regarded as a *triad,* a more politically oriented group such as the nineteenth-century Chinese Boxers. Grandmaster Walker agreed, then went on to perform narratives focussing on guerilla exploits of the Tigers that illustrated their political rather than fraternal nature. This understanding of the Ten Tigers, while it was certainly not my "discovery," was also not an obvious element of the narrative consensus. It existed as a partially validated story line, existing alongside other validated story lines that together form the mosaic of the System's "true" history.

My private discussion with Grandmaster Walker was in a sense an anomaly, because traditional transmission of knowledge is usually confined to three specific contexts: orientation, calisthenics, and philosophies.

Orientation. Each student is given an orientation to the System (lasting twenty to thirty minutes) before being instructed in the physical techniques of the art. The orientation is customarily conducted by a brown belt and involves the oral transmission of a brief history of the System, rules of conduct, and an introduction to terminology and the ranking system. The novice is given a photocopy of the general outlines of this speech, but the brown belt will also attempt an oral performance that may, like the contents of the narrative, vary depending on his or her speaking ability. In many cases, anecdotes concerning the history of the System are used to flesh out the orientation. In general, the choice of such narratives, and the decision to include them at all, are at the discretion of the brown belt charged with conducting the orientation. Obviously, this degree of instructor latitude makes for great variation in what incoming students acquire about the "official" history of the System.

Calisthenics. A portion of each two-hour class is devoted to calisthenics. Occasionally, during exercise, students are asked questions about the history of the System. Those who can supply esoteric bits of information about the System, such as meanings of terms, names of former masters, dates, and the like, may sometimes be rewarded by being excused from the next round of sit-ups or push-ups. Such occasions provide the opportunity for students to demonstrate their command of esoterica and to be taught additional bits of the group's folk history.

Philosophies. The most important context for learning the history of the System is the "philosophy" that concludes each class. A philosophy calls for the students to sit in a semicircle at the front of the instruction area facing the instructor who has conducted the class. At times a parable is narrated by one of the instructors; parables, although they may be regarded as true, are not considered to comprise elements of the history of Won Hop Loong Chuan. At the end of such a speech act, students will be asked to volunteer interpretations for the narrative. Some of these narratives are unique to the System; others are drawn from a common repertoire of (primarily Japanese and Okinawan) martial arts narratives. On other occasions, instructors will present narratives drawn from the folk history of Won Hop Loong Chuan.

In some cases, volunteers will be asked to answer questions (for example, "How many of you know the story of Kushubi's first meeting with Grandmaster Walker's father?") so that the group can construct the narrative communally. There is never a dearth of volunteers for two main reasons. First, since progress is based at least in part on knowledge of nonphysical aspects of the System, students are eager to impress on their superiors their knowledge of all elements of the art. Second, a question-and-answer session can replace rigorous exercise at the end of a gruelling workout. Typically, the highest ranking member of the group will amend any "errors" in the resulting historical account.

Because of the communal nature of this construction and because the story line is not written down, the historical accounts that emerge in these three contexts reveal both the structural stability and the sorts of variations with which students of folk narrative are familiar. The stable elements include a general observance of what Olrik long ago called the "epic laws of folk narrative."[3] To take only the most obvious example, patterns of three predominate: The Buddhist nun Ng Mui escapes with three children; Kushubi's wife is murdered by three soldiers; he takes revenge by murdering them individually on three separate occasions. Variation appears in all the familiar forms identified by Tom Burns in his classic codifications of this dramatic technique.[4] Concentration occurs, for example, when incidents are forgotten or omitted and those in attendance henceforth perpetuate attenuated versions of the story line. Other occasions may generate expanded versions, as gifted narrators flesh out spare plots by means of stock phrases and cultural clichés. Tales may also be changed to create analogies to contemporary situations.

As a result, it is virtually impossible to set down an "official" chronology of Won Hop Loong Chuan history. What I offer here is my version: a text composed of those episodes that my instructors have chosen to develop most fully and that I in turn have highlighted when giving philosophies. This history may have a basis in fact; it may be an utter fabrication by the grandmaster of Won Hop Loong Chuan. I have devoted considerable effort over almost a decade to obtaining independent corroboration of its details, but I have been unsuccessful. The lack of external corroboration for the history, however, seems to have no negative effect on students of the System. Members of Won Hop Loong Chuan are certain that the oral tradition that successfully passed along their fighting art was equally successful in faithfully perpetuating the account of its origins and development.

The System's History: One Construction

The System originated in the Sun Tzu Temple in central China approximately 2,500 years ago. The temple was devoted to the study of military strategy, history, and the martial arts; fittingly, instructors explain, *sun tzu* is translated as "war arts." Because of its reputation, the aid of the Sun Tzu monks was sought by a powerful warlord in the seventh century A.D. After the monks refused to provide assistance, the temple was destroyed in A.D. 650, and most of the monks were killed in a battle that all but destroyed the warlord's forces as well. Ng Mui, the wife of the abbot, was allowed to escape the slaughter because the victors believed that as a woman she possessed no martial knowledge and posed no threat. Ng Mui left leading a child by the hand, carrying a second in her arms, and pregnant with a third. Concealed on her person, she carried written records of the martial arts of the Sun Tzu Temple.

In time, Ng Mui gave birth to other children: a total of six daughters and ten sons, including the three children with whom she had escaped. These sons became known as the Ten Tigers. Their mother taught each one a different element of the ten fighting styles surviving from the Sun Tzu Temple, and these arts were further refined because Ng Mui arranged for the marriages of her daughters to masters of other martial arts systems. These daughters exchanged fighting systems learned from their mother for the systems of their husbands, which they passed on to Ng Mui, who then developed techniques to counter the newly acquired fighting styles, greatly enhancing the efficacy of the System.

Stories of the Ten Tigers are recounted in many of the narratives preserved by students of Won Hop Loong Chuan, and their exploits are the subject of wide variation. In the narratives collected during the course of this research, one can identify two drastically different pictures of the group.

According to a set of narratives collected primarily from brown belts from 1984 to 1986, the Ten Tigers became professional criminals who set up crossroad turnstiles as a means of extorting money from travellers. Their trade was not limited to extortion, however, and it was another talent, assassination, that led to the Tiger label. The trademark of a hit by the Ten Tigers was a mutilated corpse, ripped to shreds as if it had been mauled by a tiger.

More recently, however, Master McGlade shared with me his personal account of the Tigers. McGlade, in over twenty years as a practitioner of the art, has made a concerted effort to collect and render comprehensible the group's oral narratives. He perceives these legends as a major instrument for teaching the Won Hop Loong Chuan curriculum, and members of the System consider his knowledge in these matters as second only to that of Grandmaster A. F. Walker. According to Master McGlade, the criminality of the Tigers should be perceived as relative and socially defined. In his view, they were outlaws in the mold of Eric Hobsbawm's "social bandits,"[5] who rebelled against the authoritarian system of the warlords who destroyed the Sun Tzu Temple. They preyed on the powerful but protected the rights of the oppressed. His version of the way the Ten Tigers acquired their name attests to their social consciousness:

A master, one of the first masters outside the [Sun Tzu] Temple, he wanted to stop a warlord from pillaging a village and taking women and raping them. Because basically the warlord was doing what he wanted to do and the people didn't want that, so the master decided that he was going to give him a warning, so he sent him what's known as a blue dragon. The blue dragon was a note meaning, you know, "Stop this or I'm going to visit you." Going "to visit" him was a very polite way of saying he was going to kill him. . . . So the master was very good and he told him the day he was going to kill him. So he prepared a pit. He dug a pit and caught a couple of tigers in the pit and he put another topping over it, and he put a . . . like a vine across so he could swing across on it. Then he walked up to the gate and knocks on the gate.

They open the gate, "What do you want?"

"I am here to kill your master."

They went, "What!" And they started chasing him. And he led them on a merry chase—zigs here and zags there. And eventually they're really close to him and of course he grabs hold of that vine and swings across acting like he's running across this pit and they fall in the pit. Well, the tigers have been in there a few days and are very hungry and they're known as man-eaters anyway. They claw these people to death and then he, the master, puts a log down and lets the tigers crawl out. Goes down and collects what's left of the bodies, piles them up in front of the gate. Puts another note there, another warning. "If you don't comply, then this'll happen to you."

And basically because they looked like they were clawed by tigers (because they were)—they got mutilated pretty badly— they got known as the Tigers.

Whether the Ten Tigers are characterized as criminals or social avengers, however, there is consensus that fraternal strife between them (apparently over the Sun Tzu manuscripts and the right to lead the group) prompted a duel in which a ruthless and skillful Tiger known as Elder Brother killed his nine siblings. His success was attributed to three factors. First, he had observed his brothers' practice sessions, thus learning their styles. Second, his understanding of strategy led him to attack his brothers in the proper order—that is, in the order most likely to secure his success. Finally, his own style, "Flying Dragon," was the most effective of the ten styles and is today still regarded as the ultimate of the fighting styles of Won Hop Loong Chuan. Subsequently, Elder Brother acquired additional knowledge of the other nine fighting systems by reading manuscripts rescued from Sun Tzu.

After Elder Brother's victory, the System survived as a vagabond martial art, borrowing from and giving rise to other fighting styles, but over the centuries only the heirs of the Ten Tigers maintained the whole of the knowledge of Sun Tzu—in their memories and in written documents salvaged at the destruction of the temple. The System ultimately reached the West by the agency of a man known to students of Won Hop Loong Chuan as Mas Kushubi (one of many aliases students are told). Kushubi, half Okinawan and half Chinese, had his services sold as a small boy to a temple in exchange for food. During his indenture, he was instructed in what was known as *tode*, or *te*, the martial art that eventually developed into karate. His instructor was Itosu Yasutsune, a well-known and unarguably historical Okinawan martial arts figure who lived from 1830 to 1915. Under Yasutsune, Kushubi became the equivalent of a contemporary eighth-degree black belt, a rank at which one is recognized as a master of the highest levels of a martial art.

Leaving Okinawa for China, Kushubi was recommended to his uncle, Fu Wey (the heir to the Ten Tigers) by another family member. After passing a physically rigorous admission exam, Kushubi was accepted as a student. Kushubi held back much of his own martial arts knowledge from his uncle and other students. During Kushubi's residence with Fu Wey, China began to come under the threat of communist influence. Although specific dates are not cited for this phase of Kushubi's life, nor—with the exception of the date of Sun Tzu Temple—for any of the episodes of the history, this would probably be around the late 1920s. Because of his distaste for the communists, Kushubi asked his uncle's permission to leave the country. Denied permission and having no other means of relief from his vows, the nephew killed his uncle in a fight, which is commemorated in the first kata learned by a contemporary student of Won Hop Loong Chuan. This act left Kushubi heir to the Sun Tzu System and the custodian of the records of the art.

Following this episode, Kushubi emigrated to Burma, where he supported himself as a thief; in the narratives, he is often identified as a "second-story man." He was never brought to justice because if there were any witnesses to his crimes (as one narrator phrased it "even a pet bird or a goldfish"), Kushubi murdered them. Kushubi is said to have had a wife, who when she was pregnant with their first child was raped and murdered by three Japanese soldiers (apparently during the occupation of Burma during the Second World War). After killing the guilty parties in three different but equally brutal fashions, Kushubi continued to systematically assassinate Japanese soldiers until he was arrested and held as a "suspicious character" in an internment camp along with American prisoners of war.

While in the camp, he was seen practicing martial arts one night by an American prisoner named Walker. Walker asked him to share his knowledge, and initially Kushubi refused. Some time later, however, he saw Walker defeat a man in a fight with a single punch, using an esoteric Viking martial art identified as Bizara, which Walker had learned from his father. Kushubi then agreed to exchange knowledge with his fellow prisoner, and Walker became both Kushubi's first student and the first caucasian disciple of the art. Walker was taught only the Tiger Style, however, rather than the entire nine-style System.

After the war, Walker returned home, and later Kushubi emigrated to the United States. Walker taught his son the Tiger Style, and Kushubi eventually settled in the Los Angeles area, where his half-brother, Paul Sagawa, ran a martial arts school with a curriculum based in part on the Sun Tzu System. The details about Sagawa made available to students of Won Hop Loong Chuan are sparse. He died in the 1980s and left his school to Kushubi. Such neglect of extraneous detail, while annoying to historians, is common in folk histories.

When his son A. F. Walker was a teenager, the elder Walker suffered a permanent disability, which prevented him from teaching his son any longer. The boy was given a sealed letter and was instructed to take it to the teacher at Sagawa's Los Angeles school. Misinterpreting his father's directions, rather than taking the letter to Kushubi, young Walker gave it to a junior instructor who was leading a class when he arrived. The instructor admitted Walker to a beginner's class. During a class some weeks later, Kushubi saw his pupil's son at practice, recognized his knowledge, and asked if the boy had brought a letter with him. On being given the letter, Kushubi took the boy under his tutelage, and the younger Walker ultimately became Kushubi's heir. After Kushubi's death, Walker clinched his claim by winning a duel with a competitor for the title. As a result, he became grandmaster of the System, which he eventually organized under the name of Won Hop Loong Chuan.

During Kushubi's lifetime, Walker recruited his own cadre of students. One of these, J. W. McGlade, was invited into the group after McGlade attempted to start a fight with Walker over a pickup basketball game during their college years. McGlade proved to be Walker's most apt pupil, and since the late 1970s, he has helped organize the knowledge passed on by Kushubi into a structured curriculum.

Uses of the Narratives

The historiographic accuracy of the preceding account is not an issue in the present analysis. Certainly it is not an issue to students of Won Hop Loong Chuan. They believe that given the necessarily clandestine and subversive nature of the Tigers, it would be remarkable if the activities of the organization had been clearly documented in any verifiable records. Belief in the veracity of the narratives—with all their variations—is enhanced by the fact that the records serve identifiable functions for group members. These functions range from encouraging a sense of group pride to demonstrating the proper procedures for simple acts such as asking questions.

A comparison with invented traditions is instructive. Eric Hobsbawm and Terence Ranger contend that such traditions belong to three "overlapping types," serving the respective functions of establishing social cohesion, legitimizing institutions or "relations of authority," and socialization.[6] The historical narratives of Won Hop Loong Chuan, though they are traditions which should be regarded as consciously organized and utilized rather than "invented," serve similar ends.

This is quite consciously understood with regard to socialization. I once asked Master McGlade, for example, to explain the purpose of history to a student who just wants to learn how to fight. He responded in the following way: "There are several ways of learning how to fight. . . . The best way to do it is to teach you why you do it. . . . Well, that's what history is all about. History is a way of teaching you the mistakes of others, and what you learn from it helps you progress so that you don't have to make the same mistakes. The Sun Tzu Temple, for instance, taught our System that you should never put so much value in something that you will stay around and defend it." Master McGlade sees narratives such as his account of the origin of the name Ten Tigers as models of how to fight and why to fight. His specific allusion to the destruction of the temple is often fleshed out in philosophies as an example of holding on to the material at the cost of human life, the dangers of display of various kinds, and the virtues of hiding "what you know." In all such examples, historical narratives serve to reinforce, as Hobsbawm and Ranger put it, "the inculcation of beliefs, value systems and conventions of behavior."[7]

They also serve to legitimate the System itself. They do this primarily by providing a distinguished pedigree for the art, linking it to names well known to students of the martial arts generally, whether or

not they are familiar with Won Hop Loong Chuan. The most important names in this respect are Sun Tzu, Ng Mui, and Itosu Yasutsune.

Sun Tzu is not only the name of the temple where Won Hop
Loong Chuan is said to have originated 2,500 years ago. It is also the
nom de plume of the author (or authors) of the classic work of Asian
military strategy, *The Art of War*. By its association with Sun Tzu,
therefore, the System acquires, by self-ascription, an immediate
credibility to students apprised of this connection. Moreover, students are encouraged to study *The Art of War* and are told that the
thirteen published chapters of this work comprise only a fragment of
an original manuscript that is in the possession of Grandmaster A. F.
Walker. The knowledge of the lost manuscript, they are told, is
incorporated into the curriculum that they have been allowed to pur-
sue. Hence their involvement in Sun Tzu's System both elevates and
humbles them, inspiring them to become worthy of the honor.

Ng Mui, the woman who rescued the art after the destruction of
the temple, is known more widely as the legendary founder of another Chinese fighting style called Wing Chun. The style gained extensive publicity by its association with the late actor and martial arts
instructor Bruce Lee, who taught a modified form of it in the late
1960s. Wing Chun is regarded by many members of the System as
the martial art taught by Ng Mui to her daughters, which they
exchanged for their husbands' knowledge. Here again, Won Hop
Loong Chuan and the folk record are validated by their association
with a familiar historical figure. Equally important is the fact that the
established martial art of Wing Chun is portrayed as so inferior to the
Sun Tzu art that Ng Mui was willing to give it away to outsiders.

Itosu Yasutsune established a reputation in Okinawa at the turn of
the century as a practitioner and instructor of the precursor of modern karate. Itosu's exploits ranged from a bare-handed confrontation
with a wild bull to defeating a Japanese judo champion with a single
punch at the age of seventy-five. These and other tales have passed
into martial arts oral tradition.[8] Itosu's most famous student, Gichin
Funakoshi, has been credited with introducing karate to Japan and
founding the style known as Shotokan. His autobiography remains
one of the most widely read works on Asian martial arts.[9] Thus the
link between Kushubi and Itosu lends additional credibility to Won

Hop Loong Chuan. The reputation of the System is amplified by the belief that Kushubi apparently learned all Itosu could teach before going on to master the Sun Tzu arts.

Therefore, while gaining credibility through association with documented and legendary martial arts figures, students of the System also maintain its superiority to the arts with which these figures are associated in the public mind. The published chapters of *The Art of War* constitute an incomplete record; Wing Chun was the inferior style Ng Mui used as a means to acquire additional martial knowledge; and Kushubi went on to China to perfect his fighting skills after studying with Itosu. In all three cases, Won Hop Loong Chuan transcends and improves upon a recognized master model.

In addition to socializing students and legitimating the System, the folk history also provides emulable models of correct behavior. It conveys not only an explicit body of knowledge to be mastered, but also an implicit model for *how* this knowledge is to be acquired. It does this especially by providing a historical template which students, in their training, symbolically replicate. For example, the System teaches that before one can really become a student of Won Hop Loong Chuan, one must already be a master of another martial art. Therefore, the curriculum consists of teaching an Okinawan form of karate up until the brown belt level, at which point the student progresses to Chinese *katas*. This training pattern recapitulates Kushubi's pattern of martial education as he moved from Okinawa to China.

The use of such elements of folk history as contemporary reference points is apparent throughout the education of a student of the System. The students are often told that when they enter the training hall they are "in Japan" or "in China." The first *kata* learned, the one which constitutes the basis of the curriculum through the brown belt level, is said to be a reenactment of the battle in which Kushubi killed Fu Wey. The test for red belt rank is described as a compressed version of the ancient test which confronted applicants to Asian martial arts masters. The fact that the System does not now have a temple is explained by reference to the destruction of Sun Tzu; after that event, Ng Mui and her children were said to have vowed not to replace it until the System became strong enough to be immune to a replay of history.

With regard to this particular feature of the history, the attitude toward the past is far from simply mimetic. The lack of a temple is understood as a historical dilemma that the System replicates but must also resolve. Indeed, the current grandmaster is regarded as the symbolic "abbot" of Sun Tzu, and members of the System plan to build a new temple, which will serve as the headquarters for the art and a repository for the manuscripts rescued from the original temple. This still unrealized episode in the history of Won Hop Loong Chuan—the rebuilding of the temple—adds a final dimension to the narratives, as the group's folk history both explains present circumstances and provides strategies for the future.

It thus becomes, as Charles Hudson has observed of folk history in general, less an orthodox historical record than a sociology of knowledge that enables members to understand the present by reference to the past. A society's belief system, he suggests, "articulates not only with the present of a society . . . but also . . . with the society's folk history. . . . One could even go a step further and say that a people's belief system also articulates with their perception of the future."[10] The historical narratives of Won Hop Loong Chuan demonstrate the validity of Hudson's claims.

In addition to narratives of the temple and the Ten Tigers, which maintain an aura of mythic removal from contemporary life, the folk history of Won Hop Loong Chuan encompasses more modern narratives in which the contemporary masters of the System are both humanized and used as models for behavior. In the account of Grandmaster Walker's misinterpretation of his father's instructions and his subsequent delay in contacting Kushubi, students learn the importance of giving and receiving lucid instructions and the proper procedures for asking unambiguous questions. From the episode of Master McGlade's potentially disastrous confrontation with the grandmaster, students learn not to underestimate a potential opponent and the value of avoiding conflict. Even Kushubi, who may appear to be a sinister figure in the major narratives, is given an added and more humane dimension in minor narratives surrounding his relationship with Grandmaster Walker. For example, in the following narrative given by Master McGlade, he is shown to have a sense of humor.

Sigung [A. F. Walker] went to some tournament, and of course Kushubi did *not* like that idea—showing off for the audience. And of course he took first place and all this.

And he comes back and says, "Hey look what I won! I won this trophy!"

And Kushubi looks at it and puts the trophy down and says, "Who you think you are, Bruce Lee?" He said, "I show you what Bruce Lee is," and he proceeded to get up out of his wheel chair and kick Sigung's ass.

So I guess two weeks before Kushubi died, he just whomped on my instructor. He was 82, 5'4", maybe 120 pounds. soaking wet. My instructor's 6'2", probably weighed 185 and quick, young.

As Charles Briggs asserts in his analysis of pedagogical discourse, such texts require a dialectical unfolding during the course of per-formance.[11] Such is obviously the case with the didactic narratives of Won Hop Loong Chuan. Variants of the narrative reported here might in other contexts be used to impart lessons regarding the need to keep the art concealed, the value of humility, or Kushubi's exceptional martial arts ability. In all these contexts, however, Kushubi's criminal background, over which student opinion ranges from the intrigued to the appalled, is softened, and a more humane figure emerges. Similarly, another of McGlade's anecdotes reveals that Kushubi found it necessary to dislocate Grandmaster Walker's elbow to demonstrate a technique, but afterwards he cried for inflicting pain on his pupil. In both these examples, we see the nar-ratives humanizing the most distinguished members of an elite but potentially deadly cadre, using their experiences to teach humility as well as discipline.

Organizing Elite Experience

Richard Price, in a remarkable analysis of Surinamese oral history, has suggested that we must take seriously a culture's selection and narra-tive expansions of significant events from the general activity that constitutes the past. Historical narratives, he contends, are primary tools for a group's organization of experience.[12] Overall, it is clear that practitioners of Won Hop Loong Chuan have developed a narrative tool kit that serves the needs of the group. Clearly, these narratives are used as teaching tools within the System. Equally important, this sequence of events encourages a particular mindset among students of the art, a worldview that is conducive to extraordinary bonding. Hobsbawm and Ranger's argument that invented traditions establish or symbolize social cohesion is certainly relevant here.

That cohesion is clearly enhanced by a sense of elitism. In addition to the validation of the group's elite status provided by reference to Itosu, Sun Tzu, and Ng Mui, students frequently reminisce, or more accurately gloat, in personal experience narratives concerning former students who "couldn't handle" the curriculum or its demands on their time. Such anecdotes generally contain references to how lucky "we" are to be given the opportunity to learn a martial art of such ancient lineage and one that was formerly open only to those willing to adopt a monastic life. In this regard, Kushubi's outlaw career and the careers of the Ten Tigers undoubtedly provide an aura of romance for some students, some of whom are heard to refer to Won Hop Loong Chuan as an "assassin's art."

Related to the elitism is the function of the history in reducing the cognitive dissonance generated by the physical and psychological stress of the rigorous curriculum. Student complaints may elicit references to the previously closed nature of the System, to the "bad old days" when it was available only to Chinese students: the implication, validated by the narratives, is that modern students don't know how good they have it. The extra work expected of students who had been trained personally by Grandmaster Walker or Master McGlade—those who were "close to the hub of the wheel"—is likewise justified by reference to the narratives. For example, Kushubi's dislocation of Grandmaster Walker's elbow both explains the need for student suffering and attests to the instructor's ultimate regard for the student even when injury or ostensible "abuse" occurs.

Finally the physical movements required by the martial arts are also given a special status by way of the narratives. I have already mentioned that the first kata students learn recapitulates the death match between Kushubi and Fu Wey. Not only are students given this information as they begin to learn the kata. They are periodically reminded during practice (particularly if instructors feel their efforts lack commitment and "spirit") that the kata is a real fight to the death, and practicing it should be approached in that fashion. Because the kata constitutes a reenactment of a "sacred event" in the history of the group, it operates through the same semiotic channels as ritual reenactments such as the Christian Eucharist, which reenacts the Last Supper. Through the ritual reenactment of this central kata, the past of Won Hop Loong Chuan becomes, in Paul Connerton's evocative words, "sedimented in the body."[13] Like ritual, the kata links cognitive memory and affective impact.

Through various channels, then, a concerted effort to construct a meaningful worldview for students of Won Hop Loong Chuan is made by members of the System at all levels. Historical narratives, even as they are subject to variation and communal creativity, serve to provide a series of reference points for both the present and the future of the group. Folk history emerges as a primary vehicle for socialization even as it makes the elitism of the group palpable and its rigors bearable.

Notes

1. I am grateful to Master Jerry W. McGlade for his generous contributions of time and knowledge during the research for this article. Any mistakes and misinterpretations of the record are solely my responsibility. My analyses were influenced also by suggestions from Sylvia Grider and Tad Tuleja.

2. In 1989, the World Tae Kwon Do Federation listed its membership as in excess of 20 million. Yeon Hee Park, Yeon Hwan Park, and Jon Gerrard, *Tae Kwon Do* (New York: Facts on File, 1989), 6.

3. Axel Olrik's classic study appeared in German in 1909. It is reprinted as "Epic Laws of Folk Narrative" in *The Study of Folklore*, ed. Alan Dundes (Englewood Cliffs, N.J.: Prentice-Hall, 1965).

4. See Thomas A. Burns, with Inger H. Burns, *Doing the Wash: An Expressive Culture and Personality Study of a Joke and Its Tellers* (Norwood, Penn.: Norwood Editions, 1976); and Thomas A. Burns, "A Model for Textual Variation in Folksong," in *Folk Groups and*

Folklore Genres: A Reader, ed. Elliott Oring (Logan: Utah State University Press, 1989), 245–53.

5. Eric Hobsbawm, *Bandits* (New York: Dell, 1989).

6. Eric Hobsbawm and Terence Ranger, "Introduction," in *The Invention of Tradition* (New York: Cambridge, 1988), 9.

7. Ibid.

8. Richard Kim, *The Weaponless Warriors* (Burbank, Calif.: Ohara, 1974), 50–58.

9. Gichin Funakoshi, *Karate-Do: My Way of Life* (Tokyo: Kodansha, 1975).

10. Charles Hudson, "Folk History and Ethnohistory," *Ethnohistory* 13 (1966): 67. See also his "The Historical Approach in Anthropology," in *Handbook of Social and Cultural Anthropology*, ed. John J. Honigman (Chicago: Rand McNally, 1973), 111–41.

11. Charles Briggs, "Treasure Tales and Pedagogical Discourse in *Mexicano* New Mexico," *Journal of American Folklore* 98 (1985): 287–314.

12. Richard Price, *First Time* (Baltimore: Johns Hopkins, 1983).

13. Paul Connerton, *How Societies Remember* (Cambridge: Cambridge University Press, 1989), 72.

CHAPTER 8

Pioneers and Recapitulation in Mormon Popular Historical Expression

Eric A. Eliason

Few events serve better than a duress-induced migration to forge a people's identity and provide a defining historical touchstone for a nation. Through its representation in art and public historical displays, such a trek can galvanize generations if its drudgery is valorized, its most dramatic moments highlighted, and its embarrassing episodes forgotten. At least since the time Moses led the children of Israel to the biblical promised land, groups of individuals in various places at various times have come to see themselves as a distinct people through participation in, or shared remembrance of, a great trek.

One such group is South Africa's Boers, or Afrikaners, from whose language English acquired the word "trek." Fleeing British encroachment in 1836, the Boers left their homes near the Cape and headed for a promised land in the Transvaal. In true romantic nationalist style,[1] today's Afrikaners remember the struggles faced by their *voortrekker* ancestors as the ordeal that made them a people and gave them the character traits needed to build Africa's richest nation.[2] Afrikaners celebrate their Great Trek in art, monument, song, pageant, and parade.

175

In China, the six-thousand-mile "Long March" the People's Army made to escape the Nationalists in 1936 is likewise regarded as the event that birthed modern China. Today, the route taken by the Long Marchers is memorialized by countless trail markers and thousands of nostalgic societies who meet regularly to commemorate—and for a few of the very old, to reminisce about—significant events of the march. Stories and reenactments of the Long March still constitute an important part of the official school curriculum of "character development" for Chinese children.[3]

North America has also produced a people whose crucible of identity formation was a romanticized migration to a promised land—the Mormons. From their 1846 expulsion from Nauvoo, Illinois, to the 1869 arrival of the transcontinental railroad in Utah, Mormon pioneers performed the largest, and most persistently revered, religious migration in the history of the Western Hemisphere. Throughout the American West, the individualistic efforts of westward-moving settlers have been an important component of popular historical consciousness.[4] But in the "Mormon West,"[5] commemoration of the cooperative and purposeful Mormon pioneer migration has achieved a particularly well-developed form. Like the Afrikaner Great Trek and the Chinese Long March, the memory of the Mormon Trail has been reverently enshrined and celebrated by commemorative societies and in museums, books, monuments, trail markers, art, sculpture, sermons, dramatic productions, and parades.

This essay seeks to understand the origins of the "pioneer myth" and its contemporary place within Mormon culture.[6] First, it examines how the Mormon trek was understood by those who participated in it and how it continues to be understood by those who entertain a cultural memory of it—in romantic terms as part of a greater American historical drama, but more significantly as a "usable past" that constitutes a uniquely Mormon sacred history. Next, this essay explores the varieties of pioneer popular memory constructed by Mormons and the kinds of expressive traditions that have been mobilized to maintain, celebrate, and reinterpret the pioneers' saga. Last, this essay addresses the contestations and adaptations that the Mormon pioneer story has undergone as Utah has become more culturally heterogeneous and Mormonism has expanded outside of its traditional cultural region in the American West.

Understanding the Mormon Exodus

To understand how pioneers came to be so significant in Mormon popular historical expression, we need to go back to the religion's beginnings in Joseph Smith's visions and the coming forth of the Book of Mormon and explain these events as Mormons view them. The purpose here is neither to proselytize on behalf of Mormonism nor to "debunk" any aspect of Mormon belief. Instead, the purpose is to allow access into the sacred history of which the pioneer experience is a continuation and into the religious worldview and culture of which the pioneers and their myth are a part.

Mormonism began in the 1820s with a series of revelations to Joseph Smith, a young religious seeker in rural upstate New York. The two most important of these revelations were (1) a visitation by God the Father and Jesus Christ, who informed Joseph that he would be the medium through which the true church and the kingdom of God on Earth would be restored to a world engulfed by religious conflict and false teachings and (2) the appearance of the angel Moroni, a resurrected prophet from an ancient American civilization established by refugees who had fled from Israel before the 600 B.C. destruction of Jerusalem. Moroni presented Joseph Smith with the famous golden plates, which, after they were translated, became the Book of Mormon—a history of Moroni's people that explained (to the satisfaction of Mormons) the origins of the American Indians and recorded that Jesus had visited the Western Hemisphere after his resurrection. Armed with a divine mandate and a new book of scripture, the young prophet quickly began attracting followers, but also a great deal of antagonism.

In the early years of their church, Mormons believed that to follow their mandate to establish the kingdom of God on Earth, they needed to gather together in the same communities and participate in exclusive, communitarian economic arrangements.[7] These attitudes aroused the suspicion and hostility of their neighbors, who violently forced Joseph Smith and his Church of Jesus Christ of Latter-day Saints (LDS Church) along the fringe of the cresting wave of American westward expansion—always marginalized and continually persecuted. Having been driven off their land in the late 1830s by vigilante mobs in Ohio and in three different places in Missouri, Joseph Smith's flock, by then numbering in the tens of thousands, built the city of Nauvoo in western Illinois. It was here, during a brief hiatus from harassment, that Joseph Smith received his boldest and most distinctive revelations about the special mission of his people. The biblical restoration theme in his teachings began to markedly emphasize Old as well as New Testament motifs. For example, he initiated secret temple ordinances and began introducing a few close and trusted associates to the doctrine of plural marriage. Polygamy, as it is often called, drew inspiration from the familial arrangements of the biblical patriarchs Abraham, Isaac, and Jacob. Rumors of Joseph Smith's involvement with plural marriage began a sequence of events that led to his arrest and martyrdom in the summer of 1844 by yet another mob jealous and frightened of Mormon power.

After the prophet's death, the largest faction of the movement accepted Brigham Young's claim to church leadership and followed his lead to flee continued persecution and to search for a sanctuary in the wilderness. In 1847, Brigham Young left his followers in the temporary settlement of Winter Quarters in what is now Nebraska and led an advance company of Mormon leaders to the Rocky Mountains, where he selected the Salt Lake Valley as his people's ultimate destination. By 1848, most of Nauvoo's inhabitants who would be coming had made the trek to their promised land.

From Salt Lake City, Young immediately began sending out groups to colonize as much as they could of the Great Basin, concentrating on the valleys along the Wasatch Front of the Rocky Mountains. Highly successful Mormon proselytizing continued, especially in Great Britain and Scandinavia, where European Mormons outnumbered their American counterparts during much of the mid-nineteenth century. However, in the continuing spirit of gathering, these converts were expected to come to Zion as soon as they were able. Scores of thousands came. Most came by ship, rail, and/or riverboat to Iowa City from whence they headed to Salt Lake City by wagon. Some came by wagon from California after having rounded Cape Horn. Between 1856 and 1860, when Mormon Church money was particularly tight, some immigrants even pushed and pulled their meager belongings across the plains in handcarts.[8]

The use of wagons stopped after the completion of the transcontinental railroad in 1869, but immigrants continued to come by rail. What Mormons remember as "The Gathering" remained church policy until it began to be deemphasized at the turn of the century. At about the time of the Great Depression, the Mormon Church began to encourage its new converts not to gather physically in Utah, but to gather spiritually with nearby members and to build up the church in their homelands.

The Mormon trek to Zion drew much of its symbolic potency from the fact that its participants and their descendants understood it to be a recapitulation of the biblical Exodus. As evidenced in pioneer journals, the Mormon migration to Utah was regarded from the start as sacred history in the making.[9] While not necessarily a theological imperative, a grand recapitulation of sacred history fit nicely within the Mormon self-conception of their religion as being the restoration of all religious truths preached in both New and Old Testament times. Joseph Smith's reintroduction of other Old Testament ideas such as temple rituals and plural marriage undoubtedly prepared Mormons to heed Brigham Young's call to reenact the Exodus. In fact, Brigham Young earned the title "the American Moses" for leading the Mormons to their promised land and realizing Smith's visionary plans for a Mormon kingdom in the Rocky Mountains.[10] Under Brigham Young's direction, the bedraggled bands of refugees that left Nauvoo at gun point in 1846 became forward looking and sacred history enacting "pioneers."

Part of Young's strategy for accomplishing this feat was to use Moses's organizational model and organize the Saints into hierarchical groups of tens, fifties and hundreds.[11] Parallels with the Exodus did not end here. Mormon oral tradition and pioneer journals record that the Mississippi froze at an opportune time to allow the first pioneer wagon trains to cross, much as the Red Sea had parted to allow Moses's followers to escape Egypt. After the

Mormons crossed the Mississippi, flocks of quail miraculously wandered into pioneer camps like manna from heaven to feed the poorest of the straggling travellers. After time spent in the wilderness, the Latter-day Saints came upon a land where a river ran between a freshwater lake and a saltwater lake. It was only appropriate that the Mormons named it the Jordan River after its counterpart in Palestine. (See Figure 1.)

A factor that heightened the realism of this link with ancient Israel was that most Mormons had received "patriarchal blessings" modeled after blessings given by biblical patriarchs to their children. In these blessings, most Saints were told, by church members specially called for this purpose, that they were literal descendants of the Hebrew tribe of Ephraim through whom—according to the Bible and Joseph Smith's revelations—all the nations of the Earth would be blessed.[12] "British Israelitism," or the belief that Anglo-Saxon peoples are literal descendants of biblical Israelites, was a common notion in the mid-nineteenth century.[13] For the Mormons who recapitulated the Exodus, identification with the Israelites through their own version of British Israelitism made their chosen-ness and their "living through again" of sacred history much more literal and significant than a mere reenactment.[14]

Because the early Mormons made new sacred history by recapitulating old sacred history, they have bequeathed to today's Mormons a "usable past" that sets them apart as a new religious tradition distinct and different from the American Christian milieu out of which they emerged. This occurred in much the same way that early Christians created a new religious tradition by incorporating and reworking themes from the Hebrew religious tradition out of which they grew. Jan Shipps, a perceptive scholar of Mormonism whose interpretations of Mormon history have been highly influential in recent years, explains how the pioneers' story stands next to the sacred history of the Israelites in the Old Testament and that of Jesus and the apostles in the New Testament as a "third sacred text" to which Mormons look for guidance, instruction, and inspiration.[15]

Another key to understanding Mormon reverence for the pioneers is to place their saga within the broader context of the Romanticism that permeated American culture at the time. Several

Figure 1. *Map Showing the Striking Similarity between Palestine and Salt Lake Valley, Utah.* This Rio Grande Western Railroad map was published in William E. Smythe, *The Conquest of Arid America* (1899).

historians suggest that the content of the Mormon gospel and the
trek to establish a Godly kingdom in the West (initially outside the
boundaries of the United States) constituted a rejection of the
romantic "age of boundlessness," of American democratic and capitalist mores, and of what the Mormons viewed as the increasing disorder of ante-bellum America.[16]

However, the Mormons' self-conception of their destiny did
reflect many aspects of American Romanticism. For example, the
ancient history of the Book of Mormon, Joseph Smith's personal
religious history, and the pioneer trek together provided for
Mormons—and they hoped for the entire nation—a grand unifying
sacred history for an American culture "cursed" with a troubling a-
historicity by its newness and its cultural pluralism.[17] Also, reflecting
the Romantic notion that "primitive" civilizations must give way to
"advanced" ones,[18] Mormons fully believed—especially during the
Civil War—that America would eventually turn to them for guidance and leadership.[19] Mormons shared with the Romantics the
vision of a great, untamed wilderness waiting to be conquered by a
growing nation that God had chosen as his own. The sense of drama
this imparted to all of America's westward expansion was shared by
the Mormons, but they experienced it primarily in terms of their
own history only.

Another important contribution of Romanticism that still rever-
berates with modern Mormons is the era's historiographic
approach. At the time of the pioneer trek, historians depicted
America's past as a grand unfolding drama of the progressive triumph of superior civilization and good over ignorance and evil. If a
historian wrote detached or dispassionately and failed to convey
these truths, peers would have deemed his work as slighting the significance of the past. Truth according to popular historiography in
the nineteenth century was best illuminated through "glowing pictures" that highlighted heroism and sacrifice.[20] Mormons viewed
the telling of their own history in a similar light. In this view, God
caused the United States to be established so his true church could
be restored in a country constitutionally committed to religious
freedom. These historiographic ideas continue, in tempered form,
in Mormon circles today and inform modern Mormon celebrations

and artistic depictions of the pioneer era as a glorious achievement wrought by self-sacrificing heroes.

Genres of Pioneer Celebration

Being thus imbued with profound significance in its dual role as a recapitulation of sacred history and as the vanguard of America's prophetic destiny, the pioneer trek was charged with the potential to become a long-lasting cultural memory and the subject of generations of commemoration. In fact, the first public celebration of the pioneer trek took place on July 24, 1849, only two years to the day after Brigham Young's party entered the Salt Lake Valley. Events included a huge outdoor dinner, parades, music, and numerous speeches and sermons that focussed on the great future that lay ahead of the Saints now that they had begun to gather in Zion.[21] The pioneer era was already being celebrated when it had barely even begun.

The 1849 Pioneer Day celebration was a harbinger of things to come. From this point on, the pioneer mythos grew and shot tendrils into all aspects of Mormon cultural expression. Today, several interrelated institutions and genres of activity support and re-create pioneer memories. Ten of the most visible and significant are (1) commemorative organizations, (2) markers and statues, (3) song, (4) art, (5) literature, (6) museums, (7) dramatic presentations, (8) living history, (9) Pioneer Day parades, and (10) oral tradition.

(1) Commemorative Organizations. Of course, the Church of Jesus Christ of Latter-day Saints itself is active in maintaining pioneer memories and utilizing these stories as a means of inspiring today's Mormons to remain true to the legacy of faith bequeathed to them. Church leaders mention the pioneers in public sermons, commission works of art in their honor, support museums, and regularly use images of wagons and handcarts in their official publications. However, the LDS Church has relinquished much of its role as maintainer of popular celebrations of pioneer heritage to several voluntary organizations. The most significant of these are the Sons of the Utah Pioneers (SUP) and the generally more active and ambitious Daughters of Utah Pioneers (DUP). These groups modelled

themselves after the Daughters of the American Revolution (DAR), and like the DAR, they dedicate themselves to historical preservation of a particular event by collecting relics and documents, staffing museums, publishing books and pamphlets, and organizing commemorative occasions. Also in the spirit of the DAR, the DUP restricts its membership to women with pioneer ancestry; they are the self-appointed guardians of Mormonism's pioneer heritage by virtue of their birthright. Another group, "Days of '47 Inc.," grew out of the SUP in 1947 to take over the Pioneer Day festivities in Salt Lake City. They conceive themselves as a public interest organization responsible for planning civic events that serve the whole Salt Lake City community and not just LDS Church members.

(2) Markers and Monuments. The DUP, SUP, the Mormon Trail Association, the State of Utah, the National Park Service, the LDS Church, and other organizations erect and maintain monuments and plaques dedicated to the pioneers at various sites along the Mormon Trail and throughout the Mormon West. The most impressive and famous is the This Is the Place Monument, where Emigration Canyon empties into Salt Lake City. From atop his perch on a column of granite, a bronze Brigham Young scans the valley his people colonized and reminds today's Utahans of their legacy.

(3) Song. The pioneer period was the most fruitful hymn writing era in Mormon history. Most of the hymns unique to Mormonism were written at this time. These hymns dwelt on the hardships of the trail to Utah, the importance of leaving Babylon to gather in God's kingdom, and on the religious, political, and economic deliverance the Saints expected to find in fleeing to Zion. Many of these hymns, such as "Come, Come Ye Saints," "Israel, Israel, God Is Calling," and "High on a Mountain Top," survive to this day as Mormon favorites. Through the efforts of the Mormon Tabernacle Choir, "Come, Come Ye Saints" has even become a popular song in the hymnals of several other denominations. The song is Mormonism's chief contribution to American hymnology. Others, such as "Come Haste to the Valley," "Farewell to Thee England," and "A Word to the Saints Who Are Gathering," faded into obscurity. A hymn could survive if its theme could be reinterpreted as relevant in a post-Gathering church. In the case of the "Handcart

Song," the most famous Mormon folk tune, the words of the hymn were changed to transform it from a marching song sung by the trekkers themselves to a children's hymn that remembered their efforts.[22] The song was originally sung:

> Ye Saints that dwell on Europe's shores
> Prepare yourselves with many more
> To leave behind your native land
> For sure God's Judgments are at Hand
>
> *Chorus*:
> For some must push and some must pull
> As we go marching up the hill,
> As merrily on the way we go
> Until we reach the Valley, oh!

Today the hymn goes:

> When pioneers moved to the West
> With courage strong they met the test
> They pushed their handcarts all day long
> And as they pushed they sang this song:
>
> *Chorus*[23]

(4) Art. In the later part of the nineteenth century, the LDS Church sent some of Mormondom's most promising painters to Paris with the purpose of training them as official artists: painting portraits, decorating temples, and visually honoring Mormon history. The Paris Art Mission was an important early milestone in establishing a lasting tradition of Mormon art and a relationship of patronage between the LDS Church and Mormon artists. As might be expected, much of this art has focussed on the pioneer experience. Pioneer "high art" invariably depicts scenes of tragedy, such as the burying of those who succumbed to the elements on the trail (see Figure 2); of heroism, such as young men carrying the aged and the sick across rivers; or of triumph, such as groups of pioneers entering

Figure 2. *The Martin Handcart Company.* This painting, done in 1980 by Clark Kelley Price, depicts the burial on the trail of the artist's great-great-grandfather during the winter storms of 1856. ©The Church of Jesus Christ of Latter-day Saints. Courtesy of the Museum of Church History and Art. Used by permission.

Figure 3. *Handcart Pioneers.* C. C. A. Christensen painted this image in 1900 from personal recollection. ©The Church of Jesus Christ of Latter-day Saints. Courtesy of the Museum of Church History and Art. Used by permission.

Figure 4. *Handcart Pioneers*. The canonical image of the Mormon entry into the Salt Lake valley as painted by Minerva K. Teichert. ©The Church of Jesus Christ of Latter-day Saints. Courtesy of the Museum of Church History and Art. Used by permission.

the valley (see Figure 4). Rarely does one see depictions of the pioneers stopping for a rest or enjoying themselves around a campfire (see Figure 3 for an exception). Pioneer themes are also a distinctive feature of Utah folk and tourist art. Covered wagons and handcarts adorn products ranging from quilts to refrigerator magnets.

(5) Literature. The pioneer-trek-memorializing book and pamphlet series published by the DUP under the long and vigorous leadership of Kate B. Carter were widely read in the past but are less well known today.[24] However, internationally read official LDS Church magazines regularly recount faith-promoting episodes from pioneer history. Also, Mormon bookstores throughout the American West sell historical novels and children's books featuring pioneer themes.

(6) Museums. The LDS Church's Museum of Church History and Art houses hundreds of paintings on pioneer themes and displays pioneer artifacts in a walk-through exhibit that recapitulates pioneer chronology. The DUP's far less polished but much better stocked Pioneer Memorial Museum in Salt Lake City bills itself as the "world's largest collection of pioneer artifacts"[25] and has enshrined not only such notable items as Brigham Young's wagon but numerous pistols, blankets, toothbrushes, and other items brought by the pioneers to Utah. Scores of smaller DUP "relic halls" are scattered throughout the Mormon West.

(7) Dramatic Presentations. Mormons have long used theater as a means of transferring the memory of significant historical occurrences to those who did not live through them. Since their earliest arrival in Utah, Mormons have commemorated their trek in various dramatic productions. Since its composition in conjunction with the 1947 pioneer centennial, playwright Crawford Gates's musical *Promised Valley* has been a favorite of professional and community theater companies throughout the Mormon West. In honor of the 1997 sesquicentennial of the pioneers' arrival in Utah, the LDS Church has commissioned a new play with the intention that it be performed in local congregations worldwide.[26]

In a cultural expression similar to theater but on a grander scale, Mormon-sponsored historical pageants draw tens of thousands of Mormons and Gentiles alike to Hill Cumorah, New York; Nauvoo, Illinois; Independence, Missouri (all places with historical significance to Mormons); the temple grounds in Manti, Utah; and most recently, the country music mecca of Branson, Missouri. These extravagant spectacles employ hundreds of young Mormon volunteers as cast members and utilize spectacular pyrotechnics and visual effects. They re-create and celebrate historical episodes from the founding of America, the Book of Mormon, and, especially in the case of the Nauvoo and Branson pageants, the trek of Utah's pioneers.[27] Recently, the pioneer trek worked its way into film when it served as the climax of a big-budget, 70-millimeter film, *Legacy*, which has become a major tourist attraction in Salt Lake City.

(8) Living History. Historian Jay Anderson explains that living history is people employing the clothing, tools, and manner of a bygone era to "time travel" (or create the experiential impression of going back in time) from the mundane present to a reverenced past.[28] Time travel through living historic reenactment is a particularly attractive prospect to Mormons, whose past is not only reverenced, but sacred. Not long after the end of the pioneer period, Mormons began celebrating Pioneer Day by donning gingham dresses and sun bonnets, or straw hats and boots, in emulation of their ancestors. This practice had already begun while many trek participants were still living. (See Figure 5.) While Pioneer garb—often with doubtful resemblance to actual pioneer fashions—is sometimes worn for a party at the local church meetinghouse, in other cases it is a facet of participation in a pageant or parade where the participant also pulls a handcart, rides in a wagon, or delivers an oration in pioneer persona.

The State of Utah also honors pioneers through its maintenance of Pioneer Trail State Park, which houses a model pioneer village staffed by living history buffs. "Old Deseret" is a composite historic settlement representing Utah life from 1847 to 1869. A similar enterprise, "Sons of the Utah Pioneers Village," is an attraction at Utah's chief amusement park, Lagoon.

The most ambitious assumption of pioneer personae took place during the SUP's 1947 centennial re-creation of the advance party's journey from Nauvoo to the Salt Lake Valley. Great care was taken to include the same number of participants in the right male-to-female and child-to-adult ratios, to travel the same number of miles

Figure 5. *Pioneer Day*. At the 1922 dedication of the original This Is the Place Monument, Mormon dignitaries honor their famous forebears by donning the garb of 1840s pioneers. The slight figure at the center of the group is Lorenzo Zobieski Young, a survivor of the 1847 exodus. ©The Church of Jesus Christ of Latter-day Saints. Courtesy of the Historical Department, Archives Division. Used by permission.

per day, and to camp in the same sites as Brigham Young's party did. Unfortunately, the disruption caused by World War II scuttled plans to travel in real covered wagons, so canvas-covered automobiles adorned with plywood oxen jutting from their hoods served as substitutes.[29] For the 1997 sesquicentennial, discussions are under way to re-create the advance party trek again. This time the plan is to use real wagons and strive for authenticity down to the last detail.[30]

(9) Pioneer Day Parades. The most dramatic expressions of the pioneers' importance in Mormon cultural memory are the annual July 24 "Pioneer Day" celebrations. In honor of the pioneers, costumed re-creations of pioneer events, commemorative lectures at local church buildings, and especially parades are held on this day in

scores of towns and cities throughout the Mormon West. Sociologist Thomas O'Dea has called Pioneer Day "the greatest Mormon Holiday."[31] And rightfully so. In most towns where it is observed, Pioneer Day functions far outstrip in participation and significance even those surrounding the Fourth of July. The saga of the pioneers is especially well-suited to commemoration in a parade format. As trek reenactors parade down various main streets, they perform "micro-treks" that recapitulate in miniature the event that they honor.

Being the end point of the Mormon Trail and the geographic center of Mormondom, Salt Lake City hosts the largest celebration of pioneer heritage in North America—the annual month-long "Days of '47" civic celebration. After Pasadena's Rose Bowl Parade and New York City's Macy's Thanksgiving Day Parade, Salt Lake City's "Days of '47" celebration boasts the third largest annual parade in the United States, with 150,000 to 300,000 spectators lining the streets and simultaneous telecasts in seven states.[32] Floats with pioneer themes and pioneer reenactors riding wagons and pushing handcarts are central features of this event.

(10) Oral Tradition. Perhaps the practice most responsible for keeping the pioneers' memory alive is talking about them. It happens formally and informally at church and on special occasions such as Pioneer Day. For many Mormons, pioneer stories are part of oral family history—shared stories of heroic ancestors that bind together extended families. Traditionally, in talking about pioneers, Mormons express respect and gratitude for their accomplishments and remind themselves of their duty to live true to their memory and carry on the work they began.[33]

Through these genres of pioneer remembrance, modern Mormons appropriate their sacred past into their own experience in the present. This is important because many of today's Mormons suspect that their "living through" of sacred history ended in the nineteenth century, making their own lives rather mundane when compared to the cosmically significant pioneer endeavor. However, through recapitulations and renditions of an idealized pioneer past, modern Mormons can return to sacred time and space.[34] Mormon pioneer reverence and recapitulation are examples of the process described by Mircea Eliade in *The Myth of the Eternal Return* in which communities remember and contact an idealized "age of the gods" through the enactment of myths.[35] The pioneer era is part of the Mormon "age of the gods" and the gathering to Zion is one of its central stories.

The Construction of a Memory

Pioneer Day celebrations and Mormon historical pageants periodically emerge and dissipate in cyclical fashion; and pioneer art, museums, and monuments steadily and consistently provide inspirational touchstones for historically minded Mormons. But these genres of pioneer remembrance are by no means straightforward representations of historical events—nor are they intended as such. They are the products of a selective combing through history that has chosen certain aspects for highlighting while omitting and downplaying others. The genres of what David Glassberg calls "public historical imagery" and what Michael Kammen calls the "social production of memory" described in the previous section have been the central arenas for articulating, maintaining, and reshaping Mormon historical consciousness.[36] This section examines the content of that consciousness and the "combing process" that created it.

In discussing this process, University of Utah historian Davis Bitton draws a distinction between "history by historians," whose purpose is to instruct and "tell it all," and popular history, whose purpose is to revere, celebrate, display, and transfer cultural values. According to Bitton, ritualized popular history such as pageants, plays, and parades serve the Durkheimian function of "upholding and reaffirming at regular intervals the collective sentiments and collective ideas which make [a society's] unity and personality."[37] In performing this role, Bitton says, history is "simplified" to be made easily memorable, and it is presented in an impressive and entertaining way.[38]

Simplification implies a selective elision and highlighting of past events. It is a process with political implications and ramifications. The construction of the pioneer myth is no exception. Simplification raises questions such as Whose experience qualifies them for being reverenced as pioneers? Which parts of the pioneer past have been forgotten, and which events become draped in sacred significance for later remembrance and why? What has been the end result of nearly a hundred and fifty years of pioneer reverencing? In short, what kind of cultural memory has been produced by the interwoven activities of pioneer-honoring institutions and genres, and what does it tell us about today's Mormon and Utah communities?

Today, the time between 1847 and 1869 is understood as *the* pioneer period in Mormon history. This has not always been the case. According to late Mormon historian Eugene Campbell the "time window" in which one might be classified as a pioneer expanded in the following manner: "In the Great Basin they [the Mormons] were no longer outcasts but 'pioneers.' Although the term initially referred to members of the 1847 advance company, Mormons who made the journey later the same year also came to be known as the 'Pioneers of '47.' And by the 1870s, virtually everyone who had 'gathered to Zion' before the completion of the transcontinental railroad could lay claim to the title 'pioneer.'"[39]

The completion of the railroad in 1869 shut the time window for pioneer romance. Nevertheless, between 1869 and about 1900, tens of thousands of Mormon immigrants continued to make great sacrifices to "gather" to Utah and join their fellow Saints.[40] Because the 1869–1900 immigrants took the train, their experience does not carry the same valence for succeeding generations, and descent from them does not qualify one for membership in any special organization. (Many Mormon rail immigrants would step off the train and walk for a small portion of the journey just so they could say in jest that they too had "walked across the plains to Zion.") During the Great Depression, church leaders made a permanent policy change and encouraged Mormon converts *not* to come to Utah. Today, in fact, Mormons who have recently immigrated to Utah—far from being honored as pioneers—often feel a slight stigma associated with failing to stay abroad and help "build up the church" in places where it is new and struggling.

It should be remembered that even before the extension of rail service to Utah, many Mormon converts travelled by rail for at least part of the way to their destination. Many also took ships from

Europe or steamers up the Mississippi before reaching the destination from whence they would "walk across the plains" to Zion. The rail and waterborne stages of Mormon immigrant journeys are little celebrated and rarely appear in popular historical expression. Only the final stage of Mormon pioneer journeys has inspired much reenactment and celebration.

Of the groups that came to Utah during the 1847–1869 period, two in particular emerged as stereotypical in the Mormon imagination—Brigham Young's 1847 advance party and the handcart companies of 1856–60. Both account for only a small fraction of all immigrants during the pioneer period. The advance party numbered only 147, and the handcart pioneers accounted for fewer than 3,000 out of an estimated 85,000 pre-railroad immigrants, yet these two groups, especially the latter, are disproportionally represented in art, sculpture, and eulogy.[41] The advance company was of course important because it was first, and the handcarts stick out because of their uniqueness in American history. Two of the handcart companies became stranded in winter blizzards and were rescued only after many had perished. This tragedy, coupled with the presumed difficulty of all handcart travel, made the handcart companies ripe for romantic remembrance.[42] Yet only in the case of the first Saints expelled from Nauvoo and the two stranded handcart companies did deaths occur in uncommon numbers. Moreover, Mormon pioneers on the whole probably suffered less angst and hardship on their journeys than did their Gentile counterparts due to the atypically well organized and corporate nature of their migratory enterprise and the fact that a community of fellow believers awaited their arrival.[43] Nevertheless, the stereotype of pioneers burying their kindred dead on the trail to Zion is a particularly enduring one in Mormon popular consciousness. Because the saga of the Mormon pioneers serves as heroic, sacred history that exemplifies the spirit of sacrifice that Mormons still regard as being expected of them by God, the experiences of the least typical groups form the basis of many Mormons' mental constructions of pioneer reality.[44]

While the processes of constructing Mormon popular historical consciousness have highlighted certain parts of the pioneer experience, other episodes in Mormon history have been almost studiously forgotten. Drama and biblical parallel alone do not explain the inclusion of past events into celebrated public history. To constitute a usable past for Mormons, drama and historical recapitulation must conclude triumphantly. For example, Mormons do not commemorate their brave and resilient struggle against the United States government during the polygamy raids of the 1880s. During this time, the government confiscated all of the LDS Church's property and froze its assets; the church leadership went underground for years, and hundreds were thrown in jail for practicing plural marriage. Thousands endured hardship and ridicule to protect a way of life they felt God had required of them until, under extreme duress, the church officially discontinued the practice by revelation in 1890. Jan Shipps suggests that the polygamy raids and the eventual abandonment of the practice complete the parallel with Israelite history by providing Mormons with a "Babylonian captivity phase" and a "restitution phase."[45] However, Mormons do not exploit this potential parallel in constructing their popular historical consciousness. The martyrological potential inherent in these events, which arguably caused the Saints more suffering than the westward migration, was lost when the church officially curtailed plural marriage. To celebrate resistance now would be to memorialize a lost cause that is embarrassing to many modern Mormons—a struggle for a principle that the LDS Church now vehemently opposes. Also, Mormons have always regarded themselves as the consummate patriots, and the fact that Mormons once practiced radical civil disobedience to what they regarded as unconstitutional antipolygamy legislation is difficult to square on a popular historical level with the image Mormons hold of themselves as a people who regard obedience to civil authority as a serious religious principle. As a result, the polygamy raids, in spite of their tempting biblical parallel and heroic underdog drama, have virtually vanished from Mormon popular memory.

Traditional historical and anthropological analyses of Mormonism have interpreted public celebration of the pioneers as an expression of shared cultural values and concerns.[46] Such characterizations annoy the 230,000-member Reorganized Church of Jesus Christ of Latter Day Saints based in Independence, Missouri. RLDS historians point out that between one-third and one-half of the Mormon population of Nauvoo (some of whom later joined the RLDS Church when it was founded in 1860) chose not to follow Brigham Young to Utah.[47] In this light, the trek of the pioneers of '47 was at first not a unifier at all, but an aspect of the greatest schism and the beginning of the worst era of cultural disintegration ever faced by the Mormon people.

To say that pioneer nostalgia unifies the Salt Lake City head-quartered church is problematic as well. The most significant challenge to the unifying potential of traditional modes of pioneer commemoration has been the breakdown of the isomorphism between Mormondom's cultural region and the Church of Jesus Christ of Latter-day Saints. At one time, regional history and identity and church history and identity were virtually inseparable. This is no longer the case. Today, due to emigration and convert growth, only about twenty percent of LDS Church members reside in Utah. Most of today's nine million Mormons, particularly those in the fast growing international church, are not descendants of Utah pioneers. Also, Utah is no longer a functionally independent theocracy, but a state in a religiously pluralistic America. Today, over forty percent of Salt Lake City's population is not Mormon, with more Gentiles moving in all the time. These situations provide the multiple challenge of finding ways of celebrating the pioneer story that make it a community-building experience both for all Mormons (in and out of Utah) and for all Utahans (Mormon and non-Mormon). This has been difficult, but has resulted in creative reinterpretations of how "pioneers" should be understood in a heterogeneous Utah and a multinational diasporic Mormondom. The following sections examine how the pioneer myth has weathered these challenges.

Pioneers for All Utahans: The "Days of '47" in Salt Lake City

In her book *Parades and Power*, Susan Davis points out the inadequacy of the "common sense" way of viewing parades as "straight forward reflections" of consensual notions held by all performers and observers. What she says about Philadelphia's 1832 parade in honor of George Washington's birthday could also be said about Salt Lake

City's "Days of '47" parade. "Upon closer examination . . . the procession's meanings for performers and audience seem less unified.
This performance was a selective version of local social relationships
that hardly represented all communities [and] all points of view."[48]
In Salt Lake City as well, some do not share hegemonic interpretations of the pioneer story and feel that Pioneer Day is lacking as a
community event because it has featured only the dominant group's
collective historical memory.[49]

In the "Days of '47" parade, notions not only about social relationships but also about the sacredness of certain historical events and
the divine destiny of Utah's dominant culture have been literally
paraded in public. But as Salt Lake City's Gentile population has
increased along with Mormon sensitivity to others who call Utah
home, the "tone" of the parade has changed. Mormon themes still
dominate the Pioneer Day parade, but parade entries in recent years
have employed symbols that bridge the Mormon/Gentile divide or
are specifically non-Mormon in character.

One theme that has emerged as a "bridge" is the completion of
the transcontinental railroad.[50] As the railroad closed off the time
window of the romantic pioneer era, it opened the possibility for a
new "progressive romanticism" celebrating the modern world coming to Utah. Today the railroad is remembered as ushering in a new
age of Mormon/Gentile cooperation in Utah—a memory open for
appreciation by a larger percentage of Utahans.

The inclusion of floats that celebrate the transcontinental railroad
is, of course, antithetical to older understandings of what "Pioneer
Day" was designed to celebrate, and it is a sign that the parade is
being secularized and broadened to allow for the inclusion of more
non-Mormon participants. Other signs of the breakdown of
Mormon exclusiveness have been the inclusion of floats honoring
the establishment of Salt Lake City's Catholic cathedral and Jewish
synagogue. When speaking to the gathered crowds at the 1992
"Days of '47" celebration, LDS Church leader Loren C. Dunn
acknowledged the contributions of "pioneers of other faiths" who
also came to Utah.[51] The official theme of 1994's "Days of '47" celebration was "All Are Welcome Here." Certainly this theme was chosen, in part at least, as a corrective to the parade's past exclusivity and

Mormon-centeredness. Religious themes—while still important—have lost their dominance in Salt Lake City's "Days of '47" celebration. Floats that promote business establishments and bear corporate logos have become more prominent as well. Reasons other than the remembrance of sacred history, including fun in and of itself, are beginning to undergird the "Days of '47" celebration.[52]

These changes have coincided with shifts in responsibility for organizing the parade. In pioneer Utah, relationships between public events and authority were intimate. Mormon leaders initiated and delegated the planning and performance of Pioneer Day celebrations. Gradually, responsibility for the parade passed into the hands of the SUP and DUP, even though the church continued to provide financial support. In 1936, "Days of '47 Inc." grew out of the SUP as a nonprofit, unaffiliated organization responsible for organizing the Pioneer Day festivities. Today, church leaders no longer overtly direct Pioneer Day affairs but participate as honored guests in their important symbolic function as the living heirs and continuing administrators of Brigham Young's kingdom. Thus, even though the Pioneer Day Queen must still be a descendant of the 1847–69 pioneers and Brigham Young impersonators and representatives of the current LDS leadership still occupy important positions in the parade, community organizations have been allowed to take control of a tradition of public historical celebration once centrally controlled by the church. Mormon leaders, realizing Pioneer Day's expanded significance, have willingly released control and have encouraged inclusiveness.

Despite these developments, and much to the chagrin of the ACLU, it will probably always be impossible to completely separate church from state in public functions in Utah. Popular public expressions of significant events in Utah's history will always face the problem of Mormon dominance in that history, and Mormons will probably always see sacred significance in Utah's pioneer heritage. Also, even with a continued influx of Gentiles, demographic trends indicate that Utah will likely retain its Mormon majority (the only state with a majority of any denomination) for many years to come. There is, and will continue to be, a high correlation between prominence in Utah society and leadership in the LDS Church. For these reasons, attempts to provide public displays of history that meet the spiritual needs of Mormons as well as the community-building needs of Utah's increasingly Gentile urban areas will continue to be challenging.

Pioneers for all Mormons

The pioneer myth faces challenges abroad as well. Borne by ever-increasing legions of Mormon missionaries, the pioneer myth has escaped the bounds of the Mountain West and has become a part of a belief system that engages the members of a fast-growing, world-wide religious tradition.[53] Today, Mormonism's traditional heartland in the American West contains only about thirty percent of total church membership, and over half of all Mormons live outside the United States.[54] The increased cultural and national diversity of Mormonism has placed heavy demands upon the pioneer symbology that sprang from, and is specific to, the American West. In the worldwide Mormon community of faith, the place of the pioneers has become problematic. As many Mormons begin to question and reconceptualize the hagiographic status of the Utah pioneers, it is increasingly difficult to claim that "group consciousness" is unambiguously being maintained by honoring, celebrating, and reenacting pioneer history.

Thanks to missionary effort, the pioneer myth and its accompanying celebratory cultural practices are spreading around the world. However, intimate knowledge of pioneer history and especially elaborate forms of public pioneer reverence have not spread as fast as the Mormon gospel, and a very small percentage of today's Mormons participate in Pioneer Day festivities; some have never even heard of the celebration at all. One hundred years ago, when pioneer-honoring events formed the centerpiece expression of Mormon community identity, nonparticipation in, and unfamiliarity with, pioneer stories and celebrations would have been unthinkable for faithful Mormons. Today, as living in a nearly exclusively Mormon agricultural village in the Mountain West has become the exceptional rather than typical Mormon experience, pioneer-honoring cultural expressions have necessarily taken on new forms and new meanings for Mormons.

Part of this "pioneer problem" springs from the Mormon heartland itself and from changing perceptions of Utah in Mormon popular consciousness. Once upon a time, Utah was Zion—the place where Mormons gathered to build their social and spiritual utopia in preparation for Christ's imminent Second Coming. The land and its people were the supreme object of desire for the converts who streamed to it. Today, Utah Mormons, and pioneer descendants in general, are rightly or wrongly sometimes seen by Mormons outside of Utah not as examples of righteousness, but of self-righteousness—as too often lazily resting on the laurels of their impressive genealogy. Utah is also perceived by some as provincial and embarrassingly narrow-minded for being the center of a worldwide religion. On the other hand, others are shocked that liquor is sold in the state and that many stores are open on Sunday like anywhere else in America. Utah is still a central point of attention and all faithful Mormon eyes turn there when the prophet speaks at the tabernacle in Temple Square, but the region is by no means regarded as the idealized place of piety it once was.

The problematization of Utah and its people in the Mormon imagination has caused many to question what they regard as the overly sentimentalized, unrealistic, and "tacky" reverencing of pioneers often displayed by those whose roots in Mormonism go back generations. As the pioneer era retreats further into the past, as new generations of Mormons emerge, and as the number of people who knew pioneer grandparents diminishes, this sentiment is growing—even in Utah. Many younger Mormons view the trappings of "the cult of the pioneers" as "kitsch," "old-timey," and irrelevant. Some adults call for a more "realistic" treatment of the pioneers in Mormon discourse and historical writing. They fear that Utah's colonizers have come to represent a false ideal—superhuman paragons of a pious perfection never attainable by modern Mormons.

To some, another problem with the pioneer legacy is the fact that the honor acquired by participants in great migrations often passes on to succeeding generations of their offspring—especially in the minds of those who are themselves descendants of migrating cultural heroes. This tends to create a social distinction between those descended from cultural-historical figures and everyone else. This is certainly the case in Mormondom. In Utah especially there exists a quasi-caste system that distinguishes between (1) post–pioneer era converted Mormons and their descendants, (2) families descended from pioneers, and (3) families descended from pioneers who were also church leaders. The continued insistence by the Daughters of the Utah Pioneers on biological descent as a requisite for membership contributes to this system.[55] In prestigious social circles in Utah, the question "Who did you say your ancestors were?" occasionally serves the same function as "What do you do for a living?" would serve elsewhere. Richard Gomez, a former Catholic who converted to the LDS Church and who is the bishop of a Spanish-speaking congregation in the Salt Lake City area, feels left out "when church leaders open a 'Pioneer Day' celebration in Salt Lake City . . . by asking who among the assembled people was descended from one of the original (Anglo) founders [of Utah]."[56]

Officially, the LDS Church has sought to down-play these kinds of distinctions in recent years and has emphasized that salvation comes through faith in Jesus Christ's atonement and correct individual choices—not lineage. Nevertheless, efforts at building egalitarian sentiments on this topic are difficult to achieve without diminishing the importance of what the pioneers did in bequeathing a legacy of faith to the modern LDS Church.

Responses to the Pioneer Dilemma

Several responses have emerged to the dilemmas caused by the pioneer myth and its associated cultural practices within Mormonism. These responses have relied on the following general strategies: (1) abandonment, (2) exportation, (3) substitution, and (4) reinterpretation.

(1) Abandonment. In many ways, challenges to the pioneer myth's relevance and usefulness have already caused it to slip into popular historical unconsciousness. While once conversion required immigration to Utah and thus actual participation in pioneer sacred history, today the pioneer trek and the establishment of Zion are not even mentioned in the program of instruction that Mormon missionaries teach to potential converts. While dramatic varieties of pioneer reverence once formed a frequent and central part of virtually all

Mormons' community experience, such practices now engage only a small percentage. The further one gets from the Mormon West, the less one hears about pioneers, and it is in many of these far away places that the LDS Church is growing the fastest.

(2) Exportation. Another response to the pioneer dilemma has been for Mormondom to export the pioneer myth and its manifestations. Though it is by no means as common as in the Mormon West, children from places as diverse as Samoa and Japan have dressed up as Utah pioneers for Pioneer Day festivities. In 1993, the LDS Church's magazine reported major Pioneer Day celebrations in Papillion, Nebraska; Sacramento, California; and New York City. Four thousand people attended the church's first annual Missouri Youth Pioneer Pageant in Branson, Missouri.[57] So, public historical forms of pioneer reverence *are* expanding and growing, although not at a fast enough pace to fully penetrate all corners of an even faster growing religious tradition.

(3) Replacement. Another response to the increasing problematization of the pioneers has been to turn to an even older source for a uniquely Mormon unifying mythic history—the Book of Mormon. The ancient history recounted in the Book of Mormon, like the Bible and pioneer stories, is replete with miraculous occurrences and emulable examples of faith, obedience, and sacrifice. In the past few decades, the Book of Mormon has eclipsed the pioneer saga as the chief resource for mythic and instructive history. Recent church president Ezra Taft Benson played a pivotal role in this shift. He repeatedly emphasized the Book of Mormon's centrality in Mormon faith. He encouraged a "Book of Mormon Renaissance" by calling on Mormons to read it daily, use it as a proselytizing tool, and make it the object of increased scholarly, literary, and artistic emphasis. His call caused an upsurge in art based on Book of Mormon themes, promising to push pioneer topics to the sidelines of the Mormon art scene. A Mormon-run company produces a popular animated video series that features several stories from the Bible and the Book of Mormon, but none about the pioneers.[58]

Book of Mormon sacred history is well suited for an international religion of many cultures and regions because even though its content could be read as privileging the Western Hemisphere and

Native Americans, its history is so ancient that it is detached enough from any modern Mormon subgroup to be equally accessible to all Mormons and potential converts. The pioneer sacred history, with its close ties to Mountain West regional culture and the family memories of "ethnic" Mormons, does not provide the same equal access.

(4) Reinterpretation. The most innovative response to the pioneer dilemma has been to expand the term "pioneer" to apply not only to the traditional 1847–69 pioneer period, but to any Mormon today facing a new or difficult situation. For example, at a church social in Austin, Texas, two Mormon women performed a set of dramatic monologues entitled "Pioneers: Now and Then." One woman dressed in traditional pioneer garb and spoke of the hardships of pioneer life such as weeding the garden, preparing food, and mending clothes. The other woman wore modern clothes and discussed new challenges such as violence on television, protecting her children from drugs, and managing a busy schedule.

Mormons of African descent are a special case for pioneer designation. Since 1979, Mormons of all races have been allowed full access to the ordinances of the LDS Church. This change—instituted by prophetic revelation—reversed over a century of restricted temple access and a ban on priesthood ordination for Mormon males of African descent. Since 1979, African Americans have converted to Mormonism in unprecedented numbers and Mormon missionaries have enjoyed much success in Africa and the Caribbean. Brigham Young University historian Jessie Embry—reflecting Mormons' widespread positive attitude about the 1979 revelation—has suggested that African American Mormons are "just as much pioneers as those who crossed the plains to Zion."[59]

It has also been increasingly common to refer to converts in regions of the world new to Mormonism as pioneers. One of many examples of this appears in "Ng Kat Hing: Hong Kong Pioneer," Kellene Ricks's recent article in *The Ensign*, the LDS Church's official devotional publication.[60] This kind of reinterpretation of the term "pioneer" has been officially promoted by the church and will be the focus of its 1997 sesquicentennial celebration of the Mormon arrival in Utah.[61] These expansions of the term "pioneer" beyond its traditional designation of "those who crossed the plains" can be seen as attempts within Mormon culture to seal potential points of fissure within a community that has always valued equality and unity in faith.

Not only does the "pioneerification" of modern converts show that the Mormon leadership is sensitive to the concerns of members such as Bishop Gomez, but perhaps more important, this concept of "modern pioneers" is a way of keeping the Mormon present in sacred time—a situation where Mormons are really the most comfortable—by redeploying a symbol from a previous sacred time. This strategy helps give the Mormon present a sense of being "sacred history in the making." As new converts in Nigeria struggle to build a community of believers in the face of prejudice and misunderstanding, they recapitulate the trials of the Utah pioneers—who in their time recapitulated the trials of the Israelites. This recent reworking of the pioneer concept takes Jan Shipps's notion of the sacralization of the present through the recapitulation of a sacred past to another degree of separation. The lives of modern Mormons become sacred history in the making by living through again what is already a recapitulated sacred history. It is important to note, however, that this backward-looking aspect of Mormonism is only one aspect of the religion—the one that happens to be the subject at hand. Mormonism, more important even than being a history-reverencing religion, is a millennial religion with a progressive, forward looking stance.

Conclusions

In the last decade or so, analyzing the relationship between collective memory and group identity in large-scale societies such as nations, ethnic communities, and religious institutions has been a matter of intense interest among scholars. The temptation has existed among many to be overly cynical in their debunking of invented traditions, and they thereby perhaps damage the societies to whom they are obligated in the reciprocal ethical relationship that arises in scholar-subject interaction.[62] Historian Michael Kammen warns against cynical analyses of popular history and states that the "invention of tradition" is often done for benign reasons.[63] I would add that even in cases where we may suspect the "foisting of false consciousness," our analysis can be critical and charitable at the same time. Rather than regarding invented traditions and identities as pathological false consciousness, we can view them as creative cultural responses to new situations. I would suggest too that in painting sinister and manipulative portraits of the inventors of tradition, we may be applying historiographic assumptions and patterns of social analysis to groups whose goals and truth claims are of little relevance to those held by the observing culture. In the environment of mutual hostility that has long existed between the academy and conservative religious bodies like the Mormon Church, it is especially tempting to exploit the story of the invention of popular Mormon historical consciousness to stoke the fires of existing antagonisms and strengthen the walls of academic self-righteousness. This mistake would blind us to numerous insights attainable only through humbly trying to grasp the Mormon version of their pioneer heritage on their own terms and occasionally letting Mormons speak for themselves.

In so doing, we find that because it recapitulated biblical history and occurred in the context of America's romanticized westward expansion, the trek of the Mormon pioneers became the defining historical motif of the Mormon experience in America. As in other societies, Mormon highlighting and romanticizing of the pioneer story provided a mythic historical "rallying point" for a newly emerging cultural identity. Pioneer mythology, as it has been passed on to modern Mormons, has been shown to be a construction created, reinforced, and maintained by popular public displays and celebrations. Changing conditions in Utah and worldwide Mormonism have demonstrated that the usefulness of traditional renditions of the pioneer story are showing some wear, and its associated rituals are no longer quite—and perhaps never really were—the unifying principles some scholars have described them as being. The significance, meaning, and worth of the pioneer myth will continue to be matters of reinterpretation and discussion among members of an expanding worldwide religion and a diversifying Mormon geographic region. While the myth has slipped somewhat from its once illustrious position in Mormon thought and practice, the Mormon pioneer concept is being innovatively reworked and is showing continued vitality in the face of its challenges.

Notes

1. William A. Wilson, "Herder, Folklore, and Romantic Nationalism," in *Folk Groups and Folklore Genres,* ed. Elliot Oring (Logan: Utah State University Press, 1978).

2. Vernon February, *The Afrikaners of South Africa* (London and New York: Kegan Paul International, 1991); Allister Sparks, *The Mind of South Africa* (New York: Ballantine Books, 1990).

3. Jean Fritz, *China's Long March: 6000 Miles of Danger* (New York: G. P. Putnam's Sons, 1988).

4. John Bodnar's *Remaking America: Public Memory, Commemoration, and Patriotism in the Twentieth Century* (Princeton: Princeton University Press, 1992) examines the place of pioneers in the popular history of western states as part of a general analysis of American commemorative events and shows the centrality of the pioneer as a symbol of local historical consciousness.

5. The Mormon West, Mormon Culture Region, or "the Book of Mormon Belt" includes all of Utah, most of southeastern Idaho, the southwestern tip and western edge of Wyoming, and significant sections of eastern Nevada and northern and eastern Arizona. These areas are the legacy of Brigham Young's colonizing efforts and are still dominated and defined by Mormon culture. Through later migration and conversion, significant Mormon minorities have appeared in California (which contains the most Mormons of any state besides Utah), Colorado, and the Pacific Northwest. See especially D. W. Meinig, "The Mormon Cultural Region: Strategies and Patterns in the Geography of the American West, 1847–1964," *Annals of the Association of American Geographers* 55, no. 2 (1965).

6. Throughout this essay, I use the term "myth" not in its popular meaning as a bogus story or a widely held misconception, but in the manner common among scholars of religion. In this tradition, myths are stories defined not by their lack of credibility to outside observers or by the ostensible failure of their truth claims to withstand critical analysis, but by the sacred and ontological significance attributed to them by the cultures from which they emerge.

7. William Mulder, "The Mormon Gathering," in *Mormonism and American Culture,* ed. Marvin S. Hill and James B. Allen (New York: Harper & Row, 1972).

8. LeRoy R. Hafen and Ann W. Hafen, *Handcarts to Zion: The Story of a Unique Westward Migration, 1856–1860* (Lincoln and London: University of Nebraska Press, 1992 [1960]).

9. Wallace Stegner, *The Gathering of Zion: The Story of the Mormon Trail* (Lincoln: University of Nebraska Press, Bison Books, 1992 [1964]).

10. Leonard J. Arrington's biography *Brigham Young: American Moses* (New York: Knopf, 1985) uses this moniker as its subtitle.

11. *The Doctrine and Covenants of the Church of Jesus Christ of Latter-day Saints*, section 136.

12. Irene Bates, "Patriarchal Blessings and the Routinization of Charisma," *Dialogue: A Journal of Mormon Thought* 26, no. 3 (1993); Melodie Moench, "Nineteenth Century Mormons: The New Israel," *Dialogue: A Journal of Mormon Thought* 12 (Spring 1979).

13. John Wilson, *Our Iraelitish Origin* (Philadelphia: Daniels and Smith, 1850); Stephen Epperson, *Mormons and Jews: Early Mormon Theologies of Israel* (Salt Lake City: Signature Books, 1992).

14. The parallels between the Mormon pioneers and the biblical Exodus were so compelling that there are even unorthodox Mormon splinter groups who maintain that the pioneers of '47 were the literal reincarnation of Moses's followers. Steven L. Shields, *Divergent Paths of the Restoration* (Los Angeles: Restoration Research, 1990).

15. Jan Shipps, *Mormonism: The Story of a New Religious Tradition* (Urbana and Chicago: University of Illinois Press, 1985).

16. Klaus Hansen, *Mormonism and the American Experience* (Chicago and London: University of Chicago Press, 1981), 214; Richard L. Bushman, *Joseph Smith and the Beginnings of Mormonism* (Urbana and Chicago: University of Illinois Press, 1984), 139.

17. Michael Kammen, *Mystic Chords of Memory: The Transformation of Tradition in American Culture* (New York: Vintage Books, 1993), 50–52.

18. Ibid., 46–47.

19. Hansen, *Mormonism and the American Experience*, 210.

20. Robert W. Johannsen, *To the Halls of the Montezumas: The Mexican War in the American Imagination* (New York and Oxford: Oxford University Press, 1985), 242; David Levin, *History as Romantic Art: Bancroft, Prescott, Moteley, and Parkman* (Stanford, Calif.: Stanford University Press, 1959).

21. Eugene E. Campbell, *Establishing Zion: The Mormon Church in the American West 1847–1869* (Salt Lake City: Signature Books, 1988); Steve Olsen, "Community Celebrations and Mormon Ideology of

Place," *Sunstone* (May–June 1980); Ronald W. Walker, "'A Banner is Unfurled': Mormonism's Ensign Peak," *Dialogue: A Journal of Mormon Thought* 26, no. 4 (1993).

22. Hafen and Hafen, *Handcarts*, 257–76; Thomas E. Cheney, *Mormon Songs from the Rocky Mountains* (Austin and London: University of Texas Press, 1968).

23. "The Handcart Song," *Children's Songbook* (Salt Lake City: Corporation of the President of the Church of Jesus Christ of Latter-day Saints, 1989).

24. *Heart Throbs of the West*, 12 vol., *Treasures of Pioneer History*, 6 vol., *Our Pioneer Heritage*, 7 vol. (Salt Lake City: Daughters of the Utah Pioneers).

25. Magazine advertisement for the DUP museum in *This Is the Place: Salt Lake City Visitors Guide, 1993–94*.

26. Personal conversation with a church administrator in the Office of the Presiding Bishopric, Salt Lake City, Utah, January 1994.

27. Interestingly, Mormon pageants thrive today despite David Glassberg's assertion in his seminal work on American historical pageantry that such events had disappeared by World War II. David Glassberg, *American Historical Pageantry: The Uses of Tradition in the Early Twentieth Century* (Chapell Hill: University of North Carolina Press, 1990).

28. Jay Anderson, *Time Machines: The World of Living History* (Nashville, Tenn.: American Association for State and Local History, 1984).

29. James D. Cannon, ed., *Centennial Caravan: Story of the 1947 Centennial Reenactment of the Original Mormon Trek from Nauvoo, Illinois, to Salt Lake Valley, July 14 to 22, 1947* (Salt Lake City: Sons of the Utah Pioneers, 1948).

30. Personal conversation with a church administrator in the Office of the Presiding Bishopric, Salt Lake City, Utah, January 1994.

31. Thomas O'Dea, *The Mormons* (Chicago and London: University of Chicago Press, 1957).

32. "Saints Celebrate Pioneer Day," *The Ensign of the Church of Jesus Christ of Latter-day Saints* 10 (1993): 75; a "Days of '47 Inc." flyer in my possession.

33. Olsen, "Community Celebrations."

34. In all forms of Mormon pioneer memorialization, it is the pioneer sacred story that is the focus of the celebration—not the Israelites whose history had been recapitulated. After the Mormon arrival in Salt Lake City, the focus of recapitulative remembrance almost

immediately shifted from ancient Israel to the pioneers themselves. Thus, pioneer celebrations recapitulate an event that was itself a recapitulation. This raises the interesting question of whether recapitulations of recapitulations can be fully sustained by any culture or if one degree of removal in (re)creating sacred history is a maximum limit.

35. Mircea Eliade, *The Myth of the Eternal Return* (New York: Pantheon, 1954).

36. "Public historical imagery" is a term coined by David Glassberg to refer to popular mobilizations of historic or traditional themes in public performative events. David Glassberg, *American Historical Pageantry*, 2. Michael Kammen, *Mystic Chords of Memory*, 9.

37. Emile Durkheim, *The Elementary Forms of the Religious Life* (New York: Free Press, 1965), 474–75.

38. Davis Bitton, "The Ritualization of Mormon History," *Utah Historical Quarterly* 43 (1975).

39. Campbell, *Establishing Zion*.

40. Figures from Robert W. Sloan's *Utah Gazetteer and Directory of Logan, Ogden, Provo, and Salt Lake City for 1884* (Salt Lake City: Herald Printing, 1884) show only a slight drop in the numbers of immigrants after the 1869 completion of the transcontinental railroad.

41. Richard D. Poll, *History and Faith: Reflections of a Mormon Historian* (Salt Lake City: Signature Books, 1989).

42. Handcart nostalgia, as one might imagine, benefits from the assumption that handcart travel must have been extremely difficult compared to ox-drawn wagons. This is a debatable point; one of Brigham Young's justification for the handcart idea is that it would be easier because it eliminated the difficulties of using animals.

43. For a general examination of the myth of a perilous Mormon pioneer journey, see Richard H. Jackson's "The Overland Journey to Zion," in *The Mormon Role in the Settlement of the West*, ed. Richard H. Jackson (Provo, Utah: Brigham Young University Press, 1978). Jackson points out that most pioneer journals relate their crossing of the plains as a mixture of monotonous walking with moments of adventure and discovery, not unlike a pleasure trip or one-way family vacation.

44. The various groups of pioneers can be put into a "hagiographic hierarchy" of importance. Such a list would descend roughly as follows: handcart pioneers who died, anyone who died, handcart company members who survived, the advance company of 1847 pioneers, all 1847 pioneers, and finally anyone who crossed the plains before the railroad.

45. Shipps, *Mormonism*.

46. Especially well thought out are the works of Bitton, "Ritualization of Mormon History"; Olsen, "Community Celebrations"; Shipps, *Mormonism;* and Stegner, *The Gathering of Zion.*

47. Alma R. Blair, "The Reorganized Church of Jesus Christ of Latter Day Saints: Moderate Mormons," in *The Restoration Movement: Essays in Mormon History,* by F. Mark McKiernan, Alma R. Blair, Paul M. Edwards (Lawrence: University of Kansas Press, 1973).

48. Susan G. Davis, *Parades and Power: Street Theatre in Nineteenth-Century Philadelphia* (Philadelphia: Temple University Press, 1986), 4.

49. I once had a discussion with a non-Mormon former professor at a Utah university who claimed to have hidden in his room during the whole week of Pioneer Day because Mormon cultural displays disgusted him. Unfortunately, this man's reluctance to appreciate Utah's cultural life made his stay in Utah short and unpleasant.

50. "Saints Celebrate Pioneer Day," *The Ensign.*

51. "Pioneer Day Activities Celebrate the Heritage of Early Saints," *The Ensign of the Church of Jesus Christ of Latter-day Saints* 10 (1992).

52. Mirroring the changes made in Pioneer Day celebrations, Pioneer Trail State Park's "Old Deseret" model pioneer village and Lagoon's "Sons of the Utah Pioneers Village" downplay the "Mormonness" of the history they seek to recreate by enacting generic frontier community scenes. The perceived "secularization" of Pioneer Day celebrations is not uncontroversial to some. A community leader in San Pete County, Utah, complained to me that he regarded the demolition derby and ATC tractor pull that had become the premier Pioneer Day activities in his community as inappropriate modes of Pioneer Day celebration. His sentiment is understandable, but it ignores the long history (and still current practice) of holding rodeos and baseball tournaments on Pioneer Day. Demolition derbies are a modern version of the kind of recreational activities Mormons have always regarded as wholesome and appropriate even, and perhaps especially, when done in conjunction with pioneer remembrance.

53. Jan Shipps, *Mormonism.*

54. *Church Almanac 1993–1994* (Salt Lake City: Deseret News, 1993).

55. The kind of relationship the DUP has to Utah society is not unique to that state. In Texas, the social prestige associated with being a descendant from the former republic's first Anglo families is fostered in an aggressive manner by the Daughters of the Republic of Texas (DRT). The DUP and the DRT and their philosophy of history can be seen as regional versions of the nativism and historical "preservationism" of

the national organization of the Daughters of the American Revolution.

56. Emily Gurnon, "Latinos and Latter-day Saints: Minority Mormons," *Christian Century*, Feb. 16, 1994, p. 159.

57. "Saints Celebrate Pioneer Day," *The Ensign.*

58. This shift in emphasis toward the Book of Mormon has been so dramatic that as recently as the early 1980s, Jan Shipps could (almost accurately) leave the Book of Mormon out of her observation that modern Mormonism reflects upon the three significant historical "pillars" of the New and Old Testaments and the history of the early Mormons.

59. Jessie L. Embry, *Black Saints in a White Church: Contemporary African American Mormons* (Salt Lake City: Signature Books, 1994).

60. Kellene Ricks, "Ng Kat Hing: Hong Kong Pioneer," *The Ensign of the Church of Jesus Christ of Latter-day Saints* 22 (1992): 51, 52.

61. Personal conversation with a church administrator in the Office of the Presiding Bishopric, Salt Lake City, Utah, January 1994.

62. Richard Handler's excellent but needlessly unkind and insensitive treatment of nationalism in Quebec typifies this cynical approach to the cultural creativity expressed through "invented traditions." Richard Handler, *Nationalism and the Politics of Culture in Quebec* (Madison: University of Wisconsin Press, 1988).

63. Kammen, *Mystic Chords of Memory*, 31.

Part III

The Spirit of Place

North Americans have been among the most notoriously mobile people in modern history. Yet, as the four essays in this section show, for many of us social identity is still strongly affected by a sense of where we have come from or gotten to. This "spirit of place" is suggested in Eliason's essay, where the Utah flats are imagined as a Promised Land. Similar notions of sacred land inform many native American peoples' self-images and cosmologies, and they are of course a font of volatility around the globe, wherever conflicting religious identities create geographical "shatter zones." But even when the sacred element is lacking, the identification with locale can be powerful. It was powerful enough in the nineteenth century to cause a civil war, and it remains a significant feature of American identity long after the Appomattox stillness proclaimed it anathema.

Often the affection for locale has taken a regional turn, with citizens of the United States and Canada alike identifying themselves as denizens of the salty East or the endless plains or the jagged Rockies. Folklorists in this century have mined this vein profitably, collecting volume upon volume of regional lore that illuminated the distinctive texture of local cultures. A roster of Americanists who enlivened this literature would include such notables as Cecil Sharp, Frank C. Brown, Benjamin Botkin, Vance Randolph, Américo Paredes, and Richard Dorson.

213

Here this broad view of "locale" identity is applied by John R. Williams to the southern highlands—the area that inspired Randolph and Sharp. Williams deals with the battered consciousness of Appalachian migrants who have been wrested from their mountain womb by financial pressures and set down, identities akimbo, in spewing Cincinnati. The stories that these migrants tell about their lost mountain Edens contrast sharply with their visions of urban disharmony. The result is a layered tapestry of nostalgia and pain, vividly reflecting the affective power of homeland to those whom economic circumstance has forced into exile.

The remaining chapters in this section explore regional identity in a more circumscribed fashion, by focussing on the resonances of state and provincial attachment. In his analysis of a recently invented Newfoundland tradition, the Screech-In, Pat Byrne shows how a negatively marked identity can be creatively manipulated by its victims so that outsiders (in this case, tourists) become the butt of the joke. In this example of "parodic parry," residents of Canada's "Happy Province"—and its most impoverished—play with the literary stereotype of the island's backwardness by making their "betters" honorary "stupid Newfies." The invented ritual both confirms and denies the stereotype.

In his survey of the Atlantic lobster as a down east icon, George Lewis also deconstructs a common stereotype, showing how the animal has functioned not as a respected state emblem, but as a site of contestation over class-based values—those of the native poor versus those of outside "rusticators" who transformed a despised junk food into a status marker. Similarly, in Sylvia Grider's assessment of the Lone Star State's most resonant founding story, we see Alamo heroism not as an established fact, but as an amulet whose authenticity is periodically challenged in the lively arenas of gender, race, and class.

Common to these four chapters is an emphasis on conflict, and on the inevitability of *negotiating* community consciousness. In a pluralistic and mobile society, the meaning of "Texas" or "Newfie" is no more likely to be frozen than that of "American" or "Canadian." The essays in this section show that the spirit of place derives less from any hypothetical essence of the land than from the political and social struggles that people engage in as they forge their identities as immigrants, transients, and tenants.

CHAPTER 9

"Up Here, We Never See the Sun": Homeplace and Crime in Urban Appalachian Narratives

John R. Williams

> *I love to think back to the days we lived up in the hollow and neither Jack nor I cared what hour it was. We knew what we had to do, and we went and did it. There was the sun, of course; the sun's time was enough for us. Up here, we never see the sun.*

The speaker of these doleful lines was an Appalachian woman who had migrated north to Ohio in the 1940s. Reflecting in 1967 to sociologist Robert Coles, she registered a sense of loss that Coles found common among the displaced folk that he interviewed for *The South Goes North*.[1] Other scholars of migration have also noted the phenomenon. Indeed, migrants' anguish over having been severed from their homes—their longing to recapture a sense of community and of homeplace—has been a focal point of Appalachian studies for decades. Lewis Killian noted it in 1949 in a dissertation on Chicago's southern white workers: "Even migrants who had been in Chicago for ten years or more 'expected' or 'hoped' to return to the South to live some day. As one man who lived in the city twenty-three years put it, 'I plan to go back down there sometime, even if I go in a box!'"[2] A quarter of a century later, Ellen Steckert discovered the same sensibility in her study of southern mountaineers in Detroit. Questioning an informant about her experiences with urban doctors, Steckert found a strong affection for the "old ways"—for birthing without male doctors or medication. Like many others,

Steckert observed, the woman thought of herself "as in but not of the urban community. . . . She idolized the home community of the past."[3]

My personal experience with the southern mountaineers' strong sense of place began in the 1970s, when as a research director for *Our Appalachia: An Oral History* I interviewed a number of residents of eastern Kentucky who delighted me with stories of their Appalachian homes.[4] Throughout their personal narratives, whatever the specific theme, ran a general thread of appreciation for their home communities—a palpable sense of being firmly, and happily, rooted. That sense of personal rootedness came through vividly in the words of a self-styled philosopher, Melvin Proffitt, who had spent virtually all of his life in the same county:

> I was born and raised in the Wolfe County hills. I have been in Wolfe County the most of my life in my seventy years. I doubt if I have been out of the county four years although my brothers and sisters are all living in other states. A lot of times I thought I was born for Wolfe County or Wolfe County was allotted for me; I've gone away from the county a few times and would take a job but not for too long. I'd find myself right back at home as if I was drawn by a magnet; there never was a place anywhere that I loved like I do Wolfe County.[5]

Mr. Proffitt, like many other Appalachians that I interviewed, never considered leaving his homeplace in Kentucky, even though his life there was full of hardships and poverty. In his homespun autobiography, he wrote of the dangers of dynamiting in a deep mine and of his difficulty in finding work during the depression. Like his urban counterparts, he also repeatedly criticized the greed of landlords. Yet, regardless of his difficulties, his connection to home was essential to his identity. The mountains, a world of unique and deeply honored traditions, generated for him a secure sense of his own worth.

Other Kentuckians, however, were not so fortunate. Many were forced to leave their homes in search of work, moving like Robert Coles's migrants to the bustling northern cities. This essay assesses the experience of one such migrant group—eastern Kentuckians who resettled in inner-city Cincinnati—by examining the stories they tell about home and displacement, about the painful tension between longing and belonging.

Contrast and Nostalgia in Over-the-Rhine

The Kentuckians whose stories I relate in this essay live in the Cincinnati neighborhood of Over-the-Rhine, which is typical of many northern, inner-city neighborhoods in its congestion, racial and class tension, and escalating crime. To these working-class, first-generation migrants, the neighborhood is an area of fragmentation and displacement where they must vie for scarce resources with unfamiliar people and where there is a painful absence of the coherent religious, familial, and social customs which permeated their Appalachian experience. But they do not merely lament this sense of loss. Rather, creatively manipulating the mountains' oral traditions, they devise personal narratives that reaffirm their regional identities. Their stories and conversations reflect the power of folklore—in this case, the oral testimony of personal experience narratives—to create meaning in lives filled with confusion.

Central to their tales is the sense of the mountains as a life-affirming contrast to the city. The attitude embedded in their conversations and stories suggests deep-seated memories of the Kentucky mountains and a strong sense of identity with that place. Richard Blaustein discusses this attitude as a universal human need, which manifests itself symbolically as an idealized homeplace, "the magical kingdom in which humanity is in balance with nature, unsullied by the pressures of modern corporate industrial life."[6] Such idealization has also been noted by folklorists Barbara Allen and Thomas Schlereth in writing of the nostalgic element of regional identity.[7]

But there are more or less genuine and more or less spurious nostalgias, and it is important to keep them separate in discussing these narratives. When the residents of Over-the-Rhine speak of their homeplaces, what they recall are specific localities, not the amorphous "Appalachia" dear to scholars and reformers. One outspoken

Appalachian scholar, Allen Batteau, has even rejected the label "Appalachia" as a legitimate place name. "Appalachia is a frame of reference," he writes, "not a fact."[8] Many of my informants would likely agree that the "Appalachian" tag is an outside contrivance. "What a hell of a name," one of them told me humorously. "Who could even remember that?" To her, and to many of her fellow migrants, regional identity is a reality rooted quite concretely, not in a cultural entity invented by scholars, but in actual mountain communities—places with names like Jackson, Hazard, and Troublesome Creek.

The specificity of this connection is periodically reinforced when the residents of Over-the-Rhine go home to visit. Their nostalgia is fuelled by their proximity to the Kentucky mountains, and yet that very proximity makes it a nostalgia that is genuine and realistic rather than idealized. These migrants are in the strange position of being able continually to reassert those bonds that their daily urban reality tells them are broken.

They do this most conspicuously on Memorial Day. That day's cemetery reunions—common in eastern Kentucky—are one of the strongest traditions of community bonding in the nation. Each year thousands of urban Appalachians return home for this opportunity to visit with family and pay respects to their departed relatives. The "dinner on the grounds" serves as a time to swap stories and renew ties with the homeplace. Inevitably, these brief visits also rekindle a nostalgic sense of belonging and feed their resentment toward their inner-city existence. For these displaced people, this basic conflict in attitude toward the place they call home and the place they now live in serves to strengthen their bonds of common identity.

In the stories that are swapped at such reunions, narrators frequently allude to basic Appalachian traditions and values—values and traditions that are rooted in a specific sense of place. The bonding elements of traditional Appalachian culture—family, church, and land—are core values which were constantly reflected in our conversations. Their yearning for a traditional way of life appears frequently in their allusion to the "better life" that they enjoyed before they came north. In countless references to traditions that are not carried on in Cincinnati, they make it clear that their identity is rooted elsewhere.

Seldom is this bluntly or overtly stated. Rather, it reveals itself through pervasive allusions to folk traditions, folkloric motifs and formulae, nostalgic tales about mountain life, folk dialect, and horrible accounts of crime and violence in the city. In this last folkloric genre, the "crimelore" narrative, the mountaineers have developed an emergent form that speaks to the flexibility of oral expression and to the capacity of people under stress to redefine their traditions.

In *All That Is Native and Fine*, a spirited attack on the tendency of outside "intervenors" to promote earlier, more "authentic" forms of mountain culture, David Whisnant makes this point well. Working from preconceived hypotheses about country people and ignoring the emerging traditions of a changing society, he says, culture revivalists seek "a sanitized version of culture [that] frequently makes for a rather shallow liberal comment."[9] A focus on the neglected "emergent" is also a focus of the Hobsbawm and Ranger anthology *The Invention of Tradition*, which shows that people in societies that are undergoing cultural destabilization are prone to the creation of novel expressive practices.[10]

Over-the-Rhine nostalgia and crime stories are examples of such creative invention. That they differ from the stories told back home in no way argues against them as expressions. As the narrators left behind a structured set of traditions, they modified their tales to reflect changed conditions. In Over-the-Rhine, the most visible of those changed conditions are the congested physical environment, class and racial tensions, and crime. All of them are addressed in the migrants' narratives.

"Up the Holler and over a Hill": Memories of Space

Edna Baker came to Cincinnati in 1937, when she was seventeen. Her conversation includes frequent references to her childhood playing hide and seek in the hills, vine swings, square dances, her musical family, and the gathering of the community for work and church. All of this reveals her positive attitude to the mountains. In my interview with her, I asked her whether she and her fellow Kentuckians very often get back to the hills. Edna responded,

A lot of 'em does. . . . They go down twicet a month. The first Saturday and Sunday they go down to have church. Then the third Saturday they go down for one day, they have church one day. And Sunday, this comin' Sunday, they're going to have their reunion. . . . It's a beautiful place when you get down in there. It's a lot of them. My one cousin, now, he's got eleven there, and they've got families, and I don't know how many children they got. They have church. You see, they're Baptist. You've heard of old hard-shelled Baptist. That's what they do. And they have a foot warshin.[11]

Her references to the graveyard reunion and the foot washing ceremony, a traditional ritual in many mountain Baptist churches, show that Edna's family identifies with the mountains through a connection with distinct customs separate from their urban lives. She herself identifies with the mountains although she has lived in the city for almost fifty years.

In expressing their conflicting attitudes toward the mountains and the city, displaced Kentuckians often focus on the difference in space and spatial freedom. Once, after acknowledging that "you don't have that much space" in the city, Edna recalled the relative openness of her former home: "They, this girl and boy come runnin' in here one day, and they said somebody was chasin' them. But you could see when I was little a' growin' up at home, my brothers used to chase me a lot. I'd run all up one hill and down the other one, and up the holler and over a hill and round about." In describing two very different types of chasing, Edna succinctly identifies the contrast between the freedom of a mountain childhood and the fear of an urban one. The lack of space figures prominently in her description of the contrast. As she said later in the interview, "The kids ain't got nothin'! Nowhere to go! Only on these streets and in these alleys." Edna paints a bleak picture of life in the inner city for children. It is a place without shelter, with nowhere to run and nowhere to hide.

Jay Landin, an eighty-one-year-old farmer/moonshiner who moved to Over-the-Rhine in 1929 and took on numerous construction jobs, sums up these people's feelings about their mountain homes, remembering his father's farm: "He farmed it and put a mill on it that you could grind corn meal on. He got to making whiskey later, but most of the time he just farmed it. . . . That was some life, some life. Oh goodness, it was a wonderful life."

In 1980, crippled and bedridden from cancer, Jay was still a tough, whiskey-drinking, congenial man who could spin a yarn with the best of Dorson's bearstoppers. Jay's background is extremely varied, as is the case with many of the urban Appalachians his age. He even brags of hiding a still in the fireplace of an Over-the-Rhine tenement house during prohibition. In the mountains, he worked on his father's farm, dug coal, and made moonshine. The following memory reveals a fondness for his native Kentucky hills and, like Edna's reflection, it highlights the appeal of their rugged spaciousness:

> J.L.: I went back to Middlesboro two year ago. . . . It's up in the mountains. You turn down Laurel Fork, then you go down to Pine Creek. The way the creek runs, it must be thirty to forty miles. You can go out and throw a rock in the water and not know where you'd throwed 'cause the water just ran around like a snake through the cliffs. You know what I mean, there was a big bluff there; you couldn't hardly get down; it was rocky, steep cliffs.
> J.W.: Good place to make moonshine.
> J.L.: Oh, wonderful through there; you couldn't hardly find nothin' 'cause of the rocks. 'Course I knowed the whole thing well 'cause I's raised up and travelled it, you know, huntin'. I used to travel it a lot when I was runnin' the dogs.

Jay's home in the mountains is in direct contrast to the world of the city. In Appalachia, he could run free and develop his individuality and sense of belonging to open spaces. He was one with nature, bonding with the mountains spiritually and physically, creating a traditional sense of place that is impossible to achieve in the urban sprawl of inner-city Cincinnati. The steep, rocky cliffs and thick wooded areas—home to sinuous rivers, hunting dogs, and independent moonshiners—presented themselves as challenges rather than barriers while providing security from invaders such as revenue men.

Life for these inner-city dwellers is further complicated by the movement toward gentrification—a special instance of the city's encroachment on their space. Since the 1980s, speculators have bought up large tracts of tenements at low prices and have turned them into high-rent condominiums. The impact is bitterly described by Dave Banks, one of the most vehement spokesmen for Over-the-Rhine's urban villagers.

And people, there's six percent ownership in Over-the-Rhine, the rest of it is absentee owners. What power you have? My landlord comes in here and he says, "Well, I just sold this here building," or "I'm gonna redevelop this building." He's only required to give us a 30-day notice. And you get your ass out! And if you're not out, then he'll get an eviction notice and get ya put out. . . . And poor peoples who's been displaced all their lives when they worked ya like a dog in the fields for fifty cents a day. . . . But when everything mechanized, they thowed the people outa work, thowed 'em outa old share-croppers shacks, didn't need 'em no more. They had to come up north. And now where do the roads go through but right through your poorer sections? "Urban renewal"—all that meant to low-income people was "urban removal," 'cause you were just thowed outa your neighborhoods. So now the new thing is gentrification.

For Dave as for many other Over-the-Rhine residents, being "thowed out" is an emblem of their instability—one more embittering example of how the city limits their options by capriciously boxing them in and then setting them "free." When I asked him to relate his first impressions of Over-the-Rhine, he began by stressing these physical constraints on his freedom: "Well, I didn't think it was going to be as hard as it was. Just feelin' cramped up all the time. Couldn't get used to walkin' out in the street and feelin' like the buildings was fallin' down on top of you sometimes. And you just gotta get outa' here once in a while."

Then, however, Dave moved to a related theme of the migrants' stories—the way in which the feeling of being "cramped up" tied in with the noise and crush of urban neighborhoods, by the pressure not of falling buildings but of milling people:

> Couldn't get used to the noise or people stayin' up all hours of the night drunk, raisin' hell; these people don't go to bed until about four or five o'clock in the mornin'. Whole families stay out through the winter. Bitter cold and spittin' snow, they'll be fifteen or twenty kids leanin' against buildins out here standin' on the street corner with a coat and collar up and a hat on. There's a lot of night life out here, drug dealins and prostitution. Then there's perversions; there's queens that come down off Walnut side. Then there's women prostitutes on Vine side. So all that goes on. Then a lot of 'ems gettin' money for drugs. So they stay up all night.

The mention of drugs and "perversions" is hardly accidental. In fact, next to their pained observations about urban crowding, the fear of crime is the most common motif in these migrants' stories.

"Somebody Up to No Good"

Crime in its various forms rivets the attention of city dwellers everywhere today, and stories of criminal acts are among the chief topics of conversation and apprehension. Muggings, holdups, robberies, rapes, murders, assaults, break-ins, vandalism, thefts of cars and car parts—all breed cycles of tales that, as Richard Dorson pointed out with regard to Gary, Indiana, enjoy an ever-widening folkloric distribution.[12] The residents of Over-the-Rhine are typical in this regard. Edna Baker sums up the community sentiment when she says, "It's not home; it's not home to 'em. And when they come in here they don't sit and talk about it. All they talk about here is what somebody done in the next block. Or this 'n robbed somebody."

The urban stories of the Appalachian migrants are bleak. The city is symbolically represented as a place of evil where danger lurks around every corner. The migrants, who once listened to raconteurs tell tales with culture and family specific subject matter, now recount poignant episodes of inner-city violence, racial tension, and personal danger. Their common message is clear: No one is safe in the city. The following story, narrated by Dave Banks, illustrates this common Appalachian worldview toward inner-city Cincinnati:

They come in while I was here. That door there drags, y' know? One day, I's just moved in here about two weeks, and I heard scufflin' on the, on the stairwell, and I said, "Uh huh, there's somebody up to no good." And cause like I said, I didn't have no radio on or nuttin'; ever'thin's quiet. So, I walked from the entrance to right out here in the kitchen, and all of a sudden them door knobs is twistin', turnin'. And I was dumb enough comin' outa the mountains, you don't lock your door, especially when you're at home. Used to be you didn't even lock 'em when you were gone. You'd go off for six months and your house just like no one had left it. Well, that doorknob started twitchin' 'n' ever'thing. An' that door drags real bad; takes a football player to open it, just about. And all of a sudden the door went "bam, bam." Took about four shoves and it come in, and this boy stepped up to me, and I met him nose to nose. And then his eyes got big as a steak platter. [laughter] And he looked at me and I said, "Uh huh, what you a-huntin' for?" I said, "You found a lot more 'n you figured on findin', didn't ya?"

They didn't think nobody was in here. And they knowed my padlock was hangin' loose on the door; didn't know it wasn't locked inside. But there was another one upstairs gettin' Diane; I don't know if you know Diane and them. And she was gone to work, and they had a tire tool a-pryin' the lock offa her door up 'er ta git in on her. And I said, "What the hell y'all doin' in this buildin'? You don't live here." And I ain't got no telephone or nothin' but I said, "I'm goin' in here; I'm callin' the damn law." I said, "I'm gonna see who you are and what you're doin' up in here." Boy, that one was runnin' downstairs with that tire tool, 'n' the other one said, "He jist leaned against your door 'n' it come open." An' I said, "Boy, tell me that. It took about four tries 'fore you got in there."

Here the contrast between the mountains and the city turns on the symbolic difference between locked and unlocked doors. Back in Kentucky, you could leave your front door unlocked; in the city, you aren't secure even when it *is* locked.

The racial element in these tales is sometimes overt, which is hardly surprising given the demography of inner-city life. Yet, migrants vary in their assessment of the racial component, and many seem aware that in the everyday struggle for survival, it is the "hidden injuries of class,"[13] not just race, that feed the violence. There are certainly those who identify crime as a "nigger" problem. But others search for more sophisticated explanations. As one white migrant explained the violence to me, "Really and truly, if the whites didn't start it, it wouldn't be that much. I'm honest with you. The colored don't bother me; it's not the colored; it's the whites."

Oma Henson's experiences in Over-the-Rhine are similar to those of Dave Banks. The two of them often swap petty crime stories, as in the following excerpt that illustrates the futility of city life:

O.H.: Well, they went in an' stole my half a jar of peanut butter and I don't know what all they stoled.

D.B.: Well, Bea, y'know, they used to live underneath; they robbed her about five times before she moved. Took her Pampers, all the food outa her 'frigerator, y'know, fried chicken she had in there. They was chicken bones all up and down where they were packin' stuff outa the back windows. An' me sleepin' here and didn't even know a thing. An' none of us heared 'em. We never knowed she was gettin' robbed! And they had them at gun point. Waitin' there while they was in their beds. They was alone with four little young'ns. And got her T.V. and stereo and stuff like that. And then another time she came back, and all the bedspreads and sheets and stuff was all gone, all her clothes.

O.H.: Honey, I been cleaned out so many times in the last few year, I tell ya, it's pitiful.

D.B.: Yeah, makes ya wanta quit tryin', but you cain't. Gotta make a home.

Crimelore and Creativity: An Emerging Tradition

As Dave's philosophical conclusion indicates, in spite of the bleak picture these migrants paint, there is also a commitment to make their urban lives work, to find a meaning in the situation. That meaning is often found, or rather elicited, in the Appalachians' sharing of folklore performances themselves.

Crimelore in one form or another is a timeless genre of folklore, from the murder and banditry tales of the old Child ballads to variants of the Stagolee legend told "deep down in the jungle."[14] As the best-known scholar of the Stagolee legend, Roger Abrahams, has noted, the performance of folklore genres such as personal experience narratives can have the effect of helping to resolve community tensions. Folklore, he writes, "gives form to energies set into motion by some shared or social anxiety. . . . Power exists not in control over a problem situation itself but in the ability to objectify the situation in symbols—words, pictures, enactments."[15] This purpose is certainly served by the harrowing crime stories that are passed around and shared by these Appalachian migrants. The ability to objectify their hardships through personal experience narratives enables them to take control of the situation symbolically and to resolve their conflicts by externalizing them. The problems seem less severe when they are shared. Thus, the crime tales, no less than the more positive nostalgic reminiscences, help the migrants to reaffirm their "place" as mountain people. Indeed, some of their most creative personal narratives are generated out of their negative experiences in the urban environment.

This is particularly evident in stories I recorded from Lucy Peterson. Lucy, a strong, verbal woman who moved to Cincinnati during World War II and took a job on the loading docks, recounts her experiences working at various unskilled jobs for years until she became proprietor of a small saloon. There she was the victim of thirty-five break-ins and fifteen armed robberies. She finally put a sign in her window that read, "Please give me a break and let me make some money before you take it."

This woman's frustrations are evident, along with her incredible fortitude in the midst of seemingly overwhelming defeats. Small and frail-looking at first encounter, Lucy appears incapable of enduring the hardships that she relates in her stories. However, her delicate appearance belies a powerful drive to succeed at all costs. The following brief story illustrates both Lucy's resilient character and her negative attitude toward city life.

Well, they come in and sat down in front for a long time, and I was sittin' there watchin' them lookin' out the window; then they left. They pulled out in the car. They went down the street, and here they come back again.

They were just sittin' in the car and he was drivin' then. And they come in and that's when I asked what they wanted. And she said, "I've got a toothache, and I want to use the bathroom, and I want a dill pickle." She had that scarf all up around her mouth and she went on to the bathroom and was back there a little while. He sit there on the bar stool kinda like this [Lucy slouches over in her chair like a rag doll] and I had the T.V. on. He was sittin' there with his arm up on the bar. He had a white band on there from the hospital. And it was the middle of November; I forget what day, but it was real cool. He had this little old thin sweater and one of them thin slipovers. And I said, "Did you two just get out of the hospital?" And he said, "Yeah." And he was sittin' there about like this, just ready to fall off that bar stool. He was a dope fiend; that's what he was, a dope addict.

She came back out of the restroom and went plumb to the door and the cigarette machine set right at the door. And she said, "Hey, you come here." And I went walkin' down there and she thowed that gun up in my face and she said, "Give it to me!" And I said, "Give you what?" She said, "The money, God, the God damn money." So I just turned and went walkin' to the cash register to give her, to start givin' her the money. She was tellin' me to hurry it up. Tellin' him to take it, and he just held his hand like that now, with that band on there, holdin' his hand with his fingers spread out. And the money was just going all over the bar as I was reachin' it to him, the change, and then she told me to put it in a God damned paper bag. She

called him three times. Said, Robert, take the money. And he
didn't close his hand. The money just spilled all over the
counter. And then he went to pickin' it all up off of the bar.

In hearing this story, I could not help but compare its "Keystone
Krooks" villains with the more heroic, daredevil badmen of
Appalachian legendry. Mountain outlaws have been the subject of
numerous books and articles, and Bill Lightfoot, who collected badmen narratives in the Big Sandy region, refers to them as one of the
last real genres of extant mountain lore.[16] Once true-to-life crime
narratives, the stories of mountain badmen have been embellished
through time and repetition to the point that today one cannot tell
fact from fiction. Like the better known tales of Billy the Kid and
Jesse James, the tales of Appalachian outlaws like Bad Tom Smith
are an amalgam of Robin Hood archetypes and dime-novel
romance.[17]

The crime stories told by Appalachian urbanites, while they build
on this old tradition, are entirely lacking in the element of romance.
As the victims themselves are telling the stories, the crimes are presented as closer to present-day reality, and the perpetrators are never
larger than life. Often, in fact, the villains are so ridiculous that it is
difficult to take them seriously as badmen. Lucy's adversary in this
story is a good example. Far from maintaining the stature of social
bandit or anti-hero,[18] he is a dope fiend who does not even have the
good sense to collect the money from her. Urban criminals remain
nameless, wallowing in the bathos that accompanies their bungled
attempts to rob seemingly helpless victims. If the stories were not
real life accounts, they might evoke laughter.

In these stories, in fact, it is often the "helpless" victim who is cast
in the role of cool, collected hero. This a pattern that Richard
Dorson identified in discussing crimelore in Indiana's "land of the
millrats." Recognizing the "hallmarks of folkloric narratives" in his
urban crime tales, he noted that "clever robbers assume the guise of
tricksters; sadistic assaulters correspond to ogres and demons; valiant
and 'cool' customers who repel the criminals appear as heroes and
heroines."[19] In one urban story after another, the teller becomes the
brave protagonist who outdoes each assailant through brains or

brawn. Their clever reactions and superhuman feats are similar to those of traditional fairytale heroes. Indeed, the narrators are often tricksters themselves. Their strength of character and witty control of each situation renders them powerful adversaries for the villains they encounter.

Manipulated in this manner, the crime victim story allows the victims the unique opportunity to "re-cast themselves into heroic roles within the narrative."[20] We see this in Dave Banks's facing down his potential assailant "nose to nose" and in Lucy's sardonic please-give-me-a-break announcement. Such recastings of the actors within an established tableau suggest that the urban crime story is an emergent tradition—one that builds upon the conventions of the old victim tale but reinvents them to meet the requirements of a new situation. Like the invented traditions studied by Hobsbawm and Ranger, Over-the-Rhine personal experience narratives are "responses to novel situations which take the form of reference to old situations."[21] Like invented traditions, too, they provide their performers security in the face of adversity.

Conclusion

The crime stories and nostalgic reminiscences of Over-the-Rhine residents reflect the psychological concerns of the inner city mountain migrants who tell them. Although opposite in their expressive attitudinal core, both types of narratives serve a similar function. The migrants in this study are essentially displaced people. They experience a great deal of identity conflict in the inner city, and folk narratives that recall the nostalgic nature of their mountain home or reveal the stark reality of ethnic conflicts in the innercity provide a powerful means to assert an Appalachian identity.

In essence, these personal experience stories help the narrators come to terms with the tensions resulting from displacement. By juxtaposing nostalgic tales with crime tales we can clearly see the positive and negative modalities of their experience as urban Appalachians. In a very real sense, however, both types of narratives accentuate a positive identity. Just as the nostalgic tale asserts the narrator's positive sense of attachment to a mountain life and culture, so the crime tale enables the narrator, like the fairytale hero, to dramatically transcend the violence of urban slum life. The positive and negative strategies work together to sustain their continuity with the past through lifetimes of exile.

Notes

1. Robert Coles, *The South Goes North* (Boston: Little, Brown, 1967), 321.
2. Lewis Killian, "Southern White Laborers in Chicago's West Side" (Ph.D. dissertation, University of Chicago, 1949), 192.
3. Ellen J. Steckert, "Focus for Conflict: Southern Mountain Medical Beliefs in Detroit," in *The Urban Experience and Folk Tradition*, ed. Américo Paredes (Austin: University of Texas Press, 1971), 104.
4. Laurel Shackelford and Bill Weinberg, eds., *Our Appalachia: An Oral History* (New York: Hill and Wang, 1977).
5. Melvin Proffitt, "The Folks of the Wolfe County Hills" (unpublished biography), 1.
6. Richard Blaustein, "Regionalism and Revitalization: Toward Comparative Perspective on Appalachian Studies," in *Remembrance, Reunion, and Revival: Celebrating a Decade of Appalachian Studies*, proceedings of the 10th Annual Appalachian Studies Conference, ed. Helen Roseberry (Boone, N.C.: Appalachian Consortium Press, 1988), 8.
7. Barbara Allen and Thomas Schlereth, *Sense of Place: American Regional Cultures* (Lexington: University Press of Kentucky, 1990).
8. Allen Batteau, *The Invention of Appalachia* (Tucson: University of Arizona Press, 1990), 200.
9. David E. Whisnant, *All That Is Native and Fine* (Chapel Hill: University of North Carolina Press, 1983), 260–61.
10. Eric Hobsbawm and Terence Ranger, eds., *The Invention of Tradition* (Cambridge: Cambridge University Press, 1988), 8.
11. All comments by Over-the-Rhine residents come from interviews I conducted in the 1980s. For full references, see John R. Williams, "Appalachian Migrants in Cincinnati, Ohio: The Role of Folklore in the Reinforcement of Ethnic Identity" (Ph.D. dissertation, Indiana University, 1985).

12. Richard M. Dorson, *Land of the Millrats* (Cambridge, Mass.: Harvard University Press, 1981), 213.

13. Richard Sennett and Jonathan Cobb, *The Hidden Injuries of Class* (New York: Vintage, 1972). For an excellent study of how race and class articulate, see Douglas E. Foley, *Learning Capitalist Culture: Deep in the Heart of Tejas* (Philadelphia: University of Pennsylvania Press, 1990).

14. Roger D. Abrahams, *Deep Down in the Jungle* (Philadelphia: University of Pennsylvania Press, 1967).

15. Roger D. Abrahams, "Personal Power and Social Restraint in the Definition of Folklore," in *Toward New Perspectives in Folklore*, ed. Américo Paredes and Richard Bauman (Austin: University of Texas Press, 1972), 19.

16. William Lightfoot, "Folklore of the Big Sandy Valley of Eastern Kentucky" (Ph.D. dissertation, Indiana University, 1976), 102.

17. Charles Hayes, *The Hanging of Bad Tom Smith* (Jackson, Ky.: Breathitt County Historical Society, 1969).

18. For the classic treatment of social banditry, see Eric Hobsbawm, *Primitive Rebels* (New York: Norton, 1965), 13–29.

19. Dorson, *Millrats*, 213.

20. Eleanor Wachs, "The Code of Survival: The Crime-Victim Narrative within an Urban Context" (Ph.D. dissertation, Indiana University, 1979), 12.

21. Hobsbawm and Ranger, *Invention*, 2.

Chapter 10

Booze, Ritual, and the Invention of Tradition: The Phenomenon of the Newfoundland Screech-In

Pat Byrne

It is possible to argue that Newfoundland was for centuries a fictive world. There are those—the intrepid members of the Flat Earth Society come immediately to mind—who maintain that, like Atlantis, it remains so to the present day. Even airline booking agents in other parts of North America will route one to Finland unless one takes precautions to clarify exactly where it is one wishes to travel. One who elects to write about "this marvellous terrible place,"[1] therefore, must take a little time to acquaint potential readers with the bare facts of its existence.

"To the historian of fifty years ago, the early history of Newfoundland was a fairly simple matter. The Island had been discovered by Europeans when John Cabot, sailing for the King of England, reached it in June, 1497,"[2] just five years after the famous voyage of Christopher Columbus. It is now clear, however, that Cabot was preceded by hardy Basque and/or Portuguese fishermen and that the Norsemen, if one believes the sagas and recent archaeological evidence, were there around the year 1000. Some argue that the island was reached by St. Brendan as early as the sixth century. Be that as it may, eighty-six years after Cabot's voyage, on August 5,

1583, Sir Humphrey Gilbert sailed into the harbor at St. John's and, despite the fact that some thirty-six ships from various European countries were already at anchor there, claimed the island in Elizabeth's name. This act conferred on Newfoundland a fictive moniker and a dubious distinction as "Britain's oldest colony."

Despite its long history as a point of contact for Europeans in the New World, however, the history of Newfoundland as a fully recognized social and political entity is a relatively recent phenomenon. Sir Humphrey's earlier blusterings notwithstanding, Newfoundland was not officially recognized as a British colony until 1824. It was granted Representative Government on the Canadian maritime model in 1832, but Responsible Government (with a prime minister and a cabinet) was not achieved until 1855. Newfoundland, therefore, "did not follow the same path as did other parts of North America," where colonies "began in a positive, energetic way after the voyages of Columbus and Cartier."[3]

The difference fostered a view of Newfoundland history as the story of settlement against all obstacles and survival against all odds. According to this view, "for two centuries and more, a mere handful of renegade fisherfolk managed to eke out a miserable existence"[4] without benefit of the social institutions their North American neighbors had begun to take for granted. After 1855, the island carried on for seventy-nine years as a semi-independent colony/dominion within the British Empire. Then, in February 1934, burdened by impending bankruptcy caused by its war debt and several years of disaster in the fishery, the national government legislated itself out of existence and accepted rule by a six-man commission appointed by the British government. Fifteen years later, the people of the island voted, by the slimmest of majorities, to become a province of Canada.

Some modern scholars have argued that Lord Salisbury's well-known quip, uttered in the House of Lords in 1891, in which he described Newfoundlanders as "the sport of historic errors," displays an overly simplistic reading of their history.[5] The notion persists, however, that Newfoundlanders are "waterproof, dustproof, shock-resistant and anti-magnetic" due to the fact that "for centuries, back to the days of the first Elizabeth and our dread sovereign lord King

James, [they have] been taking [their] lumps and [have] learned a
thing or two about hanging in there."⁶ This remains the popular
reading of the past.

A Crisis of Identity

This rather cursory review of Newfoundland's history is sufficient
to illustrate the fact that a people who, in the space of one hundred
years, saw their homeland move from being considered little more
than "a great ship moored near the Grand Banks for the conve-
nience of English fishermen"⁷ to the status of a recognized colony,
to a semi-independent dominion, to a powerless ward of the
English crown to, finally, a reluctant province of still another
country were bound to experience a severe identity crisis. This
identity crisis was exacerbated by the fact that the sense of loss that
many Newfoundlanders felt at being cut adrift from Mother
England in 1949 was due to the fact that their very sense of
Englishness was based, to a large extent, on manufactured and
invented sentiment.

England had been content to treat Newfoundland as its personal
fish basket for centuries. However, "from 1832 onwards
Newfoundland was . . . a Protestant colony in the making, a 'state'
which the Colonial Office and the local elite attempted to fashion
on lines acceptable to the political, social and cultural norms of the
mother country."⁸ In 1840, however, the Newfoundland Natives'
Society was founded "to promote the interests of native-born
Newfoundlanders (the word native in this context does not mean
aborigine) in a colony that was beginning to acquire a sense of local
identity but was still dominated by an immigrant bourgeoisie."⁹ The
members of the Society were mostly middle-class, professional men
and small businessmen, and their nationalist aspirations often put
them at odds with the ruling colonial powers. At a time when political and sectarian tensions imported from the British Isles ran high,
"the British government intervened, not only instituting constitutional reforms but also 'inventing traditions' by sponsoring and
encouraging organizations and rituals which attempted to inculcate
imperial sentiment" in the local population.¹⁰

This led to one of the many paradoxes in Newfoundland's history. In a colony on the threshold of Responsible Government, "loyalty to the concept of Empire" was paramount; yet "this consciousness of being British subjects resident in a colony co-existed," and sometimes clashed, "with a strong nativist feeling."[11] It is clear in retrospect, however, that much of what came to be "regarded as immemorial Newfoundland tradition, enshrined in institutions, rituals and attitudes,"[12] at least as perceived and practiced by the middle and upper classes, had its genesis in the post-1832 era.

The success achieved in inculcating "imperial sentiment" can be measured by the lemminglike rush on the part of young Newfoundlanders to go to the aid of the mother country in World War I. By the 1930s, however, as a result of its having paid its war debt, and due to repeated failures in the fishery, combined with the general slump in the world economy, Newfoundland had become a penniless British embarrassment; by the 1940s, the British, proving to be ever-indifferent masters, "typically without consultation and too absorbed in the emergency mentality of war to give much thought to Newfoundland's tomorrow, gave the Americans *carte blanche* to use the island as a military base for as long as they needed it."[13] The same attitude, later in the decade, allowed the British government to engineer Newfoundland's entry into the Canadian Confederation, thereby ridding itself of its burdensome child forever.

Eighty years earlier, flushed with their newly acquired "imperial sentiment," Newfoundlanders had responded to proposed confederation with Canada as follows:

> Hurrah! For our own native isle, Newfoundland!
> Not a stranger shall hold one inch of its strand!
> Her face turns to Britain, her back to the Gulf.
> Come near at your peril, Canadian Wolf![14]

Now, however, it was Mother England's back which had been turned on Newfoundlanders, and they found themselves sharing the den of the same Canadian wolf. After four hundred years of facing Britain, Newfoundlanders were forced to face up to the fact that they were North Americans, but this was a role they felt ill equipped to play, either emotionally or economically. The traditional economy was undergoing rapid and radical change; the emotional adjustments took longer and were more subtle. What successive British and Newfoundland governments had failed to achieve, economic prosperity of sorts, "was brought about by war and the accident of geography."[15]

Newfoundland's strategic position at the advent of World War II meant an influx of American and Canadian military personnel, which totalled "nearly one-tenth of the country's entire population."[16] The economic windfall was immediate, but the full social and cultural impact of the presence of this North American military hoard on Newfoundland has yet to be fully assessed. The Newfoundland novelist Margaret Duley, who lived through the period, points to an essential feature that bears on the present discussion:

> At first the Newfoundland civilian was stunned. He had always had his country and his roads to himself. He could dawdle, and enjoy both in the spirit of undisturbed ownership. Now he felt dispossessed, crowded on his own streets, mowed down by the ever-increasing numbers of dun-coloured army-vehicles. The strangers were strutting, becoming the "big shots." They looked down their noses at the natives. They were disdainful of a hard old heritage. They began to call the townsfolk "the Newfies" and like Queen Victoria, the Newfoundlanders were not amused.[17]

Duley is here recording not only the reaction of the islanders to the strangers, but also the appearance of a new word in the Newfoundland lexicon. The best evidence, both written and oral, suggests that the words "Newf" and "Newfie" were coined by the newly arrived Canadian and American servicemen.[18] Another, "Newfiejohn," for St. John's, the capital city, has been attributed to the members of the Royal Canadian Navy.[19] The words were new; the stereotype they suggest, however, had been some time in the making.

The Emergence of "Newfieland"

It has been noted above that "in certain aspects of its development Newfoundland [was] eccentric and peripheral among the British North American colonies."[20] Late nineteenth and early twentieth century travellers and writers who visited the island were fond of pointing out the eccentricities of the Newfoundland dialect and the peculiarities of its folkways.[21] The vagaries of the Newfoundland climate,[22] the hardships of the seal hunt[23] and the fishery, the unusual aspects of Newfoundland foodways, and what were perceived to be peculiar and distinctive attributes of the quaint and queer Newfoundland character were all enlisted to paint a picture of the fisherfolk who inhabited "this rock within the sea"—a picture grounded more in an expedient fiction than in fact. Thus, one local writer, as early as 1904, could state:

> Newfoundland is famous for its dogs, its fogs, and its fisheries. . . . It is a region unique, with a people still more so . . . who for sheer daring and absolute endurance have no equal in the world today. . . . They are as simple as children and as guileless. . . . The Newfoundlander is his own shipwright, blacksmith and sailmaker. . . . They are addicted to tea-drinking to such an extent as to have elicited a special paper on the subject. . . . The Newfoundlanders reckon fishing above all callings, for the love of it is implanted in them. . . . Here the wearied vacationist can recuperate . . . the tourist enjoy the companionship of a people at once child-like in their trust and lion like in their courage, strong and hearty and splendid.[24]

Promoting Newfoundland as a natural paradise "peopled by childlike natives eager to act as guides and servants soon began to produce results, and as the twentieth century progressed a growing entrepreneurial class began to cash in on the influx of visitors."[25] The image of "childlike natives" was not restricted to tourist brochures. In 1934, the English headmaster of the only college on the island could say in the course of a speech before a London society—a speech delivered in defense of Newfoundlanders!—that Newfoundland "men strike me always as big children, moved by fairy tales and often superstitious, misled by the politicians who make promises . . . and led by the nose by designing men just because they have no guile in them but too much of that charity which believeth all things."[26]

Ironically—but understandably, perhaps, in the light of the identity crises noted above—at a time when an appeal to the realities of their four-hundred-year history, the fisherfolks' "hard old heritage," might have stood them in good stead, many Newfoundlanders turned neither to those realities nor to the "invented traditions" created for them by the nineteenth century minions of the Colonial Office, but to the fictive image of themselves that had been imposed upon them by outlanders and furthered by local "intellectual patriots."[27] The Newfoundland civilian's lack of amusement recorded by Duley appears to have been a temporary phenomenon; in time, a radical change in attitude occurred, and it is in the analysis of this attitudinal change that we find an explanation for the phenomenon which became known as the Newfoundland Screech-In.

Fundamental to that change was the invention of a new Newfoundland and new Newfoundlanders to replace those so recently disappeared. What began to emerge to replace the traditional culture of the fisherfolk was "Newfieland" peopled by "Newfies"—a place out of step with time, inhabited by the numskull figure of the "Newfie" joke, too stupid to realize his own ineptitude and alien status vis-à-vis mainstream North American society, but eternally happy, embarrassingly hospitable, and full of fun, deferential to his betters (read any non-Newfoundlander), but fiercely proud of his homeland and his way of life.

Having accepted this fictive image of themselves, many Newfoundlanders found it convenient and expedient to bathe it in the rosy glow of "tradition." After Confederation, Newfoundland basked in the self-imposed designation of "Canada's Happy Province,"[28] and the tourist literature promulgated an image of the Newfoundlander that is best illustrated by the immortal words of Foghorn Leghorn: "Nice boy, but dumb!" In this context the Screech-In is to be seen not as an isolated phenomenon, but as part of a calculated survival technique developed by those who "felt dispossessed," a survival technique based on turning a half-believed stereotype into a sort of personified, self-sustained *blason populaire,* which is grounded in "a kind of mystical nationalism."[29] Indeed, it has been argued that the entire concept of "a Newfoundland culture" that emerged out of that period, and has reemerged in several revivals since, is an invention born of expediency.[30]

Rum and Ritual: Ways to Screech

Hobsbawm describes invented traditions as including "both traditions actually invented, constructed and formally instituted and those emerging in a less easily traceable manner within a brief and dateable period—a matter of a few years perhaps—and establishing themselves with great rapidity."[31] The "traditions" which arose in the post-1832 era, of which McCann and others have written, are examples of the first type; the Screech-In is an example of the second. On the surface, it is simply a welcoming ceremony or a hospitality rite that revolves around the drinking of a tot of "Screech"—an imported but locally bottled rum. The origin of the practice is obscure, although its beginnings are linked to the 1940s and the influx of American and Canadian service personnel. The term, however, has a distinct sixties ring to it, reminiscent of sit-in, love-in, and the like. True to form, its origins have become part of the invention. Nevertheless, over time it evolved into a complex ceremony of initiation for visitors, complete with its own rituals and symbols designed "to establish continuity with a suitable historic past."[32]

Historians have long noted that Newfoundland history is, in part, the story of "a long battle between rum and religion."[33] The import statistics for 1815, a time when the population of the island hovered around 20,000 souls, illustrate the point: "371,000 gallons of rum and spirits were imported from the British West Indies; from other sources 443,000 gallons were imported."[34] A nineteenth-century missionary complained that "the arrival of a trading schooner among the people affords an invariable occasion for all parties . . . to get into a hopeless state of intoxication."[35]

It is not surprising, therefore, that rum would be enlisted as the ritual drink among "the happiest Canadians," who, so the reasoning goes, "for all their statistical poverty . . . enjoy life more than any other people."[36] What is worthy of note, and in keeping with what has been said above, is that rum of the cheapest variety and poorest quality is selected. A local historian, a man who, perhaps not without symbolic value, was a minister in the post-Confederation, provincial government and later a senator, describes the genesis of Screech with typical propagandistic hyperbole but without apparent irony:

> As Newfoundlanders became more affluent and sophisticated following Confederation, rum, while still the favourite alcoholic beverage of a majority of men, lost some of its centuries-old appeal. Increasingly, beer and wines became popular. During World War II, while the great bases existed, hundreds of thousands of sailors, airmen and soldiers had personal contact with Newfoundland and its hospitality. For some unexplained reason a cheap Demerara (later Jamaican) rum, brought to Newfoundland in bulk and bottled there, became part of the experience for most of these visitors. Some genius among the visitors gave the rum a name now almost a household word throughout the English-speaking world: "Screech."[37]

A promotional booklet, first distributed in the 1970s by the government-controlled liquor commission, tells a similar story but with significant embellishments:

> Long before any liquor board was created to take alcohol under its benevolent wing, Jamaican rum was a mainstay of the Newfoundland diet, with salt fish traded to the West Indies in exchange for rum. When the Government took control of the traditional liquor business in the early 20th century, it began selling the rum in an unlabelled bottle. The product might have remained permanently nameless except for the influx of American servicemen to the island during World War II. As the story goes, the commanding officer of the original detachment was having his first taste of Newfoundland hospitality and, imitating the custom of his host, downed his drink in one gulp. The American's blood-curdling howl, when he regained

his breath, brought the sympathetic and curious from miles around rushing to the house to find out what was going on. The first to arrive was a garrulous old American sergeant who pounded on the door and demanded, "What the cripes was that ungodly screech?" The taciturn Newfoundlander who had answered the door replied simply, "The Screech? 'Tis the rum, me son." Thus was born a legend. As word of the incident spread, the soldiers, determined to try this mysterious "Screech" and finding its effects as devastating as the name implies, adopted it as their favourite. The opportunistic liquor board pounced on the name and reputation and began labelling Newfoundland Screech, the most popular brand on that Island, even today.

The same booklet, appropriately titled *Ways to Screech*, offers the following version of the origin of the Screech-In:

> While Screech is available in many parts of North America, there is something in the unique character of the beverage which allows it to reach its peak only when consumed in Newfoundland. Tasted anywhere else in the world, Screech is a delightful drink; tasted in its home port, Screech is the ultimate in sensory experiences. To pay homage to those who are fortunate enough to try Screech in its birthplace, the Royal Order of Screechers was founded. Under the auspices of the Province's liquor authorities, visitors to St. John's can arrange to partake of Screech in its traditional surroundings. The occasion is solemnly recorded in the register of the Royal Order of Screechers; the successful candidate is presented with a scroll commemorating the occasion; and the Order welcomes another lifelong devotee.

This, of course, is legitimization after the fact; the liquor commission, motivated more by the love of profit than by any concern for "tradition," became involved only after the practice was well established. It is worth noting in this context the lingering "imperial sentiment" suggested by the "royal" tag. The "economically motivated connection between tourism and displays"[38] such as Screech-Ins has long been recognized, but as Bendix notes, such displays are often perceived by their originators as "an affirmation of local and national cultural identity."[39] Screech-Ins became one way to affirm the newly emerging "Newfie" identity.

The liquor commission's booklet appears to be no more than so much unabashed advertising hype until one realizes that this "solemn occasion" requires the presence of a presiding officer, the chief Screecher, who guarantees the "staged authenticity"[40] of the event. These presiders are usually middle-class professionals who, because they often travel as tourists themselves, are well aware that tourists have very definite expectations regarding the authenticity of cultural displays, whether they are mounted by Newfoundlanders or the Indians of New Mexico.[41]

The chief Screecher—usually a man, but women do sometimes preside—dresses in oilskins and salt and pepper cap or "sou'wester"—the "traditional" garb of the "Newfie" fisherman. An oar is sometimes carried as a sort of staff of office, but this appears to be optional. Invariably, however, the chief Screecher speaks a heightened form of a Newfoundland dialect, sometimes dubbed "Newfinese." The initiates, before being offered the tot of Screech (now, by the way, a perfectly palatable Jamaican dark rum) and receiving the certificate of the Royal Order of Screechers, are expected to eat a dried caplin, a morsel of uncooked bologna, and a peppermint knob. The chief Screecher takes great care to acquaint the initiates with the "traditionality" of these delicacies. In fact, a caplin is a small, smeltlike fish that was more commonly used as a bait fish or as a fertilizer than as a dietary staple in Newfoundland, although it was eaten in hard times and as a grog-bit. Bologna is a popular food item, which has earned the label "Newfie steak," and a peppermint knob is a locally produced bon-bon. The high point of the "dubious if well-meant ritual"[42] is the kissing of a codfish by the initiates; a freshly killed or salt-cured fish may be used, depending on the whim of the chief Screecher. All are then expected to kneel and repeat one or more contrived dialect phrases rattled off by the chief Screecher. This usually follows a question-and-answer format, such as the following:

Screecher: "Is we Newfies?"
Initiates: "Deed we is, me old cock, an' long may yer big jib draw."

The point is to say this as quickly and as unintelligibly as possible—to demonstrate the way "real Newfies" talk. Only after these rituals have been performed to the satisfaction of the chief Screecher are the visitors permitted to drink the tot of rum and to receive the certificate, thereby becoming members of the Royal Order of Screechers—and honorary Newfies to boot! It is customary for the chief Screecher to ask the new inductees to demonstrate their acquired "Newfieness" by chanting a prescribed response to a series of questions. For example:

Screecher: "Did ye j'st go down on yer knucks and kiss a smelly old codfish?"
Initiates: "Deed we did, me old cock."
Screecher: "Did ye j'st wrap yer chops around a piece of Newfie steak and gobble a dried caplin?"
Initiates: "Deed we did, me old cock."
Screecher: "Did ye all j'st repeat a whole lot o'tings ye don't un'erstand a-tall?"
Initiates: "Deed we did, me old cock."

This may proceed, ad nauseam, depending on the inventiveness of the chief Screecher and the tolerance/endurance of the initiates, but the chief Screecher invariably concludes with: "An' af'er all dat 'tis ye what calls we stupid Newfies?"

Contesting "Tradition"

An answer to this question is seldom forthcoming, and there the ritual remained until the summer of 1989, when, at the height of the tourist season, a public debate on the phenomenon erupted in the local print and electronic media. Those who opposed the ceremony usually did so on the grounds that "it would be a pity . . . if the province were to vulgarize itself, and trivialize its history and culture, just to make itself appealing to tourists."[43] Some were simply "appalled that the practice continues" and felt "shamed by screech-ins."[44] Its defenders saw it as no more than "an adopted custom" and maintained that "there's nothing wrong with being quaint, in fact, some visitors find it very appealing."[45] One astute commentator linked the ceremony with the Newfie stereotype, which, she noted, "has grown from a word . . . to a cultural concept."[46] The local radio and television stations interviewed opponents and proponents and conducted the mandatory "person-in-the-street-interviews," but it appeared that interest in the issue was about to fade when the lieutenant governor publicly debunked the Newfie stereotype, Newfie jokes, and Screech-Ins. They were, he maintained, "pejorative and patronizing" practices that had the end result of "subjecting ourselves to ridicule."[47]

This pronouncement by the queen's representative in the province seemed to reawaken dormant "imperial sentiment," at least in official circles. The liquor commission immediately withdrew its sponsorship of Screech-Ins and the premier of the province ordered that all remaining certificates of the Royal Order of Screechers be consigned to the shredder. This knee-jerk reaction sent Screech-Ins underground and opened the second round in the debate. One columnist dismissed the whole business as a tempest in a teapot by noting that "visitors to Newfoundland are not so deficient in their smarts as to mistake entertainment for reality."[48] He was immediately chastised by the chairperson of the Heritage Coalition of Newfoundland and Labrador, who also took the opportunity to inform the public that "the Heritage Coalition is announcing a contest for a Screech-In replacement."[49] At this point, there occurred a curious development; several people came forward and claimed credit for inventing the Screech-In ceremony and maintained that in its present form, it had become debased.[50] The deadline for submissions for the Heritage Coalition's contest was April 30, 1990. No new "tradition" appears to have been invented, the claims of the self-proclaimed originators remain unsubstantiated, and the Screech-In continues as a flourishing underground rite of passage, albeit *sans* certificates and free Screech samples!

When one considers that this ritual developed in the Canadian province that has the highest cost of living and the highest unemployment and welfare rates in the country, whose first premier

Figure 1. The Newfoundland Liquor Commission's mock certificate for those enrolled in the Royal Order of Screechers. In 1990, stung by charges that the Screech-In denigrated the island's culture, the government ordered all such documents shredded. Photo by Adriana Martinez.

under Confederation is supposed to have told fishermen to "burn their boats" and promised to "drag Newfoundland kicking and screaming into the twentieth century," where successive governments for the past forty years have subscribed to a philosophy of "develop or perish" at the expense of the traditional economy and the blithe destruction of the traditional way of life, and where every mad scheme attempted under the aegis of this philosophy has resulted in a dismal failure, the chief Screecher's cry "An' af 'er all dat 'tis ye what calls we stupid Newfies" may be no more than the local articulation of the cliché "misery loves company." On the other hand, these points may suggest that the Screech-In is no more than a Newfoundland example of folklorism understood as "a cultural reaction to specific social and economic conditions."[51] The debate continues, however, in Newfoundland and elsewhere, as to the authenticity of such displays, and, given the increase in historical and cultural tourism, it is unlikely that it will abate soon.

Notes

1. Yva Momatiuk and John Eastcott, *This Marvellous Terrible Place: Images of Newfoundland and Labrador* (Camden East, Ontario: Camden House, 1988).
2. Frederick W. Rowe, *A History of Newfoundland* (Toronto: McGraw-Hill Ryerson, 1980), 23.
3. F. L. Jackson, *Surviving Confederation* (St. John's: Harry Cuff, 1986), 66.
4. Ibid.
5. Keith Matthews, "Historical Fence Building: A Critique of Newfoundland Historiography," *The Newfoundland Quarterly* 74, no. 1 (1978): 21–30.
6. Ray Guy, *You May Know Them as Sea Urchins, Ma'am*, rev. ed., ed. Eric Norman (St. John's: Breakwater Books, 1985), 121.
7. This was a favorite metaphor used by eighteenth-century politicians to refer to Newfoundland. See C. R. Fay, *Life and Labour in Newfoundland* (Toronto: University of Toronto Press, 1956), 107.
8. Phillip McCann, "Culture, State Formation, and the Invention of Tradition: Newfoundland 1833–1855," *Journal of Canadian Studies* 23 (1988): 87.
9. Patrick O'Flaherty, "The Newfoundland Natives' Society," in *Encyclopedia of Newfoundland and Labrador*, ed. Cyril F. Poole et al. (St. John's: Harry Cuff, 1994), 3:21.
10. McCann, "Culture," 87.
11. Ibid., 98.
12. Ibid., 100. See also Cecil J. Houston and William J. Smyth, "The Impact of Fraternalism on the Landscape of Newfoundland," *The Canadian Geographer* 29 (1985): 59–65.
13. Jackson, *Surviving Confederation*, 70.
14. "An Anti-Confederation Song," in *The Penguin Book of Canadian Folk Songs*, ed. Edith Fowke (Harmondsworth: Penguin, 1973), 28.
15. Patrick O'Flaherty, *The Rock Observed: Literary Responses to Newfoundland and Its People* (Toronto: University of Toronto Press, 1979), 144.

16. Malcolm MacLeod, *Peace of the Continent: The Impact of Second World War Canadian and American Bases in Newfoundland* (St. John's: Harry Cuff, 1986), 1.

17. Margaret Duley, *The Caribou Hut: The Story of a Newfoundland Hostel* (Toronto: Ryerson Press, 1949), 11.

18. See Lester V. Berrey and Melvin Van Den Bark, *The American Thesaurus of Slang* (New York: Thomas Y. Crowell, 1942). This work makes several references to the terms but, unfortunately, makes no comment on their origins.

19. Wilfred Granville, *A Dictionary of Sailors' Slang* (London: Andre Deutsch, 1962).

20. William B. Hamilton, "Society and Schools in Newfoundland," in *Canadian Education: A History*, ed. J. Donald Wilson, Robert M. Stamp, and Louis Philippe Audet (Scarborough: Prentice-Hall Canada, 1970), 126.

21. George Patterson, "Notes on the Dialect of the People of Newfoundland," *Journal of American Folklore* 8 (1895): 27–40; 9 (1896): 19–37; 10 (1897): 203–13; and "Notes on the Folk-Lore of Newfoundland," *Journal of American Folklore* 8 (1895): 285–90; 10 (1897): 214–15.

22. Edith Blake, "On Seals and Savages," *The Nineteenth Century* 25 (1899): 513–29.

23. George Allan England, *The Greatest Hunt in the World* (Montreal: Tundra Books, 1969 [1924]).

24. P. T. McGrath, "The Fisherfolk of Newfoundland," *Outing* 44 (1904): 305–21.

25. Gerald L. Pocius, "Tourists, Health Seekers, and Sportsmen: Luring Americans to Newfoundland in the Early Twentieth Century," in *Twentieth-Century Newfoundland: Explorations*, ed. James Hiller and Peter Neary (St. John's: Breakwater Books, 1995), 70.

26. J. L. Paton, "Newfoundland: Past and Present," *International Affairs* 13 (1934): 397.

27. James Overton, "A Newfoundland Culture?" *Journal of Canadian Studies* 23 (1988): 6.

28. This phrase appeared on the province's motor vehicle license plates for a number of years. See also Joseph R. Smallwood, "Happy Province," in *The Book of Newfoundland*, ed. Joseph R. Smallwood (St. John's: Newfoundland Book Publishers, 1976), 3:1–3.

29. Overton, "Newfoundland Culture," 6.

30. Ibid.

31. Eric Hobsbawm, "Introduction: Inventing Traditions," in *The Invention of Tradition*, ed. Eric Hobsbawm and Terence Ranger (Cambridge: Cambridge University Press, 1983), 1.

32. Ibid.

33. Fay, *Life and Labour*, 43.

34. Rowe, *History*, 252–53.

35. Edward Wix, *Six Months of a Newfoundland Missionary's Journal, from February to August 1835* (London: Smith and Elder, 1836), 169–70.

36. Richard J. Needham, "The Happiest Canadians," *Maclean's Magazine* 77 (Nov. 2, 1964): 15–17, 35–39.

37. Rowe, *History*, 258.

38. Regina Bendix, "Tourism and Cultural Displays: Inventing Traditions for Whom?" *Journal of American Folklore* 102 (1989): 132.

39. Ibid.

40. Dean MacCannell, *The Tourist: A New Theory of the Leisure Class* (New York: Schocken Books, 1989), 91–109.

41. Deirdre Evans-Pritchard, "The Portal Case: Authenticity, Tourism, Traditions, and the Law," *Journal of American Folklore* 100 (1987).

42. Peter Gzowski, "Kissing the Cod," *Canadian Living*, November 1989, p. 51.

43. Editorial, "A Cautionary Word," *Evening Telegram*, July 11, 1989, p. 5.

44. M. F. Kennedy, letter, "Screech-Ins an Insult," *Evening Telegram*, July 29, 1989, p. 5.

45. Anonymous letter, "Nothing Insulting about Screech-Ins," *Evening Telegram*, August 16, 1989, p. 5.

46. Marjorie Doyle, "Let's Rid the World of 'Newfies,'" *Evening Telegram*, Nov. 19, 1989, p. 5.

47. James A. McGrath, "Notes for a Speech to the St. John's Rotary Club, January 4, 1990," manuscript, Memorial University Centre for Newfoundland Studies.

48. Philip Hiscock, "Harmless Screech-Ins Provide a Pat on the Cultural Back," *Newfoundland Signal*, March 4–10, 1990, p. 11.

49. Garfield Fizzard, letter, "Shame on You for Defending the Screech-In," *Sunday Express*, March 11, 1990, p. 8.

50. Brian Jones, "Screech-In Has Opponents and Supporters Screeming," *Evening Telegram*, March 26, 1990, p. 6.

51. Elke Dettmer, "Folklorism in Newfoundland," in *Studies in Newfoundland Folklore: Community and Process*, ed. Gerald Thomas and J. D. A. Widdowson (St. John's: Breakwater Books, 1991), 169–76.

Chapter 11

Shell Games in Vacationland: *Homarus Americanus* and the State of Maine

George H. Lewis

"I drove and drove...thinking that at any moment now I would encounter the fabled Maine of lobster pots and surf battered shores."
—Bill Bryson, *The Lost Continent: Travels in Small Town America* (1989)

I CAME TO MAINE FOR SEX AND ALL I GOT WAS LOBSTER
—Souvenir t-shirt slogan (1990)

In America, lobster means Maine. Whether one is sampling a shore dinner in New York City, Los Angeles, or Honolulu, the lobster on the plate is inevitably billed as having been flown in from the cool, fresh waters off the Maine coast. Although technically *homarus americanus* can be found all up and down the 1,300-mile stretch of the Atlantic seaboard from Cape Hatteras to Labrador and is caught, commercially sold, and shipped from many coastal American states as well as Canada,[1] the lobster has become a symbol of Maine in much the same way that maple sugar is of Vermont and potatoes are of Idaho.[2] The spiny crustacean has become a symbol—a regional icon, if you will—of the state that is called upon with light-hearted reverence (and irreverence) in observations such as this essay's two epigraphs.

Regional Character and Competing Cultural Meanings

As Howard Marshall has said in his study of special foods of Missouri, "like dialect and architecture, food traditions are a main component in the intricate and impulsive system that joins culture and geography into regional character."[3] In this way, the lobster joins with the "down east" accent, Maine humor, and the distinctive architecture of the area as a contributor to its regional character.

And a strongly defined region it is, being bounded on two sides by Canada and on one by the Atlantic Ocean. During the nineteenth century, the make-up of Maine's population remained relatively stable, with little immigration either from Canada or from the rest of New England (with the exception of some immigration from Quebec and the Maritimes in the later years of that century to a selected few manufacturing towns like Biddeford, Saco, and Lewistown).[4] Except in centers such as Portland, Maine was not thickly settled. Communities across the state were scattered and separate. As folklorist Edward Ives has pointed out, Maine's culture can be said to have developed along its own lines through this combination of isolation and stability.[5]

Interestingly, this peculiar Maine mix of culture and geography did not at first include the lobster, which was viewed by early New Englanders as cheap, low-status—even poorhouse—fare. Lobsters were many times donated to widows, orphans, and others in the spirit of public charity. Showing up in fishing nets as early as 1605 in Maine, lobsters were a common catch along the coast. However, they were so devalued as a food source that there are reports of saltwater farmers gathering them in carts after storms, when they would be piled a foot or so deep along the coast,[6] and either feeding them to the pigs or plowing them by the ton into their fields as fertilizer. Although some historians feel this usage of the lobster has been exaggerated for effect—since any food so easy to obtain and so cheap would have been consumed by thrifty Yankees—it is agreed by all that lobster *was* a low-status food at the time.[7]

This abundance of lobster, and its definition as low-status food, continued into the early 1800s. It was not until a well-defined urban market for cheap lobster began to develop in centers such as Boston that there was any real thought of creating a lobster industry. And even then, because of rapid spoilage and slow means of transportation, it was limited to coastal waters adjacent to Boston. In Maine, at the time too far away to be realistically fished for lobster for export, the lobster remained a low-status item, often used as pig feed, fertilizer, and fish bait. The fishing and ship-building industries were the important things. One ate lobster only because one could get more money at market for fish. And in a depressed economy such as that of the Maine coast, this was more than good sense. It was economic necessity.

Soon after the Civil War, two very important things occurred with respect to the lobster and Maine. First, the fishing grounds around Cape Cod and the Cape Elizabeth Islands in Massachusetts, which had been supplying the growing demand for lobster meat in Boston and New York, became depleted to the point that the overabundance of lobster off the coast of Maine began to be exploited commercially. This was made possible by the advent of the canning industry, new steam-powered technologies of transportation, and the invention of the swift lobster smack—all of which combined to allow canned and fresh Maine lobster to reach East Coast, urban markets without spoiling.[8]

By 1880, over twenty-five million pounds of lobster were being brought to New York City annually by train—some canned, but most packed tightly in large barrels of ice. Lobster smacks—boats with large pools of seawater in their holds that could handle up to eight thousand lobsters a trip—unloaded their live cargos into floating lobster cars outside the Fulton Fish Market. The "Tin Building" off Fulton Street, then the largest fish market in America, sold live lobsters in 1880 for six cents a pound. Because of its huge volume of trade, the price set on lobster by the market was the single largest factor in setting the rate per pound across the East Coast. Even today, although not as significant in price setting, the market buys and sells nearly a quarter of the total Maine lobster catch each year, moving a total of a billion pounds of all types of seafood annually.[9]

The second major impact on the wedding of the image of the lobster to that of Maine was the fact that the wealthy new national elite of the country, rising from the ashes of the Civil War on wings of monopoly capitalism, "discovered" the relatively isolated and private coast of the state and began buying up land for summer "cottages" in places such as Bar Harbor, Boothbay, Kennebunkport, and

Camden.[10] These wealthy summer people, or "rusticators," formed a distinct social group, visiting among themselves and associating with local residents mostly when in need of goods, tradespeople, or servants for their lavish summer homes. These rich summer residents, who already had fallen in love with the Maine land- and seascape, began to look for ways to set themselves apart from others in their winter worlds of Boston, New York, and Philadelphia. They brought home humorous stories of the locals and their lives,[11] imitated their accents at cocktail parties, and spoke lovingly of Maine lobster, purchased from a local fisherman and eaten freshly boiled and straight out of the shell—an experience available only to those who could afford to summer in Maine. When the rusticators discovered Maine, they appropriated the lobster along with Maine real estate as a status symbol and badge of uniqueness within their social class.[12]

Gradually, then, from the turn of the century, the significance of the lobster as a part of the regional culture of Maine was culturally negotiated and defined. But this definition was crafted more by the literate summer visitors, who had adopted the state and saw in the lobster a symbol of uniqueness, than it was by the local residents, who saw lobsters traditionally as a low-status food item, but one that was now, due to outside demand, becoming both more scarce (due to heavy fishing) and higher priced.[13] To the locals, a common symbol of their hand-to-mouth everyday existence had been taken over by outsiders and, like their land, priced beyond their means to pay. In addition, their culture was being redefined for them by these outsiders, who insisted on the lobster as a symbol of the state and its residents—an image that was firmly established by the 1930s.

For example, poet Leo Connellan called Maine "clear blue lobster country" and in 1931 entitled his first book of poetry *Death in Lobsterland*.[14] In composing his famous portraits of Maine life and people in his 1932 book *Assignment Down East*, Henry Buxton referred to small seacoast villages as "lobster hamlets."[15] By the mid-1940s, even the educated and cosmopolitan Maine poet-in-residence at Bowdoin College, Robert P. T. Coffin, had come to help redefine the lobster as part of Maine culture: "He travels fastest ahead who keeps his eyes on the past. For this thorny Yankee of the crab family goes away from you and other danger tail-end first. . . . As my best New England uncles used to do, he protects his brain by advancing with his rear into the unknown. He gazes still on tradition and authority, and goes forward backward, as best Yankees do. . . . He is the archest of arch-conservatives, the Republican of the deep. He is a Yankee, all right."[16]

Maine Residents and the Lobster

Maine has a history of being, economically, the weak sister among New England states. Even today, for many year-round residents, living takes on almost a hand-to-mouth character. On the coast, where the tourist pressure of the summer months creates a large number of temporary jobs in the service industry, locals scramble to hold two or three jobs for this short, intense period—some working up to twenty hours a day for low wages so they can "build a kitty" to hold them through the winter, when many of them may hold no job at all.[17] For those who do not live on the coast, things are generally even leaner. With the exception of some tourist industry along a few accessible lakes in western Maine and the fall hunting trade, these tourist- and leisure-oriented jobs are not available inland.

As a result, Department of Commerce figures published in 1990 show 13 percent of the state's population to be living below the poverty line. This is the highest figure in New England, and it is higher than the national average of 12.4 percent.[18] At 6.6 percent, Maine also has the highest percentage in New England of persons receiving food stamps. When one examines per capita income, a similar picture emerges. In 1988, Maine ranked twenty-sixth in the nation with a figure of $12,955. Only Vermont (twenty-seventh at $12,941) fared worse among New England states. U.S. Census figures on median housing values follow the same pattern—at less than $38,000, they are nearly $12,000 lower than the national average. And even these figures are misleading, as the urban area of Portland and the southern county of York, where a large number of the newly arrived urban professionals have located, tend to inflate them. For most of Maine, with a population classed by the U.S. Census as still

52.5 percent rural (compared with the national average of 23.4 percent) and with the highest number of citizens below the poverty line of any New England state, income and housing figures are lower still.[19]

Growing up poor along the Maine coast, as the contemporary regional writer Sanford Phippen put it, meant "eating a lot of clams we dug ourselves, and in winter a lot of deer meat. Being poor was getting a box of a summer boy's used clothes to wear to school. . . . Our house was filled with cast off furniture. My mother, who did domestic work for the rich, took in laundries, sewed, and did any other odd job she could find. . . . This Maine is frustrating; it is hard on people. It is a life of poverty, solitude, struggle, lowered aspirations, living on the edge."[20] Although there may be an element of romantic literary exaggeration to Phippen's account, there is a lot of truth to it as well. It is a life in which lobsters, with their inflated prices, are many times out of the economic reach of the people who catch and handle them. In the high season, a lobsterman has to think twice, and seriously, about dipping into his catch to put this high-priced food on his own table.

When one moves inland, away from the less economically depressed coast, one leaves the lobster—even as a relatively unattainable symbol—behind. A century and a half ago, when it was an affordable resource, technology had not been developed that would allow efficient storage and transportation of the lobster inland. By the time the lobster became redefined as a special food, and one that could be commercially transported, its price had risen so astronomically that inland Maine people, in general, could not begin to think seriously of purchasing it as a foodstuff. Today, it is seen as a symbol of the economically more affluent coast. And although most inland Mainers recognize that the year-round residents of the coast can scarcely afford to eat lobster regularly, they also are aware that, in a relative sense, the coastal economy is a stronger one than their own, and there is some feeling of resentment about that—a resentment that is, at times, focussed on the lobster if it is being used as a symbol of Maine, the state. As one inland Mainer from Aroostook County remarked in an interview: "If them tourists want to come up from Boston and pay them prices, then, by Christ, let 'em. Damn fools. Lobsters, hell, they're big cockroaches, that's what they are. You ain't gonna catch me eatin' one, even if I could afford the damn thing."[21]

The Lobster License Plate War

For this large proportion of the year-round residential population, the lobster may well serve as a constant and telling symbolic reminder of how economically disadvantaged they are in relation to the summer people and the increasingly middle-class tourist trade of the coastal areas.[22] Thus, resentment can surface whenever the lobster is utilized, officially, to serve as an icon of all the state's people. This is exactly what occurred in the mid-1980s, when the state legislature adopted a new design for the Maine license plate—one featuring a red lobster against a white background.

This design—and the explicit incorporation of the lobster as a state symbol—was inspired by a joint project undertaken by fourth grade students in the "gifted programs" of Kennebunk and Saco, relatively affluent towns on the southern Maine coast, which, along with next-door Kennebunkport, are traditional strongholds of the summer wealthy. Many of the more well-to-do citizens of Kennebunk and Saco are recent arrivals to Maine. They are likely to be white-collar professionals, trained in an urban setting such as Boston, who are looking for a quieter and simpler life. From these communities they can easily commute to Portland, the largest urban area in Maine (thirty minutes away), or, in the other direction, the Boston area (a bit over an hour away). These people, the new Maine professionals, have been brought up to see the lobster as a symbol of Maine and the coast. In addition, persons of this socioeconomic class *can* afford to eat lobster, and do. In their eyes, there could be no more appropriate symbol of the state.

For the long-time and less affluent residents, however, when the lobster became a license plate image, it took on an even more negative symbolic meaning than it had possessed before. The idea was seen to have originated among a class of persons who have long been suspicious to "native" Mainers. They have not been in the state long enough to be thought of as residents, nor do they live under the same

Figure 1. *The Maine license plate*. Legislative approval of the lobster design elicited broad opposition from state residents, and many of them protested by whiting out the symbol. One humorist chided the legislature for making Maine "the only state with a dead creature on the license plate." Photo by George Lewis.

socioeconomic conditions as the long-term residents. In addition, they are urban professionals in a traditionally rural state.

As if that weren't enough, this legislative decision, made by the central authority of a state whose residents have traditionally distrusted and resisted the power of central authority, had an immediate impact on everyone in the state who owns a vehicle. New license plates, with red lobsters imprinted on them, had to be personally affixed to all vehicles for which they were issued. Given the fact that, to many, one's automobile is a valued extension of one's self and self image, this meant the state was, in effect, forcing residents to display for all to see a symbol for which they may have had highly negative feelings.

Vocal opposition to the new plates has appeared all across Maine. Some feel the choice of the lobster as state symbol is regionally chauvinistic—that the economically better off (and more visible) coast is being celebrated at the inland's expense. Others feel there are more appropriate symbols—the potato, the pine tree, the blueberry, the chickadee, or even the mosquito. Animal protectionists object to the color of the lobster. Red means dead, they charge. If it must be a lobster, at least color it a proper, pre-cooked green. As Maine humorist Robert Skoglund has recently remarked, "We are the only state with a dead creature on the license plate. Think about it."[23]

After a legislative proposal that would give people the right to retain their old plates if they preferred was defeated, some residents, exercising their own cultural resources for resisting control, began whiting out the lobsters with paint as a protest. The state, citing a probable constitutional question involved in prosecuting such actions, has advised district attorneys it would not stand behind any decision to bring charges in instances where only the lobster is painted out and not the identifying numerals and letters of the registration plate itself.[24] Thus painting out the lobster in Maine has become a politically and legally acceptable response to the new plates—an effective cultural rejection of a manufactured identity being imposed "top down" by the state.

Although the "lobster license plate war" has been made light of by the media, there are serious class issues at stake. Proponents and opponents seem to divide along socioeconomic class lines, where one resides (coast or inland), how long one has been a resident, and whether one is urban or rural in orientation and lifestyle. In general, if one is of middle to upper socioeconomic class, a more recent arrival to Maine, urban oriented, and a coastal resident, one is most apt to see the lobster license plates as appropriate and to actually be pleased to have them on one's vehicle. On the other hand, if one is of lower socioeconomic class, a long-time resident, rural, and *especially* if one does not reside on the coast, one is most likely to be opposed to the new plates.[25]

Jim Babb, a former lobsterman from the coastal town of Searsport, concedes that "lobsters have nothing to do with inland Maine. They represent only a strip of land that's ten miles wide that stretches from New Hampshire to the Canadian border. The upcountry people feel they're completely ignored. . . . They sure as hell don't catch a hell of a lot of lobster in the Androscoggin River."[26] State Representative Mary H. MacBride, who represents Maine's largest and most northern county, Aroostook, has said that "people up in this area, a long way from the coast, feel the lobster only represents the coastal areas, and not only that, it is an advertisement for the coastal area."[27] Richard Warner, former mayor of Rockland, speaking to the economic split in lobster plate preferences, has said that "it's unfair to impose that kind of symbol on people who are having a tough go of it. It's bad enough without carrying an ad for lobsters on rusted-out cars."[28] Dorcas Gilpatrick, who was stopped by a state trooper in 1988 for whiting out the lobster on her plates, says, "Life is not that easy for most Mainers. They work hard and they don't get to go out in the sun. . . . I felt the lobster was a public relations gimmick that demeaned Maine people."[29] Gilpatrick, associate director of the Maine Civil Liberties Union, grew up in Bridgton, a rural inland town in southwestern Maine.

This breakdown of attitudes about the license plates is similar to feelings about the lobster in general. As I have pointed out, longtime residents of Maine who are more likely to be of a lower socioeconomic level, view the lobster with some degree of resentment. According to a joke common among them, "the politicians down to Augusta voted for the lobster as the state bird," underscoring both the inappropriateness of the choice and the foolishness of the choosers. The newer residents of the state, on the other hand, for the most part urban-oriented professionals, are affluent enough to afford to eat lobster and, usually prior to moving to Maine, have "bought" the image of the lobster as representative of the state. To them it indicates both a unique and local taste *and* one that, by price and reputation, has been validated by the cosmopolitan upper class of the country. Thus it fits their needs perfectly—validating their status level and pointing out the individuality of their residential choice at the same time. For these people, the media-enriched image of the lobster as identifier is both useful and appropriate.

Older Maine residents of these higher socioeconomic class levels, although few in number, share to some extent the cosmopolitan orientation of the newcomers, as they do also the economic concerns of the larger body of local residents. Being able to afford to eat lobsters themselves on special occasions, and being aware of the special status lobsters have incurred in the eyes of affluent outsiders, these people can enjoy the sense of identity the lobster gives, yet at the same time not take it as seriously as either the less economically well off, long-term residents or the newer professionals. As a local lawyer remarked, "We'll go out for lobster for special family occasions, like birthdays. And certainly order them for out-of-state visitors and business contacts. It's like I'd expect a good steak when I visit Kansas City, or Cajun food down in New Orleans. It's that kind of symbol of recognition of the area. But, other than the tourist trade, lobsters don't mean much to an awful lot of people in Maine. Sure, they know what they are, but they can't afford them. That's about it."[30]

Visitors to Maine

In the literature concerning the social impacts of tourism, there has been an effort to identify different types of visitors to vacation areas. Many of these studies focus on the changes in tourists and tourism as an area is first discovered, later visited, and still later institutionalized with the advent and spread of a tourist industry.[31] Another area of examination has been that of the socioeconomic class of the tourist. How do tourists from different class levels affect the type, quality, and impact of tourism on the visited region?[32] With respect to tourism in Maine, sociologist Peter Rose has analyzed the social structure of the summer trade, identifying groups ranging from the top "colonists" (the gentry who put the place on the social map and who expect the natives to do their bidding) to "coneheads" (who hop out of their cars only to purchase ice cream cones) and bus tourists near the bottom of the prestige ladder.[33]

From this perspective, three major—and quite different—types of summer visitors can be identified in Maine. As with the breakdown of local residents, each of these groups has its own relationship with the lobster as symbol of the state, each engaging in its own form of negotiations with *homarus americanus* to create and reinforce distinct cultural and social identities.

Those who have been visiting Maine longest, the upper socioeconomic *summer residents*, were the ones to originally develop the idea of the lobster as symbolic of Maine. The *middle-class tourist*, who comes to Maine to stay for a week or two in the summer or who perhaps visits on a prepackaged tour, represents a second form of visitor. Finally, there is the "*daytripper*," the lower socioeconomic class visitor, who comes in by car, usually for the day only—or possibly for an overnight stay on a weekend.

At the same time that the summer residents were infusing the lobster with a special, romantic significance, the more literary-prone among them were also romanticizing the year-round residents as hardy, noble, simple, rustic characters. This image was fleshed out in short stories, poems, and novels written by the "rusticators," which often focussed on the Maine lobsterman, who braved the storms of the great Atlantic to bring the lobster to market.[34] But although the image has persisted in popular literature to the present day, since the 1930s Maine has been developing as a middle-class tourist destination. No longer is the state an exclusive summer haven as it was at the turn of the century. In 1985, for example, nearly six and one half million tourists visited Maine,[35] a fact that is highly upsetting to the older summer residents. Additionally, the romance of the lobster, initially developed by these summer residents, has been successfully marketed as a pop culture image to the middle-class tourist. It, too, is no longer something special and unique to the summer resident.

So, although lobster is still eaten in the privacy of the large summer homes and in the dining rooms of the few surviving exclusive summer hotels, the lobster has lost most of its potency as a symbol of identification for these people. For many, it is now no more than an expensive regional food that, at most, evokes memories of a past when the coast was rugged, isolated, and unspoiled by the crass weight of middle-class tourism.[36]

Of T-Shirts and Tourists: Mass-Marketing the Lobster Image

With over six million tourists visiting the state annually and spending nearly 1.5 billion dollars on their visits,[37] tourism is a huge industry. For the middle-class tourist, the lobster is not only the appropriate symbol of Maine food; it is also desired in many other forms in the souvenir market. Visitors to the state arrive eagerly looking for the quaint fishing communities along the coast that they

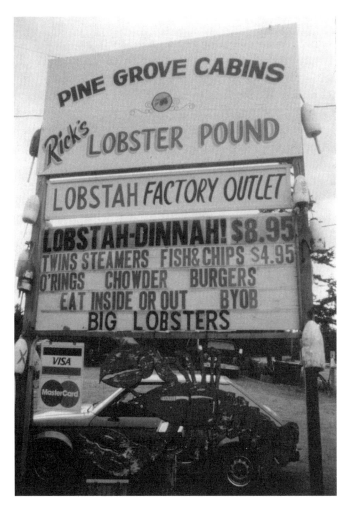

Figure 2. *"Lobstah Dinnah!"* Restaurants offering bargain rate lobster dinners are ubiquitous along Maine's fabled coast. They are a principal attraction for the heavy tourist trade. Photo by George Lewis.

remember from the full-color pictures in their down east calendars. They expect stylized lobster boats, wooden traps stacked high on rustic wharves, lobster dinners consumed in sight of the famous rocky coast. What they are more apt to get, especially in the high summer season, is a bumper-to-bumper drive up US 1, past fast food stands, souvenir shops, and factory outlet stores. The lobster is there all right, adorning roadside billboards and signs that advertise everything from shore dinners to down east craft fairs. But it is a different association and feeling than what was hoped for when the visitor rumbled over the bridge from Portsmouth, New Hampshire.

Tourists eat lobsters at summer establishments that advertise competitively on large outdoor signs, trying to lure tourists with the lowest price possible for a lobster. Sometimes, in two- or even three-lobster "specials," the price per lobster is set still lower (although one is warned that these specials "must be ordered and eaten by only one person," that is, not shared among several at the table to save money). Usually the lobsters served in these establishments are the smallest that legally can be caught and kept (three-quarters to one pound) and are not nearly the bargain the advertised price per lobster suggests. Still, if one wishes to "do Maine right," these are the least expensive places to eat the obligatory lobster dinner.

Trenton, Maine, for example, bills itself as the "cooked lobster capital of the world." This small community has five lobster "pounds" that, in the three-month summer season, sell an average of 32,725 lobster dinners each, according to the local paper.[38] Figured at 1.5 pounds per lobster, this totals nearly twenty-five tons of lobster consumed each summer in this one Maine town. (The restaurants also figure they use two and one-half tons of butter and over three tons of coleslaw per season.) Selling lobsters to tourists in Maine is clearly big business.

Another part of "lobster lore" that seems to have arisen with the middle-class tourist is the complex code of instructions for shelling the creature and eating it properly. Waiters will explain and, if necessary, help.[39] Placemats are printed with step-by-step instructions. Plastic bibs are provided to protect the tourist's clothes and to identify him or her to other diners as both financially solvent enough to afford lobster and enough of a novice to allow the "native" Maine

Figure 3. *Lobster placemat.* Tourists who partake of the obligatory lobster dinner are invited to follow a complex code of instructions. As the "eight easy steps" on this placemat suggest, the ritual has been manufactured by and for commercial interests. Photo by George Lewis.

waiter (in reality, most often an out-of-state college student) to tuck the bib—a clear symbol of infancy—under his or her chin. Thus the eating of one's first lobster serves as a commerce-driven initiation ritual, or rite of passage, for the tourist into a manufactured "culture of Maine."

These lobster-eating rituals reach their zenith each year at the three-day Maine Lobster Festival, held in Rockport on the first weekend in August. Begun in 1947, the festival now attracts close to twenty-five thousand people a year to this blue-collar, coastal community. The festival features an "eating tent" with picnic tables, benches, and the "world's largest lobster cooker," which turns out over four thousand steamed lobsters during the three-day celebration. There are children's lobster eating contests, lobster crate races, a parade featuring King Neptune, and the annual crowning of the

Maine Sea Goddess. Contestants, in order to win the title, must successfully answer a series of "lobster questions"—questions such as
"What is the maximum size of a legal lobster in Maine?" or "What is
the difference between a hard shell and a soft shell lobster?" or
"What is the green stuff found inside a lobster?"

Also situated in Rockland, in the parking lot of the Trade Winds
Motor Inn, is a fifteen-foot-high, twenty-two-foot-long metal
sculpture of a lobster, constructed from old hot water tanks and 275-
gallon oil drums. Dan Daniels, the sculptor, was a boilermaker for
twenty-five years and claims he began the sculpture "by accident,"
not realizing how big it would become. "I started with a whole oil
barrel and set it up on a 55 gallon drum. . . . I should have figured the
size by them."[40]

Daniels's lobster sculpture is not the only such roadside attraction
along the Maine coast. The Captain's Mate in Trenton has a fifteen-
foot roadside lobster made of fiberglass and chicken wire out front,
which the owner, Marlene LaBrie, bills as the world's largest. Then
there are sculptures of fishermen in bright yellow oilcloths holding
lobsters aloft, bears holding lobsters in their mouths, lobster couples
lightly touching claws as they dance—all larger than life icons raised
by the tourist industry in praise of *homarus americanus.*

The lobster image has also been appropriated by the tourist
industry as central to the souvenir business. Lobster traps are sold as
coffee tables; lobsters are found on t-shirts, as gold, silver, and pewter
jewelry, as stuffed toys, as weather vanes, as Maine "handcrafts."
John Palmer, head of Down East Crafts (which sells about two thousand products), explains why the lobster is central to what they produce: "Lobster is one of the main things people think of when they
come to Maine, and so, in our market and in our product, we try to
give them enough lobsters to keep them happy. We have a network
of home workers that assemble products for us. We give them the
materials, and specifications, and show them how to assemble products. Therein lies the handcrafted aspect of a lot of our stuff. Where
we can't get products made in this country, we do import from over-
seas—Japan, Korea and Taiwan to a certain extent."[41] These souvenirs can range in expense from art forms, sculpture, and jewelry
focussed on the upper-middle class tourist to the cheaper t-shirts

Figure 4. *Lobster t-shirts*. The lobster as an emblem of Maine appears on literally hundreds of souvenir items. The president of Down East Crafts, readily responding to tourists' expectations, says, "We try to give them enough lobsters to keep them happy." Photo by George Lewis.

and mass produced "handcrafts" of Down East Crafts, a good deal of which is geared for impulse buying in the two- to four-dollar range—lobster plaques for the wall, miniature lobster traps, Christmas ornaments ("Lobster Claus"), salt and pepper shakers. Thus because of the expense of the authentic lobster for this socioeconomic class, its perishable nature as a food item, the difficulty of transporting it home for show, and its symbolic link to Maine as almost a part of the state itself, the image of the lobster has successfully been transferred to cheaper, nonperishable, easy to transport items.[42] The authentic and ceremonial ingesting of *homarus americanus* as a part of the Maine gestalt, then, can be replaced by the purchase of a souvenir.

Not only has the image of the lobster been transferred away from the authentic object, but this image itself has begun taking on significance of its own as a symbol of "Maine-ness." Last year's t-shirt, no longer available, becomes a mark of identity, of inclusion in the category of "frequenter of Maine," as opposed to "novice traveller." For many who cannot afford to purchase *homarus americanus* itself (or are too culturally timid to attempt to eat this strange creature), the image of the lobster offers a representation of reality that can be, in ways, more compelling than the reality itself. As Stuart Ewen, in his more general discussion of style and popular culture, has remarked, "Freed from the encumbrances of matter, the *look* of the visible world can now be easily, and inexpensively, reproduced. . . . Matter as a visible object is of no great use any longer, except as the mould on which form is shaped."[43]

The cheaper of these lobster souvenirs comprise the central component of the daytripper's experience. On the lowest level of the socioeconomic scale, these people drive to Maine for the day, or possibly the weekend, if they can afford a motel for over night. Given their budgets and culturally shaped food preferences, they are more apt to purchase a crab or fried clam roll than the more expensive and exotic lobster (or lobster roll) if they venture beyond the franchised fast food stands at all. For them the souvenir market has created "Claws," an inexpensive videotape of allegedly Maine humor and lobster images, the ubiquitous t-shirt, lobster lollipops, claw-shaped harmonicas, hats with stuffed, furry lobster claws hanging from them, "Lobster Lover on Board" bumper stickers, paintings of lobsters on velvet, and racks and racks of lobster post cards.

Many of the inexpensive lobster images purchased by the daytrippers poke fun at the more traditional commercial image of the lobster. If a real lobster is too expensive and exotic for these people to experience, and if it is a symbol *both* of Maine and of gracious, upper-class living and dining, then why not, in the good old American prole tradition, have some fun with the image? Thus there are canned "lobster farts" for sale, as well as soft plastic lobster "noses" to be worn as gag masks. In such ways, as Fiske has noted in his discussion of the "producerly behavior" of consumers,[44] meaning can be twisted back, even on itself, in acts of creative exchange between objects functioning as "building blocks of reality. They are sensitive indicators of who we are, where we come from, where we intend to go."[45] This is clearly evident in images of the lobster (and the lobsterman) that have been developed over the years jointly by both insiders and outsiders.

For example, members of national media teams, sent to Maine to cover then President George Bush at his home in Kennebunkport, congregated at Noonan's—a lobster restaurant in nearby Cape Porpoise, whose weathered, unpainted board siding is decorated with colorful lobster buoys and artfully hung fishing nets. Sitting at long tables with plastic lobster bibs securely tied around their necks, these members of the nation's media cracked lobster claws, dripped butter from their chins, and joked with the waiters and waitresses—then went on camera, or put pen to paper, to pronounce this place "authentic—the real Maine." This was much to the delight of the locals, several of whom were interviewed in such media pieces and all of whom knew Noonan's as a stage built to part tourists from their dollars. Yet the image of Noonan's, contributed to by both locals and outsiders, was reinforced across the country by these "human interest" bits.[46]

For those who can afford it, not only lobsters, but the sights and experiences of lobstering in Maine are now also being made available. The *New York Times* in its travel section in the summer of 1990 noted that "several lobstermen in Maine will take along passengers while checking their traps." The *Times* recommended "Lobsta Boat

Rides" of Bass Harbor, which charged $10 a person. So, in the 1990s, not only can the tourist experience lobster, he or she can actually rent his or her own local lobsterman—and videotape the adventure for the folks back home.

As with most of the inventions of tourism, lobster boat rides are, in the main, inauthentic. Most of the "lobstermen" who take people out do not fish commercially themselves. In addition, several artfully stock their traps with lobsters each morning to assure that, later in the day, they will have contented customers.[47] David Hyde, one of the very few real Maine lobstermen who takes tourists on his boat—and who does not stock his traps—does it because he needs the income. Still, he says of what he does, "It's no different than bein' a goddamn whore."[48] Once again, the insider and the outsider have, through a process of cultural negotiation, mutually reinforced in the flesh and on videotape an image that can be traced back through this century to the stories and anecdotes of the summer rusticators.

Finally, the lobster license plate war continues in Maine. Although it is technically legal to white out the lobster, several garages along the south coast, where the new professionals are most heavily located, have begun rejecting vehicles for official state of Maine safety inspections if their plates have been altered in this way. The Maine State Police, contacted by inspectors as to the legality of the altered plates, have not been clear in their response, and so the refusals have stood.[49] Inland, inspections of such vehicles are routine, as in Bridgton, where Dorcas Gilpatrick of the Maine Civil Liberties Union has recently offered a tongue-in-cheek symbolic reconciliation of the conflict. "If we have to have something on our license plates, the only thing that'd work is a black fly. It's everywhere. It gets everybody, inland and on the coast, tourist and native, rich and poor. It's ubiquitous."[50] As such, the black fly might avoid the differential and highly charged meanings that the lobster has acquired to those who live in the state of Maine.

As Regina Bendix has pointed out in her discussion of the invention of tradition,[51] myths, icons, and traditions are defined by those involved with them in the present and in a way that makes cultural sense for their own social grouping. Icons and cultural events are, in a word, judged by whether they help symbolically to accomplish what it was intended that they accomplish. Nowhere is this more evident than with the Maine lobster, whose image has been used to reinforce social class, to define the cultural insider and outsider, and to sell status and self-esteem in the mass marketplace. The lobster has been variously praised and damned, copied and rejected, romanticized and ridiculed. It has served as fish bait, fertilizer, and gourmet food. It has appeared in literary short stories, on license plates, and on t-shirts. It has been envied and loved, steamed and boiled. But like all true cultural icons, *homarus americanus* has never been ignored.

Notes

1. In fact, Canadian lobstermen outnumber Americans by more than two to one. They provide at least half the lobster that is sold in the United States, whether or not it is sold under the name of "Maine" lobster. See Joy Dueland, *The Book of the Lobster* (Somersworth: New Hampshire Publishing, 1973), 22; and Marcia Spencer, *Lobsters Inside and Out* (Orono: University of Maine Press, 1987).

2. In both these cases, Maine has its own legitimate claim to the foodstuff. There are more maple trees tapped in Maine than in Vermont and, historically, Maine's Aroostook County was known as the potato producing capital of the country; it still accounts for a small share of the market.

3. Howard Marshall, "Meat Presentation on the Farm in Missouri's 'Little Dixie,'" *Journal of American Folklore* 92 (1979): 400.

4. Edward Ives, "Maine Folklore and the Folklore of Maine," *Maine Historical Society Quarterly* 23, no. 3 (Winter 1984): 115.

5. Ibid.

6. There is a story told on Beals Island that once, after a terrific hurricane, when people walked down to the back side of the island, they found hundreds of lobsters hanging in the fir trees—tossed there by the wind and high surf. This tale, although "tall," may not be as tall as some might think!

7. Mike Brown, *The Maine Lobster Book* (Camden: International Marine Publishing, 1986). Rollin Kelly, of Beals Island, says that when he was "a kid, my father'd take the whole family on picnics and he'd take a little dip net and go around the rocks and dip up lobsters

enough for dinner. . . . He told us there were so many lobsters they used to use them for fertilizer in the fields." Susan White, ed., *A Lobster in Every Pot* (Camden, Maine: Yankee, 1990), 56.

8. Carol Bryant et al., *The Cultural Feast* (New York: West Publishing, 1985), 58–59. In some ways, this shift in consumption patterns, based as it was in shifts in the transportation technologies, recalls the post–Civil War adoption of prairie-raised beef as "traditional" American fare. See Eric Ross, *Beyond The Myths of Culture* (New York: Academic Press, 1980).

9. Bruce Ballenger, *The Lobster Almanac* (Chester, Conn.: Globe Pequot Press, 1988), 43.

10. George Lewis, "Mass Society and the Resort Town: A Case Study of Bar Harbor, Maine" (master's thesis, University of Oregon, 1968), 13–28; George Street, *Mount Desert: A History* (Boston: Houghton Mifflin, 1905); Hyatt Verrill, *Along New England Shores* (New York: Putnam's Sons, 1936), 220–98; Richard J. Hale, *Story of Bar Harbor* (New York: Ives Washburn, 1949), 52–60.

11. An example of this sort of story (which usually pitted the local against the rusticator) is of the lobsterman out off lower Penobscot Bay in treacherous shoal water filled with kelp that obscured any view under water. The lobsterman was patiently pulling his traps when a rusticator in a fancy sailboat approached and, worried about the water depth, asked the lobsterman, "How much water do we have here?" The lobsterman glanced over at the rusticator, spat tobacco in the water, and said, "Plenty. All you got to do is stay in it." White, *A Lobster in Every Pot*, 68.

12. See Edward Ives, "Maine Folklore and the Folklore of Maine," for an account of this phenomenon, especially with respect to the development of the down east "accent," the image of the Maine rustic, and "Maine" humor by the wealthy summer people of that time. See also Richard J. Hale, *Story of Bar Harbor* for how Bar Harbor's summer colony interacted with the natives. How the Maine summer folk set themselves off from others of their socioeconomic class is reflected in Louis Auchincloss's story "Greg's Peg," in which the summer colony in Bar Harbor is visited by "outside" yachtspeople: "I noticed several young men who were not in evening dress and others whose evening clothes had obviously been borrowed, strong, ruddy, husky young men. It was the cruise season, and the comfortable, easy atmosphere of overdressed but companionable 'Anchor Harbor' was stiffened by an infiltration of moneyed athleticism and arrogance from the distant

smartness of Long Island." Reprinted in *The Best Maine Stories* (Augusta, Maine: Lance Tapley, 1986), 125–26.

13. At the turn of the century, the total U.S. lobster catch—most of it from Maine—totalled 30 million pounds per year. Ballenger, *The Lobster Almanac*, 44.

14. "Clear Blue Lobster Country" is reprinted in *Maine Speaks* (Brunswick, Maine: Maine Writers and Publishers Alliance, 1989), 161.

15. Henry Buxton, *Assignment Down East* (Brattleboro, Vt.: Stephen Daye Press, 1938).

16. Robert P. Tristram Coffin, *Mainstays of Maine* (New York: Macmillan, 1944), 1–2.

17. Personal observation and interviews along the Maine coast, 1955 to 1990. In addition, see the more formal data contained in *Maine Tourism Study,1884–85*, vol. 2 (Augusta, Maine: State Development Office).

18. Poverty, income, and housing value data are drawn from the Bureau of the Census on-file data disk, Atlanta, Ga., August 26, 1988, as well as from information contained in the 1990 Statistical Abstract of the United States (Washington, D.C.: U.S. Dept. of Commerce).

19. That the growing affluence of the new urban professionals of the Portland/York County area has been a large factor in raising the per capita income level of the state can be seen by the national ranking of Maine in this category from thirty-ninth in 1980 to thirty-second in 1988. This period coincides with the move of young professionals to the southern urban areas of the state.

20. Sanford Phippen, "The People of Winter," in *The Best Maine Stories*, ed. Sanford Phippen (Augusta, Maine: Lance Tapley, 1986), 311–12.

21. Author interview with George Hoag, South Portland, Maine, July 1988.

22. Although the people of Maine are disadvantaged economically in comparison to the summer residents and tourists, this does not at all imply any feelings of inferiority or lack of self-esteem on their part. Indeed, most "Mainiacs" would not swap places with urban tourists for all the lobsters in the Atlantic. Although life in Maine is, by comparison, sparse and spare, most natives like it that way and see it as morally and emotionally a better life than that to be found in the city. As Draper Liscomb, a long-time resident of Town Hill, Maine, said about moving back to the state after a time spent in Connecticut, where he was economically forced to go look for work: "I didn't want

to raise my kids down in that god damn mess, you know. Yeah, that was one of the big reasons I came back home. . . . I really like to go outdoors and piss holes in the snow. . . . You know, all those doctors and lawyers work their hearts out, so they can come up here and live like I do." Interview conducted by Bethany Aronow, summer 1981, SALT Cultural Studies Archives, Portland, Maine.

23. Robert Skogland, on "Stories from the Kitchen," Maine Public TV, 1990.

24. *Bangor Daily News*, November 2, 1988, p. 31.

25. Joining with these people in opposition, but for different reasons, are the small percentage of young, educated, liberal leaning activists who view a cooked lobster on the registration plate as a symbol of capitalist exploitation of natural resources.

26. Quoted in Christopher Cox, "License to Kill," *Boston Sunday Herald*, October 21, 1990, p. 13.

27. Ibid.

28. Ibid.

29. Ibid.

30. Author interview with Merle Carroll, Brewer, Maine, October 1988.

31. See Edward Cohen, "Toward a Sociology of International Tourism," *Social Research* 39 (1972): 164–82; and David Nash, "Tourism as a Form of Imperialism" (paper delivered at the American Anthropological Association annual meeting, 1974).

32. See David Greenwood, "Tourism as an Agent of Change," *Ethnology* 9 (1970): 80–90; and Dean MacCannell, *The Tourist: A New Theory of the Leisure Class* (New York: Schocken, 1976).

33. Peter Rose, "Colonists and Coneheads," *Salt: Journal of New England Studies* 30, no. 2 (1987): 6.

34. See the works of Sara Orne Jewett and Elisabeth Ogilvie as examples. See also Rachel Field, *Time out of Mind* (New York: Macmillan, 1935) and Mary Ellen Chase, *A Goodly Heritage* (New York: Henry Holt, 1932).

35. *Maine Tourism Study, 1984–85*, vol. 1 (Augusta, Maine: State Development Office).

36. Discussions with guests at the exclusive Colony Hotel, Kennebunkport, Maine, July 1988 and June 1989.

37. *Maine Tourism Study.*

38. *Ellsworth American: Out and About*, July 1989, p. 11.

39. For more on restaurant ritual, see Joanne Finkelstein, *Dining Out* (New York: New York University Press, 1989).

40. Interview by Lou Brown, Rockland, Maine, July 1988, SALT Cultural Studies Archives, Portland, Maine.

41. Interview by Lou Brown, Trenton, Maine, July 1988, SALT Cultural Studies Archives, Portland, Maine.

42. For the upper-middle class tourist, lobsters are available—live and boxed to travel—in the major Maine (and Boston) airports. Thus, for a fairly steep price, the air traveller who takes less than twenty-four hours to reach his or her destination can take lobsters home—though they must be cooked and consumed immediately and thus are not durable as souvenirs nor as proof of a Maine experience.

43. Stuart Ewen, *All Consuming Images* (New York: Basic Books, 1988), 25.

44. John Fiske, *Understanding Popular Culture* (Boston: Unwin Hyman, 1989).

45. Marshall Fishwick, "Icons of America," in *Icons of America*, ed. R. Browne and M. Fishwick (Bowling Green, Ohio: Popular Press, 1978), 8.

46. Some of the research on which this essay is based was, when first collected, picked up by the *Washington Post*. I was interviewed by Don Oldenberg and the material, with Oldenberg's interpretation, was published in an article entitled "Lobster Mania" on May 30, 1990. This article (and material drawn from it) also appeared in newspapers as far afield as the *Miami Herald*, the *San Francisco Chronicle*, and the *International Herald Tribune*.

47. Brett Jenks, "Selling the Folk," *Salt: Journal of New England Culture* 39 (1990): 48.

48. Ibid.

49. Martha Engler, "Folks Unable to Get Cars Inspected," *Kennebec Journal* 39 (1991): 1, 10.

50. Christopher Cox, "License to Kill," 11.

51. Regina Bendix, "Tourism and Cultural Displays: Inventing Traditions for Whom?" *Journal of American Folklore* 162 (1989): 131–46.

CHAPTER 12

How Texans Remember the Alamo

Sylvia Ann Grider

"When the fact becomes legend, print the legend."
—A newspaper editor in *The Man Who Shot Liberty Valance*

In part because of the way Texas history has been taught in the public schools, the record of Texas's legendary past is more familiar to many Texans than the actual historical record.[1] For nearly a century, much to the despair of professional historians, Texas children have been fed a steady diet of legend, celebrating especially the heroic exploits of the Anglo-Americans who fought and won a revolution against Mexico.[2] This canonical schoolbook history— really a kind of invented tradition—has maintained an ethno-historical or folk version of what can aptly be called the Texas Mystique.[3]

The Alamo and the Texas Mystique

The decade of the Texas Republic (1836–1845) is always presented as the golden age of the Texas Mystique, with the Battle of the Alamo its memorable centerpiece. According to oral tradition, in March of 1836, 180 Texans, surrounded by thousands of Mexican troops, made a conscious decision to remain in the San Antonio fortress and willingly fought to their deaths, to the last man. A pantheon of special heroes emerged from this battle: Colonel William B. Travis, the leader of the Texans, who drew a line in the sand and asked those willing to die for freedom to step over it and join him;[4] Davy Crockett, already famous as congressman and backwoodsman, who defended the ramparts with his trusted Kentucky long rifle, Old Betsy;[5] and Jim Bowie, who was bayonetted on his sickbed after killing scores of attacking Mexicans with his famous "Arkansas toothpick."[6] The legend conveniently omits any mention of the Tejanos, or Texas-Mexicans, who sided with the Anglos and died fighting with instead of against them.

The earliest textbook glorification of this event is from Anna Pennybacker's 1888 *New History for Texas Schools*. Throughout the day of March 4, she writes, the Mexicans "kept up a terrible cannonade."

> Just before sunset, this suddenly ceased, and Santa Anna ordered his men to withdraw some distance from the Alamo. The weary Texans, who, for ten days and nights, had toiled like giants, sank down to snatch a few moments' rest. Travis seemed to know that this was the lull before the last fury of storm that was to destroy them all; he ordered his men to parade in single file. Then followed one of the grandest scenes history records. In a voice trembling with emotion, Travis told his men that death was inevitable and showed that he had detained them thus long, hoping for reinforcements.[7]

In a footnote, Pennybacker quotes Travis's alleged speech to his men, with the caveat, "Some unknown author has written the following imaginary speech of Travis." That imaginary but much-quoted speech preceded Travis's next legendary action. "When Travis had finished, the silence of the grave reigned over all. Drawing his sword, he drew a line in front of his men, and cried, 'Those who wish to die like heroes and patriots, come over to me.' There was no hesitation. In a few minutes, every soldier, save one, had crossed."[8] Again, Pennybacker offers a footnote: "The student may wonder, if none escaped from the Alamo, how we know the above to be true. The story runs, that this one man, Rose by name, who refused to step over the line, did make his escape that night. He reported the events. . . .

While some historians doubt the truth of the story, we deem it to the interest of the student to let him investigate the matter for himself."[9]

This alleged drawing of the line in the dust by Travis, whether it really happened or not, soon became the most famous episode of the Battle of the Alamo. First published by William P. Zuber in the *Texas Almanac* of 1873 and later reprinted in the *Quarterly of the Texas State Historical Association*, the story has been the subject of spirited controversy ever since.[10] So many visitors to the Alamo monument have asked about this line that the Daughters of the Republic of Texas, the official custodians of the Alamo, have embedded a brass strip in the sidewalk just in front of the main entrance. Tourists by the thousands have had their photographs taken standing on this strip and have gone away believing that it really does mark the fortress commander's "line in the sand."

The Line and the Revisionists

While historians grow weary of pointing out that the famous episode probably did not take place, movies, schoolbooks, and oral tradition continue to keep the story alive.[11] Even though Zuber himself admitted that he had embellished the story, the image of Travis drawing the line in the dust with his sword has taken on a life of its own, and it seems largely impervious to the attacks of revisionist historians. The emotional reason why is expressed broadly in the most often quoted defense of the line legend, that of J. Frank Dobie, himself something of a legend to many Texans:

> It is a line that nor all the piety nor wit of research will ever blot out. It is a Grand Canyon cut into the bedrock of human emotions and heroical impulses. It may be expurgated from histories, but it can no more be expunged from popular imagination than the damned spots on Lady Macbeth's hands. Teachers of children dramatize it in school rooms; orators on holidays silver and gild it; the tellers of historical anecdotes—and there are many of them in Texas—sitting around hotel lobbies speculate on it and say, "Well, we'll believe it whether it's true or not."[12]

Dobie's comment recalls not only the newspaper editor's quip in John Ford's *Liberty Valance*, but also Warren G. Harding's nearly as famous observation about an earlier American hero: "I love the story of Paul Revere, whether he rode or not."[13] In these cases, as in the story of the Alamo, it is the emotional utility of the legend that sustains it, no matter how brazenly or how frequently the "facts" may belie it. As folklorist William Wilson has put it, "What actually happened is often less important than what we think happened. We are motivated not by actual fact but by what we believe to be fact. And if we believe something to be true, that belief will have consequences in our lives and in the lives of others."[14] Cultural theorist David Lowenthal expresses a similar sentiment: "The more strenuously we build a desired past, the more we convince ourselves that things really were that way; what ought to have happened becomes what did happen. If we profess only to rectify our predecessors' prejudices and errors and to restore pre-existing conditions, we fail to see that today's past is as much a thing of today as it is that of the past; to bolster faith that the past originally existed in the form we now devise, we minimize or forget our own alterations."[15] This process has certainly been at work on the Alamo legend.

To highlight one notable example, consider *Texas History Movies*. Off and on since 1926, young Texans have been learning their legendary state history from this *Dallas Morning News* comic strip, written by drama critic John Rosenfield and illustrated by editorial cartoonist Jack Patton. The comic strip was once so popular that it was reissued in booklet form and long distributed free to the state's schoolchildren; an abbreviated version is currently available from the Texas State Historical Association.[16] Over the years, the booklet was edited to remove racist and sexist panels considered inappropriate for use in public schools. No attempt was ever made, however, to correct the legendary depiction of Travis's line in the sand. Indeed, that panel embellishes the cover of the most recent reprint.

Movies, comic books, pulp novels, and other popular culture concoctions have consistently reinforced the legend.[17] As a result, some researchers are beginning to suspect that most Texans know little accurate state history but know and believe instead the more colorful fictions that they have picked up from the mass-media and oral

Figure 1. The cover of *Texas History Movies*, depicting the drawing of Alamo commander William B. Travis's famous line. Courtesy of the Texas State Historical Association.

tradition. In 1988, Richard Shenkman published a good-natured revisionist survey entitled *Legends, Lies, and Cherished Myths of American History*. In an introductory note, he states, "Americans, despite everything you hear, know plenty of history. They know that the Pilgrims landed on Plymouth Rock, that Teddy Roosevelt charged up San Juan Hill, that Columbus discovered the world is round, and that Eli Whitney invented the cotton gin. The punchline, of course, is that Americans know all of these things but that none of them are true. . . . many of the best-known stories from history are false."[18] Among those stories, Shenkman observes, is "the essential fact that the defenders of the Alamo fought to the last man."[19] In Texas, both oral tradition and most older history textbooks assert this "fact," paying particular attention to Davy Crockett's last stand. In the canonical version, Crockett dies a hero's death on the ramparts, falling only after his rifle, Old Betsy, jams and he is forced to use it as a club as he goes down swinging.

The historical record left behind by some of Santa Anna's soldiers says otherwise. For example, José Enrique de la Peña, a lieutenant colonel in the Mexican army, kept a detailed diary that was not published in English in the United States until 1975. This is from his account of the aftermath of the Battle of the Alamo:

> Some seven men had survived the general carnage and, under the protection of General Castrillón, they were brought before Santa Anna. Among them was one of great stature, well-proportioned, with regular features, in whose face there was the imprint of adversity, but in whom one also noticed a degree of resignation and nobility that did him honor. He was the naturalist David Crockett, well-known in North America for his unusual adventures, who had undertaken to explore the country and who, finding himself in Béjar [San Antonio] at the very moment of surprise, had taken refuge in the Alamo, fearing that his status as a foreigner might not be respected. Santa Anna answered Castrillón's intervention in Crockett's behalf with a gesture of indignation and, addressing himself to the sappers, the troops closest to him, ordered his execution. The commanders and officers were outraged at this action and did

not support the order, hoping that once the fury of the moment had blown over these men would be spared; but several officers who were around the president and who, perhaps, had not been present during the moment of danger, became noteworthy by an infamous deed, surpassing the soldiers in cruelty. They thrust themselves forward, in order to flatter their commander, and with swords in hand, fell upon these unfortunate, defenseless men just as a tiger leaps upon his prey. Though tortured before they were killed, these unfortunates died without complaining and without humiliating themselves before their torturers. . . . I turned away horrified in order not to witness such a barbaric scene.[20]

Many Texans were infuriated by the publication of this translated diary, and serious threats were phoned and mailed to the translator. Then, in 1977, Dan Kilgore published "How Did Davy Die?"—his revisionist presidential address to the Texas State Historical Association.[21] After summarizing all of the historical accounts, he concluded that Crockett had in fact been executed after the battle. The Texas press and the general public again flew into an uproar. Kilgore was personally threatened by anonymous and outraged Texans who wanted to believe in the legendary Crockett instead of the revisionist version.

A Local Example: The Great Travis Debacle

Texans are even quicker to defend their legendary history and its heroes when the detractors are not Texans themselves. In cases like this, the local media, more often than not, side with the legendary accounts. One example of this process occurred in the otherwise lazy summer of 1989, when Texas newspapers whipped the public into a frenzy over an isolated local episode that residents of Bryan, Texas, now refer to as "the Great Travis Debacle."

Meetings of the Bryan Independent School District board are usually so dull that few citizens bother to attend. The June 1989 meeting promised to be no different. One perfunctory item of business dealt with the closing of the old and structurally unsound

William B. Travis Elementary School and its replacement with a new building. A senior member of the board, banker Travis Bryan, proposed that the traditional name be kept and that the new school also be named the William B. Travis Elementary School.

This was hardly an uncharacteristic suggestion, given the fact that Bryan was not only the great-great-grandson of the town's founder, but also a descendant of Stephen F. Austin *and* the Alamo commander's namesake. Nor was it a radical suggestion. The naming of public schools after state heroes is commonplace in Texas, and practically every county in the state has a school named for one of the great Republic quartet: Austin, Travis, Crockett, and Sam Houston. The favored modern equivalents include Lyndon Johnson and Sam Rayburn.

In this case, however, the school renaming was unexpectedly complicated by issues of race, class, gender, and regional chauvinism. Recognizing the tremendous demographic and social changes that had taken place in Bryan since the original Travis School was opened in 1929, some community members proposed a new name. One school board member, who was also a member of the Texas A&M history faculty and a native of Michigan, proposed that the new school be named in honor of Mary Branch, an African American woman who became the first woman college president in Texas when she assumed the leadership of what is today Huston-Tillotson College in the state capital.[22] Another A&M history professor, a fifth-generation Texan, spoke on behalf of the Branch proposal and, as part of his remarks, summarized the reasons why she would be a better role model than William B. Travis for the predominantly Hispanic and African American children who would attend the school: Travis he described bluntly as "a ne'er do well who in two weeks' time happened to do something wonderful."[23]

At this point in the proceedings, another board member, who hailed from Connecticut, elaborated on the shortcomings in Travis's character, pointing out that, according to Travis's own diary, he was a womanizing slaveholder—not exactly an ideal role model for African American girls. In doing this, the board member was doing little more than disclosing an open secret, for the Travis diary is well known in Texas, as is the fact that its author indiscreetly kept score of his sexual exploits among San Antonio's Mexican prostitutes. Most Texans, however, have a tendency to overlook the flaws in Travis's character that the diary reveals, and it was hardly comforting to have this dirty laundry aired in public by a mere Yankee—especially one who commented that "other than dying at the Alamo, the rest of his life was not very exemplary."[24]

The Yankee logic, though, carried the day. The school board voted four to three in favor of naming the new school after Branch, and it went on with its other business as usual. That, however, was only the start of the story. Things soon began to heat up in public when the local paper reported the meeting in glaring and, for Texas, incendiary front-page headlines: "BISD rejects Travis, names school for black educator."[25] This opened an irresolvable dialectic between empirical historical fact and the beloved Texas Mystique.[26] The battle lines were drawn between those who believed in the Travis of legend—the gallant, martyred commander of the Alamo—and those who had just found out about the historical Travis—the soldier of fortune who, in coming to Texas, had left behind him in Alabama a wife, a child, and possibly a murder charge.

The state press predictably sided with the legend by interpreting the school board's vote as anti-Travis rather than pro-Branch. For example, the headline in the *San Antonio Express-News* stated, "Alamo's hero Travis loses battle of Bryan";[27] according to the *Dallas Morning News,* "Travis furor divides town";[28] and the *Houston Chronicle* reported, "School bypasses name of slave owner Travis."[29] Later the *Chronicle* followed up on the story with a half-page, illustrated feature under the headline, "Travis's halo fades as board reinterprets legend."[30] The major Texas newspapers, as a rule, have no interest whatsoever in the mundane business of small-town school boards. But the rejection of one of the state's founding fathers instantly became front-page copy throughout the state.

What started out as a local human-interest story was then picked up by Paul Harvey and the national wire services and eventually was reported as far away as London. Adding to the uproar, it turned out that the local reporter who wrote the first story on the board meeting had misidentified the historian who testified against Travis as the president of the Texas State Historical Association. That bit of seemingly irrelevant misinformation caused some anxious days for the association's staff, who had to field irate calls and letters from Texans around the state who wanted to know "just what in the hell is going on." Some historians began to fear another anti-intellectual, antihistorian backlash such as had emerged during the "How Did Davy Die?" controversy. The Texas A&M history department came in for its share of abuse, too, primarily in the form of anonymous and hostile calls casting aspersions on the qualifications of the faculty. Most of them, for the duration of the uproar, refused to take further unscreened calls.

The controversy continued throughout the summer, played out publicly in the editorial and feature pages of the state's newspapers and privately in the hate mail and telephone calls received by the school board members who had voted for Branch over Travis. Editors, columnists, and especially writers of letters to the editor fulminated against the iniquity of calling Travis's honor into question. The woman school board member who had dared to speak out against him in the first place was singled out as the primary target, not so much because she was a woman, but because she was from out of state. In an apparent attempt to keep the controversy newsworthy, some more conservative papers pointed out that as a Connecticut Yankee she had no right to any opinion regarding Texas heroes. Historians who recalled the Connecticut origins of Stephen F. Austin's own family discreetly kept quiet.

The general tone of the Travis controversy in Bryan was almost as hostile as the earlier Davy Crockett controversy, and the racist and sexist overtones of the pro-Travis faction threatened to polarize the community. The elementary school in question served a largely lower socioeconomic, ethnic student body. The school board members were all Anglo. The calumny directed toward the woman on the board who had precipitated the controversy inflamed many, not just women, who had personally experienced the macho persona of the state. Few knew anything about the eponymous Mary Branch, and this ignorance further illustrated the fact that a subtext of the entire episode was "discrimination by exclusion."

A few weeks after the conflicting Travis and Branch proposals were presented, the school board finally resolved the issue with a compromise. The new school would still be named after Branch (thus holding to the original four-to-three vote), but the Bryan school district's general administration building would be renamed for Travis.[31] The night that the board passed this motion, the room was packed with spectators, a considerable number of whom, both black and white, were Branch supporters. The community seemed satisfied with the compromise: Travis's reputation emerged unscathed (the Texas memory is very selective); the dog days of summer ended; and the local media sought other, less controversial human-interest stories. In all of the uproar, nobody seemed to notice that Bryan already had a Travis Street, a Travis Landing shopping center, and a Travis House apartment complex.

Appropriating a Family Saga

Folklore provides us with a conceptual framework for understanding the emotional allegiance Texans feel for their legendary history. Mody Boatright, an internationally known literary scholar and Texas folklorist, first recognized a distinct category of traditional narrative that he named the family saga.[32] According to Boatright, families enshrine in formulaic narratives those past episodes and ancestors that embody characteristics that later generations regard as distinctive and memorable. These narratives can be jocular, heroic, obscene, esoteric, or absurd, but their fundamental characteristic is that they are intended for a private audience, the limited family circle, rather than for a wider audience of strangers.

Because they are kept alive primarily in oral tradition, the actual facts of these family stories are often rearranged over time, as new facts and ancestors are invented, if necessary, to enhance the point being made or the dramatic appeal of the story. For example, Lyndon B. Johnson proudly described to the biographer Doris Kearns how his great-great-grandfather had died a hero at the Battle of San Jacinto, at the end of Texas's war for independence. Later research revealed that this particular ancestor was a real estate trader who died at home in bed. Kearns concluded that Johnson "wanted an heroic relative so badly that he simply created the tale, and after retelling it dozens of times, the grandfather really came to exist in Johnson's mind."[33]

The empirical truth of such stories, then, is largely irrelevant. Intended for the family audience, they are accepted at face value there and not openly questioned, because to do so would be to question the family itself. Many such sagas are so important to the emotional cohesion of the family, in fact, that they are only told on special occasions, such as family reunions, or by certain individuals who have great status within the family.[34]

Because many of the legends Texans keep alive through the media and oral tradition suggest that Texans are "one big happy family," it is useful to consider them parts of a collective family saga. The story of Travis's line in the sand provides a clear example of how these "family" stories become embedded in the general psyche. William Zuber's published version of his family's encounter with Moses Rose, the defector from the Alamo, and the story Rose allegedly told about his escape, were clearly elements of an individual family saga that had been preserved orally and creatively modified over the years. Later Texans collectively appropriated those parts of the story dealing with events inside the Alamo, especially the episodes of Travis's speech, his line, and Rose's defection. The details dealing specifically with the role of Zuber's family have dropped out of the collective version.

As is so often the case with family sagas, the story was for many years under the custodianship of a family elder—in this case Zuber's mother. In fact, Mary Ann Zuber's control over the story was so strong that her son's account of it in the *Texas Almanac* contains the following affidavit, dated May 9, 1871: "I have carefully examined the foregoing letter of my son, William P. Zuber, and feel that I can endorse it with the greatest propriety. The arrival of Moses Rose at our residence, his condition when he came, what transpired during his stay, and the tidings that we afterwards heard of him, are all correctly stated. The part which purports to be Rose's statement of what he saw and heard in the Alamo, of his escape, and of what befell him afterwards is precisely the substance of what Rose stated to my husband and myself."[35]

Too naive to realize the consequences of his publishing the story, Zuber openly admitted how he had rearranged, embellished, and invented passages to create the version of the speech that appeared in the *Almanac*. Zuber's actions really are not that surprising. As

Lowenthal has observed, "Those who remake the past as it ought to have been, as distinct from what it presumably was, are more keenly aware of tampering with its residues. They deliberately improve on history, memory, and relics to give the past's true nature better or fuller expression than it could attain in its own time."[36] This point is quite in keeping with Zuber's own account, where he states that he "wrote the sentiments of the speech in what I imagined to be Travis's style, but was careful not to change the sense. I devoted several weeks of time to successive rewritings and transpositions of the parts of that speech. This done, I was surprised at the geometrical neatness with which the parts fitted together. Of course it is not pretended that Colonel Travis's speech is reported literally, but the ideas are precisely those he advanced, and most of the language is also nearly the same."[37]

By exposing his embellished version to an objective and critical public readership, Zuber lost control of this priceless family heirloom, which had been kept alive by oral tradition. Such transformation of traditional materials from a private to a public arena is not uncommon. As Wilson states, "No matter what the origin of a folklore item, it will, if it is to survive, move from the individual expression of its originator to the communal expression of those who preserve it, sloughing off as it passes from person to person and through time and space the marks of individual invention, and in a short time reflecting quite accurately the consensus of the group."[38] Once it was published, this private family saga was thus transformed into a public legend, which continues to exert considerable influence on how Texans and the mass-media interpret and "remember" the Alamo.

Conclusions

The popular legend surrounding the Alamo borders on the sacred in Texas because it expresses, or validates, the mystique that Anglo Texans have of themselves as independent, self-sacrificing, brave, and patriotic.[39] Countless retellings of the legend in schoolbooks, movies, at family gatherings, and state celebrations venerate the forging of the Republic of Texas in the crucible of the Alamo. The martyred heroes of the Alamo have taken on sacred proportions. To reduce the Battle of the Alamo to the dry empirical facts of body count and political consequences is to deprive the saga of Texas independence of its meaning to contemporary Texans.

Just as family sagas recount family history as it ought to have been or might have been, the historical legend is a barometer of contemporary public opinions and values, and not necessarily an empirical record of past events. The constituency or bearers of a historical legend are those who like the tale the way it is because it validates their own culture's mores and aspirations. Because of the emotional investment that legend bearers thus have in their inventions, to attack or contradict a legend—especially one with such a sacred aura as that of the Alamo—is to risk an immediate and heated counterattack. As the quotation from Dobie makes clear, no amount of revisionist research will change the opinions and emotional commitment of the legend's supporters. Provable facts are irrelevant because the legend operates on the emotional or symbolic level, not on the rational level.

The dialectic among empirical historical facts, oral history, legend, invented tradition, and family saga is a dynamic one, especially when an episode such as the Battle of the Alamo is rendered in several of these genres or rhetorical forms simultaneously. As the examples cited here show, history and tradition energize each other. Disputed historical legends give revisionist historians raw material and subject matter to work with. The more empirical details historians uncover, however, the stronger becomes the emotional defense of the legends under attack. Then support of the legends in turn spawns alternative or variant forms, which intermingle with and draw from one another. Whenever historical legends are involved, with their functional emphasis on validating the present, the historically questionable may become a psychological imperative. Thus Texans remember an Alamo that never was.

Notes

1. See Margaret Swett Henson, "Texas History and the Public Schools: An Appraisal," *Southwestern Historical Quarterly* 82 (1979): 403–15; and David McComb, "Texas History Textbooks in Texas Schools," *Southwestern Historical Quarterly* 93 (1989): 191–96.
2. The first Texas history textbook to be used throughout the public schools was privately printed in several editions by a patriotic teacher. The first edition is Mrs. Anna J. Hardwicke Pennybacker, *A New History for Texas for Schools* (Tyler, Tex.: privately printed, 1888). All subsequent references are to this edition.
3. See Eric Hobsbawm, "Introduction: Inventing Traditions," in *The Invention of Tradition*, ed. Eric Hobsbawm and Terence Ranger (Cambridge: Cambridge University Press, 1983), 1–14.
4. The standard biography of Travis is Archie McDonald, *William Barret Travis: A Biography* (Austin: Eakin Press, 1976).
5. For in-depth studies of Crockett, see Michael Lofaro, ed., *Davy Crockett: The Man, The Legend, The Legacy, 1786–1986* (Knoxville: University of Tennessee Press, 1985).
6. The folklore surrounding Bowie's death is recalled in Edward G. Rohrbough, "How Jim Bowie Died," *Publications of the Texas Folklore Society* 15 (1939): 48–58.
7. Pennybacker, *New History*, 73.
8. Ibid., 74–75.
9. Ibid.
10. Zuber's tale of Moses Rose has been widely discussed. See, for example, R. B. Blake, "A Vindication of Rose and His Story," *Publications of the Texas Folklore Society* 15 (1939): 27–42; J. Frank Dobie, "The Line That Travis Drew," *Publications of the Texas Folklore Society* 15 (1939): 9–16; Llerena Friend, "Historiography of the Account of Moses Rose and the Line That Travis Drew," appendix in *My Eighty Years in Texas*, by W. P. Zuber (Austin: University of Texas Press, 1971), 255–62; Perry McWilliams, "The Alamo Story: From Fact to Fable," *Journal of the Folklore Institute* 15 (1978): 221–34; W. P. Zuber to Charlie Jeffries, "Inventing Stories about the Alamo," *Publications of the Texas Folklore Society* 15 (1939): 42–48. Whether or not Rose was a real historical character is also widely debated among Texas historians.
11. The Alamo has been the subject of literally hundreds of books and articles. Two recent summaries of the scholarly and popular writings are Wallace O. Chariton, *Exploring the Alamo Legends* (Plano, Tex.:

WordWare, 1990); and Wallace O. Chariton, *Forget the Alamo* (Plano, Tex.: WordWare, 1990). Another indispensable study for anyone interested in the symbolic and metaphoric significance of the Alamo is Susan Prendergast Schoelwer, *Alamo Images: Changing Perceptions of a Texas Experience* (Dallas: Southern Methodist University Press and DeGolyer Library, 1985).

12. Dobie, "The Line," 14.

13. Richard Shenkman, *I Love Paul Revere, Whether He Rode or Not* (New York: HarperCollins, 1991), vii.

14. William B. Wilson, "Folklore and History: Fact amid the Legends," in *Readings in American Folklore*, ed. Jan Harold Brunvand (New York: W. W. Norton, 1979), 462.

15. David Lowenthal, *The Past Is a Foreign Country* (Cambridge: Cambridge University Press, 1985), 326.

16. John Rosenfeld and Jack Patton, *Texas History Movies* (Austin: Texas State Historical Association, 1986).

17. The best study of the Texas Mystique in the media is Don Graham, *Cowboys and Cadillacs: How Hollywood Looks at Texas* (Austin: Texas Monthly Press, 1983).

18. Richard Shenkman, *Legends, Lies, and Cherished Myths of American History* (New York: William Morrow, 1988), 11–12.

19. Ibid., 89–90.

20. José Enrique de la Peña, *With Santa Anna in Texas: A Personal Narrative of the Revolution*, ed. and trans. Carmen Perry (College Station: Texas A&M University Press, 1975), 53.

21. Dan Kilgore, *How Did Davy Die?* (College Station: Texas A&M University Press, 1978).

22. For Mary Branch, see Olive D. Brown and Michael R. Heintze, "Mary Branch: Private College Educator," in *Black Leaders: Texans for Their Times*, ed. Alwyn Barr and Robert A. Calvert (Austin: Texas State Historical Association, 1981), 113–28; and Michele Stanush, "Mary Branch Made History as Texas's First Black Female College President," *Austin American-Statesman*, March 29, 1993.

23. *Bryan Eagle*, June 13, 1989.

24. Ibid.

25. Ibid.

26. For the concept of the dialectic in legend formation and performance, see Linda Dégh, "The Dialectics of the Legend," Folklore Preprint Series #6 (Bloomington, Ind., 1973).

27. *San Antonio Express-News*, June 14, 1989.

28. *Dallas Morning News*, July 9, 1989.
29. *Houston Chronicle*, June 14, 1989.
30. *Houston Chronicle*, June 18, 1989.
31. *Bryan Eagle*, July 11, 1989.
32. See Mody Boatright, "The Family Saga as a Form of Folklore," in *Mody Boatright, Folklorist*, ed. Ernest Speck (Austin: University of Texas Press, 1973), 124–44.
33. Doris Kearns, "Angles of Vision," in *Telling Lives: The Biographer's Art* (Philadelphia: University of Pennsylvania Press, 1979), 90–103.
34. See Steven Zeitlin, Amy Kotkin, and Holly Baker, eds., *A Celebration of American Family Folklore* (New York: Pantheon, 1982).
35. This passage is quoted in W. P. Zuber, "An Escape from the Alamo," *Publications of the Texas Folklore Society* 15 (1939): 27.
36. Lowenthal, *Foreign Country*, 328.
37. Zuber, "Escape," 27.
38. Wilson, "Folklore and History," 456.
39. Discussions of the Texas Mystique and the distinctiveness of Texan culture can be found in Joseph Leach, *The Typical Texan: Biography of an American Myth* (Dallas: Southern Methodist University Press, 1952); David McComb, *Texas: A Modern History* (Austin: University of Texas Press, 1989); and D. W. Meinig, *Imperial Texas: An Interpretive Essay in Cultural Geography* (Austin: University of Texas Press, 1969).

Part IV

National Perspectives

We close this volume with a pair of "top down," or nation level, studies. Since the national perspective also informed the studies collected by Hobsbawm and Ranger, it is appropriate that "inventedness" here is clearly marked. Indeed, the invention in both cases may be precisely dated. The Mountie Stetson discussed by Robert MacGregor was widely adopted at the end of the nineteenth century and only made official in 1902. The yellow ribbon phenomenon addressed in my paper first arose during the Iranian hostage crisis (1979–81) and came to its fullest flower during the Gulf War (1991). Both are examples of traditions that, as Hobsbawm and Ranger put it, emerge within "a brief and dateable period" and succeed in "establishing themselves with great rapidity."

Again like the colonial examples in Hobsbawm and Ranger, these two North American traditions were deployed—although not, strictly speaking, "constructed"—as the expressive symbols of centrist political moods. In the Canadian case, the deployment was deeply embedded in the public image of the nation as a tamer of wildness: the Stetson, like royal scarlet, meant law and order. Yellow ribbons signalled a different effacement of friction: they were deployed, and consciously promoted, as emblems of "resolve."

Yet, in both these cases, the consolidating power of the emblem was undermined, and eventually modified, by plural voices. As MacGregor shows, a Sikh Mountie's resistance to the Anglo Stetson

291

forced a modification of the dress code on behalf of his coreligionists and, not incidentally, a "resetting of the symbolic order." And while yellow ribbons were certainly touted at the center, a variety of peripheral voices contested their meaning, their purportedly transparent, pro-administration message. In each case, a national tradition was subtly denationalized—reinscribed at the margins with resistant affect.

At the same time, the new inscriptions reframed history. The acceptance of turbanned Mounties was a tacit acknowledgment that the peoples beyond Suez had also made Canada, that their contributions to the mosaic were worthy of record. In the case of yellow ribbons, the reframing was complicated, indeed frustrated, by the positioning of the 1991 war as a redemption of Vietnam. But in each case, the public debate over expressive practices revealed their intimate links to usable pasts—pasts that continue to resonate as sites of contestation.

CHAPTER 13

"Kamell Dung": A Challenge to Canada's National Icon

Robert M. MacGregor

For well over a century, the Royal Canadian Mounted Police have been featured in public images to symbolize the dignified strength of a united Canada. The familiar scarlet-coated "Mountie" began to appear in national immigration pamphlets and tourist advertisements as early as the 1880s, when the RCMP itself was only a decade old, and by the late 1890s, the scarlet uniform had already achieved iconic status both within and outside of Canada. Before the turn of the century, a New York State sandpaper manufacturer, Behr-Manning, was using the uniform as a promotional cut-out costume that children could place over the company "mascot," a tiny bear.[1] About 100 years later, in December of 1990, Canada's consul-general to the United States, Tom McMillan, created a controversy when he publicly criticized Moosehead Beer's "Share the Wilderness" advertising campaign. The campaign, which was aimed at U.S. beer drinkers, incorporated images of moose, mountains, and Mounties in a way that, according to McMillan, reinforced Americans' "macho" and "stereotypical" image of their northern neighbor.[2]

293

Figure 1. *The iconic Mountie.* A 1990s Canadian tourism poster. The association of "scarlet" with national pride has existed since about the 1890s. Courtesy of the Royal Canadian Mounted Police.

McMillan protested in vain. At the end of the twentieth century, the Mountie has become as universal a Canadian icon as the cowboy has become an icon of the United States. Today, we see the symbol being used on the back of the Canadian fifty-dollar bill, in a British beer campaign featuring "Malcolm the Mountie," in the Mount Allison University athletic teams' designation as "Mounties," in a Mountie waiter serving a "moosehead" entree in the film *Gremlins II*, and in numerous examples of both national and provincial tourism. To say that the image of the Mountie has been universally disseminated for over a century would be an understatement.

In 1989, the visual integrity of this national symbol was challenged by a young Sikh policeman named Baltej Singh Dhillon. His request that he be permitted to wear his religion's required turban rather than the regulation RCMP Stetson set off a wave of soul-searching throughout the nation and led, in 1990, to the "reimagining" of the Mounties' traditional uniform. In this essay, I explore the origins of the RCMP uniform, show how it came to be a totemic emblem of Eurocentric Canada, discuss the Dhillon incident as a challenge to white Canadians' national identity, and argue that his eventual acceptance as a turbanned Mountie involved a resetting of the existing symbolic order.

The Evolution of the Force's Uniform

The force that we know today as the RCMP was established in 1873 as the North-West Mounted Police. Its original mission was to patrol on horseback the vast western territory that had been acquired by the 1867 Confederation and specifically to encourage treaties with the Indian tribes whose animosity was being exacerbated by whiskey traders. After enabling legislation was put into effect in Ottawa in the summer of 1873, the first recruits set out to winter in Fort Garry, at present-day Winnipeg.[3] In the next decade, the force established posts throughout the wilderness and began for the first time to make the central government's influence felt among the native peoples.

Photographs, surviving articles of clothing, and the Official Dress Regulations give us some idea of what the first Mounties wore.

There seemed little uniformity in the matter and certainly no uniform. Before the August Force set out for Fort Garry, dress variations caused by personal preference or sheer necessity appeared to have been the rule rather than the exception. Like others on the frontier, many of the policemen favored leather chaps, buckskin jackets, and buffalo-skin trousers. Early on, the force was refreshingly free of British-style military rigidity.

One exception to this rule—or rather lack of rule—was the gradual appearance of British scarlet as a dominant color. Reports about conditions in the North West Territories frequently stressed the symbolic significance for the Indians of the British army's traditional uniform, and so the Mounties soon adopted a scarlet tunic and blue trousers. Prime Minister Sir John A. MacDonald was insistent that the dominant note in the uniform should be scarlet, since he was convinced that this color would elicit the most respect for "the Queen's soldiers."

Since the RCMP scarlet tunic has come to stand so vividly for Canada, it is thus interesting to recall that at the outset it stood just as vividly for the British army. The conscious logic of red, in fact, was to highlight the British military aspect of the force and to distinguish its members from blue-coated American soldiers. In an 1872 report to the prime minister, Colonel Patrick Robertson-Ross had made the point explicit: "I ascertained that some prejudice existed among the Indians against the colour of the uniform worn by the men of the Provincial Battalion. Many of the Indians had said, 'Who are those soldiers at Red River wearing dark clothes? Our old brothers who formerly lived there [H. M. Sixth Regiment] wore red coats. We know that the soldiers of our Great Mother wear red coats and are our friends.'"[4] Among the Indians, evidently, the impression had long existed that men in red could be trusted: the scarlet coat meant honesty, fairness, courage, and square dealing.[5] Hence the British-style tunic was one of the great secrets of the Mounted Police in dealing with the plains tribes, and the force's first prescribed uniform was calculated to symbolize a British presence. As one journalist put it, "There is nothing Canadian about a Mountie uniform. Even the stiff-brimmed Stetson, popularized by Lord Baden-Powell, found most of its customers among British settlers who did not know any better."[6]

Since Dhillon's challenge to the uniform code focussed on the Stetson, we should recall that this item was originally just as "un-Canadian" as the red tunic—and that, as far as "traditions" go, it had a far shorter history than the coat. The first Mountie headgear was not a Stetson at all, but rather a helmet for dress and parade uses and a forage cap for everyday wear. The helmet, popularized on the British Empire's eastern front, was the familiar cork or pith helmet in off-white or grey. It was worn with a chin strap, sometimes a helmet plate and a brass spike, and often a *puggree*, or yellow muslin scarf, wrapped around it with the loose ends hanging behind; the more ceremonially minded might sport a horsehair plume, varying in color according to rank. The forage cap was a blue cloth pillbox with a white band for enlisted men, a gold one for officers. In the winter, virtually everyone wore fur caps.[7]

Changes in headgear design came early. In 1880, Colonel James Macleod, the retiring commissioner, wrote in his annual report: "Future issue of the helmet should be buff or brown leather. It would be better, also, if they were not so tall as the present pattern, which presents an unnecessary surface to the wind on the prairie, and is thereby rendered very uncomfortable to the wearer. . . . I think that a light grey felt hat would be preferable to the helmet. Very few wear the latter unless obliged to. On trips they are almost invariably carried in the wagons, and get greatly damaged by the knocking about. The men always wear felt hats when they can."[8] Before the issue was settled, they also wore an Ashantee pattern white cock helmet, a white universal pattern helmet with spike, a peaked forage cap, and a soft felt deerstalker hat. The Stetson came into general use only in the mid-1890s, and although it was worn in 1897 by the NWMP contingent to Queen Victoria's Diamond Jubilee, at that time it was still only one of a variety of wide-brimmed felt "prairie hats" used by the force. The style gained in popularity during the South African War of 1899–1902, and the hero of Mafeking, Lord Baden-Powell, later introduced it to both the South African constabulary and the Boy Scouts. But it was not officially adopted by the force until the summer of 1902.

That July, a Board of Officers at Regina inspected a consignment of the American-made hats shipped through Montreal and concluded that their weight, texture, and quality made them suitable for police use. The draft of dress regulations submitted to the comptroller the following summer contained the first official description of the hat. It read: "Stetson Hat, cowboy pattern, with brown leather band 1³⁄₈ inch buckle, leather covered. Hat to be secured to head by ¼ inch strap worn at the back of the head. Four dents in crown dividing crown equally front and rear and sides."[9] The official adoption of this "cowboy" hat thus ended a twenty-five-year search for a serviceable military headgear. The choice proved popular with members of the force and has been an RCMP emblem ever since.

Turbans, the RCMP, and Politics

In 1988, a twenty-three-year-old Alberta university student, Baltej Singh ("Bill") Dhillon, passed the examinations required of RCMP aspirants before they can be admitted to recruit school in Regina. For the previous two summers he had worked for a British Columbia detachment of the force helping to improve police relations with the Sikh community, and he had long dreamed of the day when he could don the famous red tunic. There was only one obstacle. As an orthodox Sikh, he was required by his religion to wear a turban. In 1989, Bill Dhillon's request that he be permitted to wear this religious headgear instead of the RCMP Stetson or work cap threatened to keep him forever out of the Mounties.

The turban issue had surfaced as early as five years before, when Vancouver Sikhs had asked RCMP commissioner Norman Inkster to consider bending the dress regulations. Originally, he had refused the request, but further investigation of Canada's changing ethnic composition forced him to revise his opinion. By the mid-1980s, he later reflected, the first language of an approximate 3.5 million Canadians was something other than either French or English; of the 130,000 immigrants who entered the country in 1988 alone, forty-eight percent spoke neither of these languages. Inkster believed, therefore, that the changing ethnic mosaic required not only recognition but adjustment by the RCMP.

There were legal as well as ethical reasons for his change of mind. The Canadian Human Rights Act and the Canadian Charter of Rights and Freedoms prohibited job discrimination based on religion, and denying Sikhs the right to wear the turban could be construed as an abridgment of their rights. Faced with that possibility, Inkster coyly recalled, "I came to my own conclusion that it would not be helpful for me to engage the RCMP in an argument that involved human rights, knowing at the outset we would lose this argument." He therefore recommended that the wearing of the turban be permitted.[10]

But it was one thing for the RCMP officially to recognize the turban and quite another for Sikh Mounties to actually wear it. Even though permission had been granted, in 1989 the few Sikh members of the force were bending their religious views rather than the regulations, by wearing the Stetson. Similar accommodation had occurred in Edmonton a decade earlier, when turbans for the city police, officially approved, stayed on the shelves. When Dhillon actually set about to wear the "exotic" headgear, he generated a storm of controversy.

Public objections to Mounties wearing turbans focussed around a grassroots group called Defenders of RCMP Tradition, which by November of 1989 had collected 150,000 signatures from across Canada indicating opposition to any change in the force's dress code. The group was started by three Alberta women opposed to "compromise" on "Canada's unique heritage," but it reflected social resentments that far outstripped the uniform issue. It was hardly surprising that the group arose in Alberta, for the province is known for ultra-conservative, nationalist, and racist sentiments. It is a stronghold, for example, of the anti-immigration Reform Party and of the nativist Canadian Cultural Society, whose members denounce the supposed mistreatment of white Canadians and oppose publicly funded multicultural programs. It was an Albertan, Calgary MP Bobbie Sparrow, who introduced a bill into the Ottawa parliament that would have made the RCMP uniform an official symbol of national sovereignty. "The RCMP," she said, "represents part of the basic fabric, foundation, and formation of Canada." Change the uniform, she implied, and you would threaten that solidity. The bill had little chance of passage, but it certainly reflected the attitude of many Albertans over what was, and what was not, Canadian.[11]

It would be wrong to assume that the opposition to Dhillon's move was confined to fringe elements among the "unenlightened" right. In February of 1990, antidiscrimination forces uttered a collective groan at the results of a University of Calgary poll. Of 284 university students surveyed, over seventy percent said they did not want the RCMP opened to Sikhs wearing turbans.[12] A concurrent national poll, conducted by the Angus Reid/Southan polling company, found that fifty-nine percent of all Canadians believed it was more important for minorities to change their customs and attitudes than for the country to adjust to their presence.[13] Clearly, Albertans opposed to Sikh turbans mirrored the attitudes of other Canadians struggling to deal with a rapidly changing ethnic demography.

Enter "Sgt. Kamell Dung"

While the turban debate raged, a number of racist items appeared in some western provinces that added fuel to the fire. Four items in particular had wide distribution.

First was a t-shirt ridiculing the very idea of RCMP Sikh officers. The shirt showed a circle of Mounties on horseback, most of them wearing turbans and sporting beards, along with the caption "Musical Ride 1995. Say It Ain't So, Brian." (The reference was to Prime Minister Brian Mulroney.) Novelty distributor Kelly Fulmore, the shirt's designer, called it a "light-hearted political cartoon" and "just the opinion of a Canadian concerned about the heritage of the RCMP." "What kind of respect will the RCMP get," she mused, "when they stop a car full of drunks and get laughed at because they're wearing turbans?"[14]

The second item was an enamelled metal pin that depicted a black, an Oriental, and a Sikh surrounding a worried-looking white man; the caption read, "Who is the minority in Canada?" The pin was created by Calgary businessman Peter Kouda, who himself immigrated from Czechoslovakia in 1968, and it was sold at flea markets throughout the province. At Calgary's Crossroads Fleamarket, Kouda provided a booklet for customers to inscribe their reactions. Among the comments were the following:

- It's time to start standing up for Canada. Mulroney has sold us out.
- Real Canadians are in the minority. Right on. Say it as it is.

- Wake up people. Look at what's happening to our country.
- This is more than a pin. It's the truth.
- We have the RCMP, which is our only symbol outside of Canada. You shouldn't have a little group coming into the country and trying to change it.
- I'm sorry. White people don't have any rights and we are in the minority.[15]

With an assimilationist fervor that is not uncommon among second generation immigrants, Kouda opposed more recent (and darker) minorities with the same logic as his nativist Anglo customers: "When less than 2 percent of Canadians get special privileges," he commented, "it shows that this country is going down the drain."[16]

In the third item, a lapel button, the figure of a turbanned Mountie is slashed with a diagonal, and the caption reads, "Keep the RCMP Canadian." The designer of this button, Bill Hipson, had designed similar buttons announcing, "Don't mess with the dress." He believed that his creations were meant to provoke debate on the changing nature of Canadian society and, more precisely, to protest against "reverse discrimination against white people." Denying that the stereotypical images were meant to be slanderous, he nonetheless revealed his own racial bias in his description: the buttons, he said, were meant to show "jungle persons from the outer regions of the world taking advantage of the immigration policies."[17] They were also meant, of course, to turn a profit, and that they did. Such was the animosity against "jungle persons" in Anglo Canada at the beginning of the 1990s that Hipson admitted he had stumbled upon a "lucrative field."[18]

The fourth, and most notoriously insulting, of the items was a poster-sized 1990 wall calendar depicting a saber-carrying Mountie in a turban and Turkish slippers and bearing the legend "Sgt. Kamell Dung. Is This Canadian or Does This Make You Sikh?" The creation of a husband and wife team, Herman and Linda Bittner, the calendar sold in the thousands in western province bars. Herman Bittner, who posed for the photo caricature, believed he was performing a "vital public service." "I'm doing a job the politicians

Figure 2. *Lapel button* (1990). The designer, Bill Hipson, sold the button to protest "reverse discrimination against white people." Another Hipson button read "Don't Mess with the Dress." Line drawing by Alan Gibbs. Photo by Adriana Martinez.

should be doing. They're supposed to be representing the views of the majority."[19]

Reactions to the pins, t-shirts, and calendar were swift and widespread. Government and civil rights spokespeople expressed outrage. The message conveyed by the items, said Secretary of State Gerry Weiner, "is one of intolerance and blatant prejudice, if not outright racism, and is completely unacceptable."[20] Prime Minister Mulroney angrily denounced the Alberta-born artifacts, likening them to the sinister hoods of the Ku Klux Klan.[21] Similar outrage was voiced by, for example, the Alberta Human Rights Commission, the Canadian Ethnocultural Council, the World Sikh Organization, Citizens Against Racial and Religious Discrimination, the Manitoba

Figure 3. *Calendar* (1990). The notorious "Kamell Dung" calendar, suggesting Anglo Canada's fear of "jungle persons." Its creators, Linda and Herman Bittner, sold thousands of the calendars in the Western provinces. Line drawing by Alan Gibbs. Photo by Adriana Martinez.

Association of Rights and Liberties, and the B'Nai Brith Canada League for Human Rights.[22]

But the official unanimity concealed a more complex public response. Especially among white Canadians of middle to lower economic and social status, the popularity of the items suggested a strong concern about the changing racial composition of the country and about government policies that encouraged, or at least did not discourage, Third World immigration. The Angus Reid/Southan poll that revealed general resentment of nonwhite minorities also showed mixed reactions to the blatantly racist material. University graduates opposed the pins and calendars three to one, but among high-school dropouts, the opinions were dead even for and against. Overall, the survey found that one in three people surveyed expressed some degree of support for the racist viewpoints.[23]

Perhaps this should not have come as a surprise. Three years before the appearance of the items, polls were already revealing the felt threat to "Canadian" identity among Anglo Canadians confronting Third World immigration. A 1986 Gallup poll conducted in British Columbia found that twenty-five percent of majority respondents felt that Indo-Canadians were not acceptable in "their" community, whether they were born in India or in Canada. A Saskatoon study the same year found that over fifty percent of those polled opposed all East Indian immigration, and twenty-six percent favored cutting off further Chinese entry.[24] The Alberta paraphernalia reflected a crisis of identity among white, and predominantly working class, Canadians. It did not create that crisis.

The groundswell opposition to the turban, which peaked in the opening months of 1990, was rendered moot in the spring of that year, when the federal government made the turban official dress. On April 24, the RCMP's manual of dress reflected the decision by authorizing the force commissioner "to exempt any member from wearing any item of the significant uniform of the RCMP on the basis of the member's religious beliefs." For Sikh members, an RCMP-issued turban was given specific sanction under the changed regulations, "provided it conceals the hair and is neat," while a handkerchief-sized "patka" cloth was additionally allowed for some aspects of the training program. The style of turban was, not surprisingly, bureaucratically controlled: As of 1990, Sikh Mounties who wished to wear a turban or patka cloth had to secure these items from the Material Management Branch. There was even a special form for making the request.[25]

The decision to allow the turban, said Solicitor-General Pierre Cadieux, finally brought the RCMP into compliance with the nationally endorsed Charter of Rights and Freedoms. The brouhaha subsided, although it remains to be seen whether the official recognition of "Sikh identity within Canadian identity" will settle the matter or merely move it underground. Alberta MP Louise Feltham, reacting to the approval of the turban, spoke for many when she said that the decision would be challenged all the way to the Supreme Court and when she moaned that the situation was "not good enough."[26]

"Allocation of Symbolic Resources"

The virulent debate over what might be seen as a minor change in a dress code suggests that what was at stake in the Kamell Dung episode was not headgear, but the sense of identity embodied in the traditions of a "Canadian" icon. As Trevor-Roper pointed out in his study of "Celtic" dress, the fact that an allegedly traditional item of clothing has been actually invented for nationalistic purposes in no way diminishes its import as a symbolic emblem or its utility as the politically charged embodiment of certain values.[27] In any society, symbolic resources are a cultural capital, which may be spent in an international arena like other capital, and into which society's members invest more or less of their common identities. A threat to the symbol, then, can be construed as a threat to identity. In addition, symbols that are clearly defined and seemingly immutable may not only reflect but actually contribute to social solidarity.

That this process is frequently reflected in symbolic clothing is suggested by much research on the "language" of dress. Several investigators have explored the symbolic and practical imports of staff uniforms in health establishments. A typical finding is that a white uniform symbolizes one or more of the necessary leadership virtues, such as authority, dignity, respectability, efficiency, and reliability.[28]

Most commonly, the white uniform is seen as eliciting respect. It provides a symbolic assurance that the wearer is to be trusted and must be taken seriously. Beeson made a similar point about the need for corporate employees to "dress for success" in the "grey flannel mold," and Bickman explored the social power of uniforms in general.[29] As Kelly Fulmore's rhetorical jibe makes explicit, respect was a symbolic issue in the turban episode as well.

But uniforms may also serve internal purposes. Joseph and Alex analyzed the uniform as a device for resolving certain dilemmas of complex organizations, particularly the need to define internal boundaries, to ensure that members conform to common goals, and to eliminate conflict in their members' "status sets."[30] Thus issues of collective identity, symbolic interests, and social status are all closely linked to uniforms as "symbolic resources." In a "mosaic" environment such as Canada, however, such symbolic resources may speak in different languages to different people and may even be contested between groups of different social identities. Such was the case in the 1989 turban episode, as established Canadians and more recent arrivals wrangled bitterly over who "owned" the cultural resource of the Mountie uniform.

For "tradition"-minded, white Canadians, ownership of the icon was clear. To them, the long historical association of the RCMP with English Canada was a significant element in the cultural-symbolic capital of Canadian society. As one Canadian put it after watching a public appearance of Mounties on Capitol Hill, "There was something special about scarlet. Watching the Mounties I thought about my country, its history and the important role the RCMP had played in its development. The constables on the Hill that day were a living, breathing, and moving symbol of that past."[31] For many Anglo Canadians, in other words, the Mountie uniform—and especially the New World Stetson—served to focus a collective identity of transplanted Englishness in much the same way that the *topi*, or pith helmet, had done in British India.[32]

For others, however, the glorious past was less homogeneous. Although the popular figure of the Mountie as an image of Canada was held collectively, it was not universal, and among some

Canadians—well before Bill Dhillon came to the fore—the red tunic indicated a quite different, less happy, history.

French Canada, for example, has never been uniformly impressed by the RCMP. Its resistance to the symbolic resource lies not only in language differences, but in the concrete historical fact of the 1885 Riel Rebellion, when French-blood Metis were overcome by scarlet Mounties. Walden has said that French antipathy to the Mounted Police also partakes of a Gallic resistance to British imperialism, with its often racist depiction of non-Anglo-Saxons as treacherous and villainous.[33] The Kamell Dung episode was a modern version of this tension, and indeed in one widely circulated image from the turban debate, the two threats to Anglo identity merged in a single figure—a Sikh Mountie uttering the greeting "Bonjour." This may seem socially fantastic, but the symbolic import to a "threatened" white "minority" is perfectly clear.

Breton pointed out that in the forging of Canadian identity, the form and style of public institutions such as the RCMP played a critical role in the "production and allocation of symbolic resources."[34] The proposed changes to the uniform in 1989 entailed not only a restructuring of white Canada's collective identity, but a realignment of the nation's symbolic order. To those of a Eurocentric bias, the state's endorsement of that realignment made them feel that their society was being wrested from them. The 210,000 signers of the petition to keep the RCMP traditions, the purchasers of the racist items, Tory MPs, and various segments of the Canadian public perceived the change as a dismantling of institutional forms—forms without which their sense of themselves was put in jeopardy.

The dark-bearded, turbanned Sikh thus was perceived not only as a physical outsider, but as alien to the existing symbolic order. The result might be expressed as a "contradiction in status," evoking uncertainty and resentment among those privileged ethnic groups whose master status was being symbolically undermined.[35] The reaction, predictably, was to reaffirm the threatened solidarity by proclaiming the inviolability of its symbolic emblems.

That the Anglo majority failed to maintain this inviolability testifies to immigration patterns that, over the past few decades, have challenged both the "traditional" Canadian mosaic and its symbolic representations. Members of a collectivity that was historically of a low social status started to demand a restructuring of the collective identity and a redistribution of social recognition. This met with a combination of official approval and popular ambivalence. The case of Dhillon and the RCMP clearly highlighted this ambivalence.

Notes

1. Barbara Whitton Jendrick, *Antique Advertising Paper Dolls* (New York: Dover, 1981), 12.
2. Sandra Porteus, "U.S. Moosehead Ads Seen to Present Poor Canadian Image," *Marketing,* Dec. 10, 1990, pp. 1, 4.
3. S. W. Horrall, "Historic Document Recalls Establishment of the Force," *RCMP Quarterly* (January 1971): 28.
4. A. L. Haydon, *The Riders of the Plains* (Toronto: Copp Clark, 1911), 28.
5. See, for example, J. G. A. Creighton, "The Northwest Mounted Police of Canada," *Scribner's Magazine* 14 (Oct. 1893): 399–417; and John Peter Turner, *The North-West Mounted Police 1873–1893* (Ottawa: Edmond Cloutier, 1950).
6. Graeme Decarie, "Mountie Turban Looks Fine," *The Gazette*, March 18, 1990, p. B2.
7. See David Ross, "Uniforms of the NWMP," *RCMP Quarterly* (Summer 1980): 4, 19; and James J. Boulton, *Uniforms of the Canadian Mounted Police* (North Battleford, Saskatchewan: Turner-Warwick, 1990). For an interesting discussion of how the U.S. movie industry has misconstrued RCMP apparel, especially the Stetson, see Pierre Berton, *Hollywood's Canada: The Americanization of Our National Image* (Toronto: McClelland and Stewart, 1975), 120–21.
8. Haydon, *Riders of the Plains*, 344.
9. Boulton, *Uniforms*, 146.
10. "The Turban Issue—The Commissioner's Response," *Pony Express*, July 1989, p. 4. This was a special edition of the RCMP staff relations branch newsletter.
11. Sparrow is quoted in Ashley Geddes, "MP Says Ottawa's Turban Move Is a Bad Decision," *Calgary Herald*, March 15, 1990, p. A3.
12. Lorraine Locherty, "Students Reject Turbans in RCMP," *Calgary Herald*, Feb. 2, 1990, p. B2.

13. Lorraine Locherty, "Racial Bias Trend Grows," *Calgary Herald*, Feb. 25, 1990, p. A1.
14. "Manitoba Eyes Changes over Anti-Turban T-Shirt," *Calgary Herald*, Feb. 12, 1990, p. A11.
15. Quoted in Bob Bergen, "'Racist' Pins Selling Fast," *Calgary Herald*, Oct. 31, 1989, p. B1.
16. Quoted in "Turban Foes Vow to Fight on in Court," *The Gazette*, March 16, 1990, p. B8.
17. Quoted in Lorraine Locherty, "Controversy Flares over Pin," *Calgary Herald*, Dec. 29, 1989, p. A1.
18. Quoted in Lorraine Locherty, "Lapel Pin May Face New Fight in Court," *Calgary Herald*, March 21, 1990, p. B1.
19. "Sikh Calendar Defended," *Calgary Herald*, Feb. 4, 1990, p. B3.
20. Quoted in "Ottawa Slams 'Racist' Pins," *Calgary Herald*, Jan. 13, 1990, p. D1.
21. William Gold, "Mulroney Takes Long Overdue Swipe at Pin Pedlars," *Calgary Herald*, March 10, 1990, p. A5.
22. For the general outcry, see Sheldon Alberts, "Rights Commission Steps Up War on Minority Pin," *Calgary Herald*, Feb. 9, 1990, p. B2; Roman Cooney, "Mayor Threatens Firm over 'Minority' Pins," *Calgary Herald*, Jan. 5, 1990, p. B1; Anthony Johnson and Goeff White, "Fight Far from Over on Turban," *Calgary Herald*, March 16, 1990, p. A1.
23. Locherty, "Racial Bias," A1.
24. Frances Henry, *Race Relations Research in Canada Today: A 'State of the Art' Review* (Ottawa: Canadian Human Rights Commission, 1986).
25. Bulletin UDM-38 provides for "members of the Sikh religion" to request an official exemption from the dress code. The application form is included as an appendix.
26. Ross Howard, "Cadieux Gives Sikh Mounties Right to Wear Turbans on Duty," *The Globe and Mail*, March 16, 1990, pp. A1–A2.
27. Hugh Trevor-Roper, "The Invention of Tradition: The Highland Tradition of Scotland," in *The Invention of Tradition*, ed. Eric Hobsbawm and Terence Ranger (Cambridge: Cambridge University Press, 1983), 15–41.
28. See Dan W. Blumhagen, "The Doctor's White Coat," *Annals of Internal Medicine* 91 (1979): 111–16; Arnold Goldberg, Daniel Offer, and Leonard Schatzmann, "The Role of the Uniform in a Psychiatric Hospital," *Comparative Psychology* 2 (1961): 25–43; Jeanne Howe, "What's All This about Colored Uniforms?" *American Journal of*

Nursing 69 (1969): 1665–67; Joseph P. Kriss, "Sounding Board: On White Coats and Other Matters," *New England Journal of Medicine* 292 (1975): 1024–25; Helen K. Lafferty and Lois E. Dickey, "Clothing Symbolism and the Changing Role of Nurses," *Home Economics Research* 8 (1980): 294–381.

29. Marianne Beeson, "In the Gray Flannel Mold," in *Dimensions of Dress and Adornment: A Book of Readings*, ed. Lois M. Gurel and Marianne Beeson (Dubuque, Iowa: Kendall/Hunt, 1979), 128–32; and Leonard Bickman, "The Social Power of a Uniform," *Journal of Applied Social Psychology* 4 (1947): 47–61.

30. Nathan Joseph and Nicholas Alex, "The Uniform: A Sociological Perspective," *American Journal of Sociology* 77 (1974): 719–30.

31. Jerry Dan Kovacs, "Kudos for the Force: Something Special about Scarlet," *RCMP Quarterly* (April 1984): 27.

32. Francis DeCaro and Rosan Jordan, "The Wrong Topi: Personal Narratives, Ritual, and the Sun Helmet as a Symbol," *Western Folklore* 43 (1984): 233–48.

33. Keith Walden, *Visions of Order* (Toronto: Butterworth, 1982).

34. Raymond Breton, "The Production and Allocation of Symbolic Resources: An Analysis of the Linguistic and Ethnocultural Fields of Canada," *Canadian Review of Sociology and Anthropology* 21 (1984): 123–44.

35. Joint Committee on Justice, *Proceedings*, June 1, 1989 (Ottawa: Queen's Printer), 1–4.

CHAPTER 14

Closing the Circle: Yellow Ribbons and the Redemption of the Past

Tad Tuleja

In the explosion of public patriotism that accompanied the 1991 Gulf War, the most visible symbol of troop support was not the Stars and Stripes—although flags were profusely evident—but a recently invented tradition, the yellow ribbon. The practice of tying these mini-banners around trees had first surfaced during the 1979–81 hostage crisis as a sign of sympathy for embassy victims of the Iranian revolution. Its resuscitation ten years later, as nearly half a million troops flew to the Middle East, symbolically linked U.S. civilian and military personnel not only to each other, but to a home front that viewed their endeavors with pride and foreboding.

Ribbon display during the Iran crisis can be traced to a Maryland woman, Penne Laingen, whose husband Bruce had been *charge d'affaires* at the Teheran embassy and who, after its capture, edited a newsletter for hostage families. In the 1973 pop song "Tie a Yellow Ribbon Round the Ole Oak Tree" a beribboned tree had symbolized a woman's fidelity to her absent husband, and Laingen promoted the idea in speeches and newsletter columns. Ribbons quickly sprouted around the country, and the song itself acquired a patriotic sheen. As commiserative emblems, the ribbons amply illustrated Hobsbawm

311

and Ranger's observation that traditions are invented, in many instances, as salves for cries.[1]

But if it was the hostage crisis that sparked the instant tradition, it took a more elaborate and desperate crisis—the war against Saddam Hussein—to develop its potential. Even before the first bombs began to drop on Baghdad in January of 1991, yellow ribbons were being touted as symbols of national resolve, and the country was awash in a virtual "blizzard of satin and acetate."[2] Lassoed trees weren't the half of it. Homeowners hung ribbons on fences, flag-poles, and doors, often in concert with seasonal emblems as "folk assemblages."[3] The business community, which had rallied to a national cause in the 1930s by displaying blue eagles, now featured yellow bows in their windows and advertisements. Supermarkets decorated their coupon inserts with the supportive emblems and adopted yellow register tapes. Newspapers and magazines ran the ribbons up their mastheads. Local governments sprinkled them throughout municipal buildings and public spaces. Churches expressed their sympathy with Desert Storm troops, if not with their mission, by adding satin bows to seasonal wreaths. Florists incorpo-rated yellow ribbons into their arrangements. Novelty companies produced yellow ribbon bumper stickers, decals, buttons, pins, gimme hats, t-shirts, and coffee mugs. One need not be unduly cyn-ical to observe that, on the home front, the six-week war was a small-business bonanza.[4]

Nor did the yellowing of America come to a halt with the February cease-fire. As Desert Storm troops began to trickle home, the ribbons continued to advertise national solidarity. The tenor of bumper stick-er philosophy moved from "Kick ass" to "Welcome home," but the yellow symbols remained as prominent as ever. An "Archie" comic book featuring the story "When Johnny *and* Jenny Come Marching Home Again" was littered equally with yellow bows and traditional bunting. The United States Postal Service issued a stamp honoring "those who served" with a slender ribbon snaking decoratively through its ads. Troops disembarking at air force bases were "decorat-ed" with citizens' versions of the campaign ribbon.[5] In Austin, Texas, a July 4 salute to Texas troops—sponsored by mogul Ross Perot and billed modestly as "the biggest celebration in history"—included a

Figure 1. Popular support for the troops of Desert Storm was reflected by yellow ribbons on individual homes as well as government-sponsored displays. This ribbon adorned a tree on a Massachusetts community's town common as well as the cover of its 1990 annual budget report.. Photo by Jim Gambaro.

Figure 2. Bumper sticker sold to promote the Austin, Texas, welcome-home celebration for Gulf War troops. The "biggest celebration in history" included, as illustrated, the wrapping of the Capitol dome with a giant yellow ribbon. Photo by Adriana Martinez.

project that would have turned artist Christo green: A San Antonio engineer wrapped the capitol building in yellow metal as part of a Texas-sized "Operation Yellow Ribbon."[6] Twelve months after Saddam Hussein surrendered, a million ribbons still fluttered in the breeze of a "reborn" America.

That this occurred is an empirical fact. Why it occurred, to what extent it was a homogeneous phenomenon, and what symbolic capital was being expended during the yellowing of America—these still open questions are the subject of this essay.

A Homogeneity of Mood?

The establishment view was that yellow ribbons reflected national solidarity—a mood that, however beset it may have been with apprehension, was overwhelmingly one of support for the "liberation of Kuwait." Not only the ubiquity of ribbons themselves but George

Bush's eighty-three percent approval rating suggested that ribbon display, like flag display, was a sign of unity. According to this "bottom up" interpretation of the symbol, it rose up—naturally and spontaneously—out of a deep well of national pride and love of country. Critics of Bush's Gulf policy saw this equation between ribbons and unity as facile and tendentious. Reflecting Hobsbawm and Ranger's view of traditions as state-manufactured and state-serving formulations, they saw the yellow ribbon phenomenon as a hegemonic stratagem, imposed "top down" and designed to generate, in Raymond Williams's phrase, a "structure of feeling" that was as unnatural as it was nonreflective.[7] According to this reading, yellow ribbons were an obscurationist cover—a principal means by which the power bloc concealed dissent.

While these two interpretations of the ribbon phenomenon may seem mutually exclusive, they actually share a conceptually critical assumption: the belief in congruence between such "dominant symbols"[8] and "collective consciousness." Neither the president's supporters, who applauded the ribbons as expressions of pride, nor his detractors, who derided them as flickers of false consciousness, doubted the consensual mood they were said to represent. Eighty-three percent is an impressive figure after all, and for at least as long as the war lasted, most observers agreed, there was a virtual homogeneity of mood in support of the president. The fluttering ribbons were merely its objective correlate.

It would be fruitless to deny that Desert Storm generated *some* kind of national mood swing or that yellow ribbons were, by and large, expressions of resolve. Yet "homogeneity" puts too simple a cast on a complex picture. It glosses over the unresolved features of symbol formation, and it ignores the sensibilities of millions of Americans—including many ribbon wearers themselves—who read the patriotic symbol as anything but totalizing. Such discordant sensibilities come to the foreground in this essay. The success of yellow ribbons as an instant tradition, I will try to show, ultimately had less to do with national oneness—either top down or bottom up—than with contestation.

That the meaning of symbols may be publicly contested has been noted frequently, most articulately perhaps in the works of Victor

Turner. Public symbols, Turner wrote, are best examined as "positive forces" in an "activity field." Far from evoking only one set of responses, they are "dynamic entities" continually being negotiated and redefined. Even the milk tree, which Turner calls "at its highest level of abstraction" a symbol of "the unity and continuity of Ndembu society," represents at another level "aspects of social differential and even opposition between the components of a society which it is supposed to symbolize as a harmonious whole."[9] Other students of symbolism have drawn similar conclusions. Cohen, for example, suggests that it may be the "very essence of the symbolic process to perform a multiplicity of functions with economy of symbolic formation."[10] Similarly, "The expressive value of what is called a collective symbol may lie in fact in a set of variations on a common theme rather than in any uniform conceptualization."[11] Seeing public symbols, then, as icons of unity—whether naturally upwelling or imposed—misreads their dynamic *availability* to parties in conflict.

This is important to keep in mind with regard to Desert Storm, for throughout that conflict, both the variations and the common theme were continually contested. Debate over subtexts supposedly inscribed in the "homogenizing" ribbons not only reflected the multivocality common to all symbols. It also dramatized an ongoing debate about the meaning of America—about what it means, in the twentieth century, to be an American. That dramatization was staged simultaneously in two historical moments—the past of Vietnam and the present of Desert Storm—so that the semantic debate became a conflicted assessment of history itself.

Evolution and Ambiguity

That yellow ribbons should have served as touchstones for this debate might have been predicted from their own conflicted history. From their first appearance in the nineteenth century as signs of affection for U.S. cavalrymen, their semantic load had been charged with ambiguity. As Turner, Firth, and Cohen agree, this is true to a great extent of virtually all symbols. It becomes particularly salient when a symbol is noniconic—when, to use Saussure's famous term, its "arbitrariness" invites a multitude of interpretations. This is certainly the case with regard to color, and the inherent openness of yellow ribbons rests in part on the historical fact that "yellow" itself is connotatively fluid.

Countless examples of this can be found in dictionaries of symbolism,[12] but consider only the valences of yellow in American popular culture. The dominant (one is tempted to say hegemonic) sense is that of cowardice ("yellow streak," "yellow belly"), but depending on context the term can also connote sensationalism ("yellow journalism"), anti-unionism ("yellow dog contract"), regional pride ("yellow rose of Texas"), or racial typing ("high yellow," "yellow peril," and George "Yellowhair" Custer). The symbolic burden is as undecided as it is rich.

Connotative variation also attends the yellow ribbon's more iconic "half": the knotting or tying that anchors the symbol to its display site. Throughout the world, knotting symbolizes both danger and protection. Ambivalence is so embedded in this symbol that only the conceptual stance of the knotter toward the power of binding can reveal whether a given knot is aggressive or apotropaic.[13]

When you fuse these two malleable elements into a single symbol, you get, not surprisingly, more rather than less malleability. As Soens shows in an excellent historical survey, a resulting ambivalence has informed yellow ribbon wearing from the very beginning.[14] When U.S. cavalrymen's sweethearts wore ribbons around their necks in the nineteenth century, the symbolic signal was not simply one of affection. The yellow band also served as a combined property tag and off-limits sign—a signal to other service branches that the girl was "cavalry goods" and also possibly infectious (yellow being the color of the quarantine flag). This nicely supplements Eliade's observation about the ambivalence of "protection."

By the turn of the century, soldiers—reflecting this somewhat bawdy tradition—had adopted a music hall ballad called "She Wore a Yellow Ribbon," which found its way into the twentieth century's first reshaping of the custom, John Ford's 1949 cavalry drama *She Wore a Yellow Ribbon*. Here, as in the Tin Pan Alley song, the negative resonances of ribbon wearing ("hands off" and VD) were submerged, and the custom became sanitized enough to provide an emblematic flourish to the movie's romantic subplot. Shorn of its sexual connotations, the theme song went on to become a Hit

Parade favorite, first for the Andrews Sisters and then, in 1961, for Mitch Miller.

The next recasting of the cavalry custom came in 1973, when Tony Orlando and Dawn recorded a sentimental ballad, "Tie a Yellow Ribbon Round the Ole Oak Tree," which became, obliquely enough, the year's biggest hit. I say obliquely because while the song's lump-in-the-throat message—stand by your man even if he's done wrong—framed the story of a released convict's homecoming, the encoded referent for the prison scenario was clearly Vietnam. In 1973, with "Vietnamization" virtually complete and the Paris Accords signed, those returning home after having "done their time" were not convicts but conscripts. That they were being repatriated to something less than open arms lent the ballad a poignant undertone that explains its success. The song functioned as metaphorical expiation at a time when straightforward gratitude was still politically unfashionable.

The yellow ribbon custom's burgeoning political valence next made itself felt in 1979, after the fall of Teheran created a new crop of American scapegoats. During the Iranian hostage crisis, the Tony Orlando vehicle resurfaced on mainstream radio, both reflecting and actively encouraging the display of ribbons as a sign of support for the civilian victims of militant Islam. By that time, as we have seen, the custom had already acquired a sedimented history of quasi-patriotic affect, and its enlistment as an emblem of support for "prisoners of policy" must be viewed against that gradually evolving, and consistently contestable, symbolic backdrop.

But with a difference. What Penne Laingen's modification of the custom did was to, blatantly and precisely, nationalize its affect. The link between returning Vietnam veterans and the prisoner of the 1973 song may have been indistinct; not so the fusion of embassy hostages and yellow ribbons. And, since the hostages were cast as victims whose only crime was American citizenship, they and "their" ribbons came to represent not just a foreign policy, but the nation itself—the nation as an embodiment of what Lawrence has nicely called the "moral hegemony of victimization."[15] During the 444 days of the hostage crisis, it was not they who were being held captive, but the United States. *Time, Newsweek,* and their sister magazines made the point explicit. The ongoing story ran under the banner "America Held Hostage."

Given this background, it was practically inevitable that the next time the nation went to war, yellow ribbons would be trotted out as the "traditional" emblem of homefront solidarity. It was also inevitable, however, that the administration's attempt to freeze its meaning would be incomplete and that the debate about who owned America would rumble on.

"Just Another Battleground"

Political symbols resonate at three levels: the cognitive, the affective, and the behavioral. To nurture commonality, they must work at all these levels simultaneously, and with the same saliency for at least a majority in the polity involved. But because symbols typically *condense* both ideas and images, the fusion of the three levels is seldom complete. Turner's distinction between the ideological and sensory "poles" of ritual activity suggests an uneasy alliance that is also present in symbol formation.[16] Firth makes the related point that semantic loading can as easily disrupt as reinforce commonality. Condensation, he notes, may actually "hamper communication by clogging the channels—by providing too many alternatives for interpretation."[17]

If those alternatives do not cohere—if political leaders cannot make them cohere—then the resultant clogging may hamper more than communication. If the manipulation of symbols by those in power is successful, writes Kertzer, public ritual "creates an emotional state that makes the message uncontestable. . . . It presents a picture of the world that is so emotionally compelling that it is beyond debate."[18] But when it does not work that neatly, we get a rhetorical firestorm of "nomadic subjectivities."[19] For political leaders attempting to enhance solidarity through symbolic messages, then, "there is always the danger that ambiguity gives way to open conflict about the meaning of the rites. In such cases, rather than producing political unity, the rites can become just another battleground."[20] This was exactly what happened during Desert Storm.

Not that the battle over meaning was terribly visible. To judge from network and CNN coverage of the war, Bush's eighty-three percent approval rating was a timid estimate. Commentators made almost as much of "national consensus" as did the administration itself, and the depiction of war protestors consistently stressed their isolation. Thus the yellow ribbon was effectively colonized by administration supporters; concern for the troops was represented as support for policy; dissent was defined as crankiness, if not outright disloyalty; and being American was comfortably defined as "standing with the president." Precisely the same techniques had marginalized dissenters during the long ordeal of Vietnam.

But the polls and the acetate blizzard aside, this patriotic fix did not entirely take. A few examples from the liberal wilds of Massachusetts, where I was living when the "liberation of Kuwait" was under way.

- In February of 1991, journalist Monica Collins, after interviewing ribbon wearers in a Boston suburb, found that the patriotic symbols revealed not universal support for the administration master plan, but rather a "rainbow of messages." "Do yellow ribbons signal support for the troops?" she asked. "Support for the war? Support for peace? Support for President Bush? Support for smart bombs? Do yellow ribbons unite us in nationalism? Or divide us?" The answer, she found, was, "All and none of the above."[21]
- Later that month, ninety miles to the west, students debated the meaning of the ribbons in the University of Massachusetts paper, the *Daily Collegian*. Student columnist Gayle Long, countering the consensus view that wearing a ribbon was pro war, said that her ribbon expressed her hope for a swift conclusion—for "the thought of life and peace in the Middle East and the rest of the world."[22] Linda Babcock, responding under the headline "Bloody, Yellow Ribbons," condemned Long's "naiveté about the symbolism of war." "For most who wear ribbons, support for the troops necessarily means supporting the soldiers' duty: to enforce American foreign policy. . . . Life? Peace? You've got to be kidding."[23]
- On February 18, while Desert Storm troops were preparing for a ground offensive, a war protestor named Gregory Levey

burned himself to death on the Amherst common. An impromptu shrine grew up on the site where he died, sympathizers set up a round-the-clock vigil, and the ground was showered for the following month with memorial offerings. Among the gifts presented to the young man's spirit were numerous peace poems, sheaves of flowers—and yellow ribbons.[24]

Such counterhegemonic displays were hardly surprising in Amherst, an enclave of gentrified hippies whose largest institution of higher learning is known locally as "UMarx." But a similar display of disparate meanings also obtained eleven miles down the road, in the more conservative, working-class community of Belchertown. Officially, the town was so committed to yellow ribbons—whatever they meant—that public buildings and the common itself displayed them prominently. So of course did many homes. But the knee-jerk patriotism that cynics might have seen in this display was not borne out in my interviews with Belchertown homeowners.

To my initial query about the meaning of their ribbons, the homeowners' virtually unanimous response was "support for our troops." Yet, this affective concord was not matched cognitively or behaviorally—that is, in terms of political understanding or desired action. A few ribbon displayers had friends or relatives in the Gulf, although most did not, and their linkage of the troops with policy was anything but uniform. Some endorsed our military actions uncritically, but others equated "support for the troops" with the less aggressive desire to "bring them home safely." Still others expressed confusion or ignorance about "what's going on over there." One man, when I asked his opinion of our Middle East policy, gave a frustrated reply: "What policy?" Another criticized the American role of "world policeman." One woman, the wife of a disabled Vietnam veteran, called their yellow ribbon a traditional "symbol of peace." Some people, she said, were planting "peace gardens" of yellow flowers.

Clearly, the meaning of yellow ribbons in this conservative community was no more frozen than in yuppie, leftist Amherst. In both communities, the symbol—open and negotiable by definition—became a social text that people manipulated for private

Figure 3. A "producerly" reaction to the yellow ribbon mania. This yellow peace ribbon decorated the spot on the Amherst, Massachusetts, town common where Gregory Levey immolated himself to protest the Gulf War. Photo by Tad Tuleja.

purposes. Probably it is going too far to imagine that such manipulation, in the majority of cases, was oppositional. Yet, none of the ribbon wearers I encountered was supinely deferential either. Perhaps Fiske comes closest to defining what was going on. Building on de Certeau's idea that popular "poaching" raids can disrupt the hegemonic, Fiske stresses the "contra" in the contradictions of popular culture and insists that "producerly" remakings of the culture's givens hint at opposition.[25] Placing a yellow ribbon on a peace martyr's grave is not revolutionary activity, to be sure. But perhaps, with Fiske's "optimistic skepticism," we might call it "protopolitical": It displays what Foley, acknowledging the ambivalence of adolescent ritual, calls "the potential of popular culture practices to be progressive."[26]

However dimly realized that potential may have been, surely something like producerly behavior occurred during Desert Storm. The dreams of White House flacks notwithstanding, yellow ribbons were not fully "appropriated by any particular group."[27] Instead the nation engaged in a communicative display of "capture the ribbon," fighting over symbolic capital in a rainbow of stances toward the war. The ribbons meant neither war nor hope nor peace—and they meant all of these things. The fluttering indices of a "solidarity without consensus,"[28] they proved the Gramscian point that the struggle for hegemony is never-ending—a dialectical, "open-ended process of contestation."[29]

"Burying Vietnam"

So much for homogeneity of mood with regard to the ribbons' immediate valence. But the immediate valence was not the only one; nor, I believe, was it the most important one. What was really at stake in the game of "capture the ribbon" was Americans' relation not to the present, but to the past. I have said that in the negotiation of symbolic capital that attended Desert Storm, there were two arenas of political conflict under siege. I want to conclude by examining the older, and more conflicted arena—the war in Vietnam, which Desert Storm was supposed to "resolve."

The ghosts of Vietnam, our national revenants, haunted the Gulf engagement even before it became Desert Storm. The entire January debate about moving from a defensive posture into open war could be seen as a public airing of two enmeshed fears: "another Munich" versus "another Vietnam." Even though the Munich card took the trick, that did not allay public apprehension about a possible replay of the Asian debacle. If one recalls the constantly reiterated promise, before the first sorties began on January 16, that *this* incursion would be decisive, fully supported, and most of all brief, one realizes how essential the administration felt it was to discount comparisons. Mr. Bush himself promised it bluntly: "This will not be another Vietnam."

But Desert Storm was to be not only unlike Vietnam; it was to *redeem* the old war's failings, not only by restoring America's status as a world power, but also by extending the thanks of a grateful nation to the "boys abroad" who, a generation ago, had undertaken its thwarted mission. Vietnam veterans would not be thanked directly, of course, but they could still bask in the gratitude extended to their Gulf War counterparts. Thus, by the time-honored process of "regeneration through violence,"[30] the nation would finally make up for what had "gone wrong" in Southeast Asia.

This positioning of Desert Storm as a redemptive effort was not simply a collusive pipe dream of the nation's leaders. Making up for the past was a dominant theme in discussions of the war from start to finish, and it became a recurrent leitmotif in analyses of yellow ribbons. Penne Laingen herself acknowledged that the public "this time is making amends for neglecting Vietnam veterans."[31]

A Maine veteran, recalling how he was spit upon when he returned from Vietnam, commented, "We feel we need to make up for the wrongs of the past. I know I wish I could have been greeted like this."[32] My Belchertown neighbors, with extraordinary frequency, echoed this sentiment. They displayed ribbons to show that "I don't want these guys to go through the same thing as the Vietnam vets," because "I felt sorry for the fellows and hope it doesn't happen again," and because the Vietnam vets "got a dirty, rotten deal." The most pointed, and richly ambiguous, comment came from a middle-aged man who had tied his ribbon to the pole of a front porch Old Glory: "Maybe we'll finally bury Vietnam."

Burying can mean confronting and getting it behind you, or it can mean sweeping it under the rug. Desert Storm, I suggest, helped us to do the latter. The episode's semantic tragedy, ritually masked in the nationwide triumph, was that it decoratively disguised, rather than coming to terms with, the wounds of the past. Because yellow ribbons allowed us to "correct" a mistake without identifying or taking responsibility for it, they enabled us to bury Vietnam before it was really dead. Rather than serving to recall and "re-member" a savaged past, then, Desert Storm actually encouraged us to forget.

The decorative disguise was evident throughout the conflict, but it reached its full potential upon Saddam's surrender, as the nation mounted a victory celebration of Roman proportions. Journalists were blithely confident that this triumph would bury Vietnam by giving our new heroes the beribboned plaudits that the others had missed. Lance Morrow, writing in *Time*, proclaimed "the end of the old American depression called the Vietnam syndrome—the compulsive pessimism, the need to look for downsides and dooms."[33] In the same magazine, two women issued a generic "Dear Soldier" letter, explaining to Desert Storm veterans what they would find upon their return: "You will find signs that you're returning to a different country than the one you left in August: proud, resolute, united and overwhelmed with national purpose. You will be lavished with honors, medals and ribbons, streets named after you, Desert Storm ice cream flavors. You who wrote to us of your fears of coming home should not worry. No one will spit on you. You will not be called baby killers, and we promise that you will not grow old holding a sign in a subway station: I'm a veteran. Can you spare some change?"[34] The undercurrent here speaks louder than the surface calm, as the writers' exuberance merely highlights the country's anguish. Perhaps in some Durkheimian paradise yet to be discovered the American people will be "proud, resolute, united, and overwhelmed with national purpose." That was certainly not the sense of the streets in 1991, as the writers' shrill palliatives ironically implied. "You will not be called baby killers." Indeed. When the nation truly comes to terms with the "hurts of history,"[35] we will no longer require such grotesque assurances.

"Coming Full Circle"

To come to terms, however, would require a feat of memory for which the American people have thus far shown meager aptitude. Many students of history and memory have already noted this. Lipsitz defines as "the constitutive problem of our time" a "crisis of historical memory" that turns away from the painful.[36] Thelen suggests that a national unwillingness to recall and talk *through* (rather than around) our checkered past dooms us, Sisyphuslike, to an "endless conversation."[37] Most vividly, Frisch quotes a Nigerian friend who claims that Americans are simply uninterested in recalling history; what we want—and what our historians typically give us—is "a pretty carpet that can be rolled out on ceremonial occasions to cover all those bloodstains on the stairs." The predictable result is "a present that seems to float in time—unencumbered, unconstrained, and uninstructed by any active sense of how it came to be."[38]

A less scholarly, but no less apposite, gloss on our unremembered (and thus unusable) past comes from Vietnam veteran and newsletter editor Greg Kleven. "Why are Vietnam veterans still talking about the war?" he asks in *Vietnam Echoes*. "Because America didn't go to Vietnam, and never had to come home. . . . We are still talking about the war because the war isn't over and won't be until this society, led by veterans, goes full circle."[39]

Indeed, no one seems more aware of how far we are from closing the circle than Vietnam veterans. Veterans who were involved in Austin's "Operation Yellow Ribbon" could not escape being reminded of that fact. The promoters of the "Capitol Salute to the Troops" did afford them a special reviewing stand; a Vietnam float joined the victory parade; and the capitol grounds contained a "Moving Wall" replica of the Vietnam Memorial. Yet, if these symbolic gestures were designed to incorporate the Vietnam experience into the national back-patting, they succeeded only ironically, by displaying a dramatic difference in representational scale and public attendance. "By sponsoring the Moving Wall," a local radio station wrote in the Capitol Salute program, "B93 hopes to complete the circle in honoring a group for which the proper recognition is long overdue—our Vietnam Veterans. We hope you will spend a few moments at the Memorial remembering."[40] In fact, the number of people who spent those moments was miniscule compared to the thousands who lined Congress Avenue to cheer on the tanks. The hope of a memorial to Austin's Asian war vets remained a dream.[41] The loss of 58,000 young men and women in the Asian quagmire receded into the shadows of the live oaks, while the eyes of the town, and of the nation, were on the heroes of Kuwait.

Because yellow ribbons tried so hard, and failed so significantly, to tie up the loose ends of the past, it may be useful to see the custom as a gesture not of celebration but of desperate, unfulfilled compensation. "A society continually threatened with disintegration," writes Kertzer, "is continually performing reintegrative ritual"—acts of symbolic no less than moral compensation in which the demons of fissure may be temporarily contained.[42] Military adventures can be especially productive in this regard, since they facilitate the muting of personal skepticism by collective action.[43] Popular entertainment can also play a part, as in the "suturing" provided a wounded body politic by the Rambo films.[44] On the home front, ritual dramas such as ribbon display and (on a grander scale) Operation Yellow Ribbon help us to "do something about situations otherwise felt to be unendurable." Such collective wish fulfillments utilize social fantasy as "an attempt to bridge a felt gap between means and ends by imaginative construction."[45]

I have tried to show in this essay that in the case of yellow ribbons, the construction remained incomplete for three reasons: the inherent openness of symbolism in general, public misgivings about administration policy in the Persian Gulf, and—most of all—a national failure to identify clearly, and thus to exorcise, the demons of Vietnam.

Those demons had, and still have, much to do with the nation's rejection of its Vietnam veterans, a marginalized cadre long scapegoated for the "wrongs of the past." Resolving our ambivalence about those warriors, and helping them to heal, would be a first, essential step in putting the ghosts to rest. But there is more, and more painful, work to be done. To truly "come full circle," as Kleven notes, the nation would have to confront the "hurts" not only of our own people, but also of those countless Southeast Asians whom American military policy left shattered and gasping. This would mean, for example, normalizing relations with our former enemy—a process that has finally been started by the Clinton presidency—supporting veterans who want to return to the site of their travail and, not least of all, acknowledging that our presence in Vietnam cost the lives not only of 58,000 Americans but of more Vietnamese (including children) than could possibly be numbered. It would mean seeing that all of us were simultaneously victims and victimizers. "Like it or not," writes Kleven, "Vietnam is part of the medicine that American society needs in order to get over its self-inflicted wounds."[46] It was this hard fact that the yellowing of America (almost) concealed.

Epilogue: Poaching Redux

That the yellow ribbon tradition obscured dissent seems obvious enough, given the acetate blizzard and Mr. Bush's eighty-three percent approval rating. That the symbol remained open to interpretation may have been less obvious, but it was no less true. Three postwar examples, unrelated to the conflict, make the point.

- Several days after the Persian Gulf cease-fire, an Exeter, New Hampshire, jury convicted schoolteacher Pamela Smart of manipulating her student boyfriend into killing her husband. Smart's mother, during the trial, had worn a yellow ribbon, "symbolizing her belief that her daughter [was] a hostage of the judicial system."[47]
- Six months later, in Killeen, Texas, a man killed twenty-four patrons of a Luby's cafeteria in the worst nonmilitary mass murder in U.S. history. Television news reports of the incident mentioned two signs of mourning: flags flown at half-mast and yellow ribbons.
- More recently, young Vashon McQueen of Bryan, Texas, became the hapless victim of a drive-by shooting. Friends of the slain teenager attended his funeral wearing yellow ribbons inscribed, "In Loving Memory."[48]

As counterculture kids of the 1960s "poached" on one dominant symbol, the American flag, by unpatriotically reassembling it into clothing, so the grieving citizens of Exeter, Killeen, and Bryan transformed the recently nationalized yellow ribbons, lifting them into their own worlds of private meaning. Such "producerly" responses should keep us alert to how variously evocative—and how impervious to fixing—traditions can be.

Notes

1. Eric Hobsbawm and Terence Ranger, eds., *The Invention of Tradition* (Cambridge: Cambridge University Press, 1988).
2. Monica Collins, "There's a Rainbow of Messages Tied Up in Yellow Ribbons," Boston *Sunday Herald*, February 10, 1991, p. 28.
3. Jack Santino, "Yellow Ribbons and Seasonal Flags: The Folk Assemblage of War," *Journal of American Folklore* 105 (1992): 19–33.
4. Kate Ballen, "America Ties on Yellow Ribbon," *Fortune*, March 11, 1991, p. 14.
5. Michael Brosnan, "Operation Welcome Home," *Down East* (July 1991): 12.
6. History's "biggest celebration," described by Governor Ann Richards as "one giant Texas-size party," was announced exuberantly in the flyer *Parade Line*, produced by the ad hoc Governor's Committee to Salute the Troops. Perot was its finance chairman.
7. Raymond Williams, *Marxism and Literature* (Oxford: Oxford University Press, 1977), 128–41.
8. Victor Turner, *The Forest of Symbols: Aspects of Ndembu Ritual* (Ithaca, N.Y.: Cornell University Press, 1967), 20–25.
9. Ibid.
10. Abner Cohen, *Two-Dimensional Man* (Berkeley: University of California Press, 1974), 32.
11. Raymond Firth, *Symbols: Public and Private* (Ithaca, N.Y.: Cornell University Press, 1973), 79.
12. See, for example, Henry Dreyfuss, *Symbol Sourcebook* (New York: McGraw-Hill, 1972).
13. Mircea Eliade, *Images and Symbols: Studies in Religious Symbolism* (New York: Sheed and Ward, 1961), 110–12.
14. A. L. Soens, "The Yellow Ribbon: The Bawdy Balladry behind the Manufactured Popular Piety" (paper presented at Popular Culture Association meeting, Louisville, Kentucky, March 19, 1992).
15. John Lawrence, "The Disappearance of the Civilian Hostage during the Gulf Conflict" (paper presented at Popular Culture Association meeting, Louisville, Kentucky, March 20, 1992).
16. Turner, *Forest of Symbols*, 28.
17. Firth, *Symbols*, 81.
18. David Kertzer, *Ritual, Politics, and Power* (New Haven, Conn.: Yale University Press, 1988), 99–101.

19. John Fiske, *Understanding Popular Culture* (Boston: Unwin Hyman, 1989), 24.
20. Kertzer, *Ritual*, 71.
21. Collins, "Rainbow of Messages," 28.
22. Gayle Long, "I Wear Yellow Ribbons to Show My Hope for Life, Not War," University of Massachusetts *Collegian*, February 20, 1991, p. 5.
23. Linda Babcock, "Bloody, Yellow Ribbons," letter to the editor, University of Massachusetts *Collegian*, February 25, 1991, p. 5.
24. Meredith O'Brien, "Levey Vigil Continues," University of Massachusetts *Collegian*, February 25, 1991, p. 1.
25. Fiske, *Popular Culture*, 105.
26. Douglas E. Foley, *Learning Capitalist Culture: Deep in the Heart of Tejas* (Philadelphia: University of Pennsylvania Press, 1990), 200.
27. Alice McQuillan, "Yellow Ribbons Go Back Decades," *Boston Sunday Herald*, February 10, 1991, p. 4.
28. Kertzer, *Ritual*, 67–75.
29. James Brow, "Notes on Community, Hegemony, and the Uses of the Past," *Anthropological Quarterly* 63 (1990): 1–5.
30. Richard Slotkin, *Regeneration through Violence: The Mythology of the American Frontier* (Middletown, Conn: Wesleyan University Press, 1973).
31. McQuillan, "Yellow Ribbons," 4.
32. Brosnan, "Welcome Home," 13.
33. Lance Morrow, "Triumphant Return," *Time*, March 18, 1991, pp. 19–23.
34. Nancy Gibbs and Priscilla Painton, "And While You Were Gone," *Time*, March 18, 1991, p. 27.
35. George Lipsitz, *Time Passages: Collective Memory and American Popular Culture* (Minneapolis: University of Minnesota Press, 1990), 27.
36. Ibid.
37. David Thelen, "Memory and American History," *Journal of American History* 75 (1989): 1117–29.
38. Michael Frisch, "The Memory of History," in *Presenting the Past: Essays on History and the Public*, ed. Susan Benson, Stephen Brier, and Roy Rosenzweig (Philadelphia: Temple University Press, 1986), 7–10.
39. Greg Kleven, "Why Are Vietnam Veterans Still Talking about the War?" *Vietnam Echos* 8 (1991): 1–3.
40. "Capitol Salute to Texas Troops," program brochure for Austin, Texas, celebration, June 29–July 4, 1991.

41. Debbie Graves, "Monument to Vietnam, Korea Vets Still a Dream," *Austin American-Statesman*, June 24, 1991, p. A1.

42. Kertzer, *Ritual*, 63.

43. Firth, *Symbols*, 78.

44. William Warren, "Spectacular Action: Rambo and the Popular Pleasures of Pain," in *Cultural Studies*, ed. Lawrence Grossberg, Cary Nelson, and Paula Treichler (New York: Routledge, 1992).

45. Firth, *Symbols*, 200n.

46. Kleven, "Still Talking," 3.

47. "Pamela Smart Found Guilty of Murder-Conspiracy," *Northampton Daily Hampshire Gazette*, March 23, 1991, p. 1.

48. Yvonne Salce, "Minister Challenges Mourners to Give Meaning to Youth's Death," *Bryan–College Station Eagle*, December 9, 1993, p. A1.

About the Contributors

PAT BYRNE, who has a B.A. from Iona College and an M.A. and Ph.D. from Memorial University of Newfoundland, is an associate professor in the departments of English and folklore at Memorial University of Newfoundland. A published poet and songwriter, he has performed at numerous folk festivals. His academic interests include short fiction, Newfoundland literature and folklore, Shakespeare, and modern American fiction. He has published articles on the influence of the McNulty family on Newfoundland music and on the manifestations of the tall tale in Newfoundland literature.

ERIC A. ELIASON is completing his Ph.D. in American studies at the University of Texas at Austin. During the 1994-95 school year, he taught folklore in the Brigham Young University English department. The author of several articles and encyclopedia entries on Mormon, Western, and folklore topics, he is currently editing a volume of essays in Mormon studies and writing a book on the drawn threadwork tradition of the Dutch Caribbean island of Saba. Eliason lives in Austin with wife Stephanie and their children Shelby and Caleb.

THOMAS A. GREEN, who holds the Ph.D. in anthropology from the University of Texas at Austin, is associate professor of anthropology at Texas A&M University; he taught previously at Texas, Delaware, and Idaho State. His research is in folklore, native American cultures, and ethnohistory; he is currently editing *Folklore: An Encyclopedia of Forms, Methods, and History.* Green has been involved in the martial arts for thirty years, including five years as a student and instructor in Won Hop Loong Chuan, the style he discusses in this volume.

Sylvia Ann Grider is associate professor of anthropology at Texas A&M University, where she teaches folklore and Texas cultural history. She has a doctorate in folklore from Indiana University at Bloomington and an M.A. and B.A. from the University of Texas at Austin. A former president of both the American Folklore Society and the Texas Folklore Society, she has published widely on topics ranging from children's ghost stories to Elvis Presley. Her latest book is the forthcoming *Texas Women Writers,* edited with Lou Rodenberger.

George H. Lewis is professor of sociology and anthropology at the University of the Pacific. He has published on the symbolic meaning of cultural artifacts in journals ranging from *Food and Foodways* and *American Music* to *Theory, Culture, and Society.* His books include *Sidesaddle on the Golden Calf: Popular Culture and Social Structure in America* (1972), *Symbols of Significance* (1983), and *All That Glitters* (1993). He is presently at work on an essay collection on the diffusion of culture in the Pacific Rim region. Although born in Maine, he likes lobster anyway.

Robert M. MacGregor is professor of marketing at Bishop's University in Quebec. His research interests include cultural analysis and the use of racial and ethnic stereotypes in advertising. His paper "The Eva and Topsy Dichotomy in Advertising" appeared in *Images of the Child* (1994), edited by Harry Eiss.

Jerrilyn McGregory is assistant professor of English at Florida State University. Born in Indiana, she holds a master's degree in English from Purdue, a second master's in Africana studies from Cornell, and a Ph.D. in folklore and folklife from the University of

Pennsylvania. The author of *Wiregrass Country*, a holistic study of folklife in a little known region of the South, McGregory is currently writing an ethnography of that region's sacred music tradition, focussing on the culture- and community-building roles of African American women.

JAY MECHLING is professor of American studies at the University of California at Davis. He received his B.A. (1967) in American studies from Stetson University and his graduate degrees (M.A. 1968, Ph.D. 1971) in American civilization from the University of Pennsylvania. He has written over seventy papers on topics that include his native Florida, the Boy Scouts, the animal rights debate, children's lives, and Cold War America. A past editor of *Western Folklore*, he received a Distinguished Teaching Award in 1993 from the faculty senate at Davis.

MARIO MONTAÑO received his doctorate from the folklore and folklife department at the University of Pennsylvania. His research interests are in the Texas-Mexico border region, where he grew up and where his work focusses on Mexican foodways and the anthropology of education of Mexican migrant children. He is chair of the department of anthropology at The Colorado College.

NANCY PEAKE moved from New York City to Corrales, New Mexico, where she became enamored of the Southwest and its tricultural history. She holds a Ph.D. in American studies from the University of New Mexico, where she focused on the relationships between Native Americans and Anglo Americans in the late nineteenth and early twentieth centuries. In addition to writing about Navajo material culture, particularly weaving, she has published work on the lives of Anglo urban and reservation Indian traders, which illuminates their role as cultural brokers.

JOEL SAXE teaches video at Greenfield Community College in Massachusetts. For several years, he has been conducting a folklore documentation project on Yiddish culture and Jewish radicalism in Miami and New York. He has also produced documentaries on

Yiddish culture and issues related to cultural diversity in education. Saxe received a B.A. in filmmaking from Hampshire College and a master's in communication and multicultural education from the University of Massachusetts at Amherst. His doctoral dissertation for Massachusetts is on the Yiddish culture of Miami Beach.

Deborah Anders Silverman received the Ph.D. in English from the State University of New York at Buffalo in 1996, with a dissertation in Polish American folklore. She holds a B.M. in music education, summa cum laude, and an M.A. in English from the State University of New York College at Fredonia. She teaches English at Fredonia and at Daemen College. The 1995 recipient of the Bertrand H. Bronson Prize from the American Folklore Society's Music and Song Section, she is currently working on a book about Polish American folk celebrations, music, and foodways.

Tad Tuleja took a B.A. at Yale and master's degrees at Cornell and the University of Sussex. A freelance writer for the past twenty years, he has published widely on American topics. His scholarly papers have examined calendar customs, folk etymology, and the tooth fairy, while his recent books include *Curious Customs* (1987), *American History in 100 Nutshells* (1992), and *The New York Public Library Book of Popular Americana* (1994). He is completing a doctorate in anthropology and folklore at the University of Texas at Austin.

John R. Williams, professor of English at Spartanburg Methodist College, holds a bachelor's degree from Centre College, a master's degree in English from the University of Kentucky, and a Ph.D. in folklore from Indiana University. A Kentucky native keenly interested in Appalachian culture, he has taught high school English in Jackson, Kentucky, and served as director of the Appalachian Oral History Project. Married with three children, he is researching the oral traditions of South Carolina mill villages and the blues history of the Piedmont.